Encyclopedia
of **Practical**
Photography

Volume **5**
Dev-Edis

Edited by and published for
EASTMAN KODAK COMPANY

AMPHOTO
American Photographic Book Publishing Company
Garden City, New York

Note on Photography

The cover photos and the photos of letters that appear elsewhere in this encyclopedia were taken by Chris Maggio.

Library of Congress Cataloging in Publication Data

Amphoto, New York.
　Encyclopedia of practical photography.

　Includes bibliographical references and index.
　1. Photography—Dictionaries. I. Eastman
Kodak Company. II. Title.
TR9.A46　　770'.3　　77–22562

ISBN 0–8174–3050–4 Trade Edition—Whole Set
ISBN 0–8174–3200–0 Library Edition—Whole Set
ISBN 0–8174–3055–5 Trade Edition—Volume 5
ISBN 0–8174–3230–2 Library Edition—Volume 5

Manufactured in the United States of America

Editorial Board

The *Encyclopedia of Practical Photography* was compiled and edited jointly by Eastman Kodak Company and American Photographic Book Publishing Co., Inc. (Amphoto). The comprehensive archives, vast resources, and technical staffs of both companies, as well as the published works of Kodak, were used as the basis for most of the information contained in this encyclopedia.

Symbol Identification

 Audiovisual

 Biography

 Black-and-White Materials

 Black-and-White Processing and Printing

 Business and Legal Aspects

 Chemicals

 Color Materials

 Color Processing and Printing

 Equipment and Facilities

 Exposure

 History

 Lighting

 Motion Picture

 Optics

 Picture-Making Techniques

 Scientific Photography

 Special Effects and Techniques

 Special Interests

 Storage and Care

 Theory of Photography

 Vision

Guide for the Reader

Use this encyclopedia as you would any good encyclopedia or dictionary. Look for the subject desired as it first occurs to you—most often you will locate it immediately. The shorter articles begin with a dictionary-style definition, and the longer articles begin with a short paragraph that summarizes the article that follows. Either of these should tell you if the information you need is in the article. The longer articles are then broken down by series of headings and sub-headings to aid further in locating specific information.

Cross References

If you do not find the specific information you are seeking in the article first consulted, use the cross references (within the article and at the end of it) to lead you to more information. The cross references can lead you from a general article to the more detailed articles into which the subject is divided. Cross references are printed in capital letters so that you can easily recognize them.
Example: *See also:* ZONE SYSTEM.

Index

If the initial article you turn to does not supply you with the information you seek, and the cross references do not lead you to it, use the index in the last volume. The index contains thousands of entries to help you identify and locate any subject you seek.

Symbols

To further aid you in locating information, the articles throughout have been organized into major photographic categories. Each category is represented by a symbol displayed on the opposite page. By using only the symbols, you can scan each volume and locate all the information under any of the general categories. Thus, if you wish to read all about lighting, simply locate the lighting symbols and read the articles under them.

Reading Lists

Most of the longer articles are followed by reading lists citing useful sources for further information. Should you require additional sources, check the cross-referenced articles for additional reading lists.

Metric Measurement

Both the U.S. Customary System of measurement and the International System (SI) are used throughout this encyclopedia. In most cases, the metric measurement is given first with the U.S. customary equivalent following in parenthesis. When equivalent measurements are given, they will be rounded off to the nearest whole unit or a tenth of a unit, unless precise measurement is important. When a measurement is considered a "standard," equivalents will not be given. For example: 35 mm film, 200 mm lens, 4″ × 5″ negative, and 8″ × 10″ prints will not be given with their customary or metric equivalents.

How Articles are Alphabetized

Article titles are alphabetized by letter sequence, with word breaks and hyphens not considered. Example:

> Archer, Frederick Scott
> Architectural Photography
> Archival Processing
> Arc Lamps

Abbreviations are alphabetized according to the letters of the abbreviations, not by the words the letters stand for. Example:

> Artificial Light
> ASA Speed

Contents

Developers and Developing

A developer is a chemical solution used to turn the invisible latent image that exposure creates in a photographic emulsion into a visible image. Developing, in a practical sense, is the process of using a developer to bring out the visible image in a controlled way. The chemical reactions that take place during this process are discussed in the articles DEVELOPMENT and CHEMISTRY OF PHOTOGRAPHY. This article covers general procedures for developing, the composition of black-and-white film and paper developers, and the formulas and use of a number of standard and special-purpose developers. Additional important information is included in the articles CONTRAST and FORMULAS FOR BLACK-AND-WHITE PROCESSING, as well as in those listed at the end of this article.

It is generally not practical for the individual photographer to attempt to formulate his own color developers because of their chemical complexity, and because of the expense and difficulty of obtaining some ingredients, especially color developing agents. The use of color developers is covered in COLOR FILM PROCESSING and the related articles listed there.

Developing Procedures and Materials

Black-and-white developing is one of the three major steps in film and paper processing:

1. A developer brings out the image.
2. A stop bath halts developer action at the appropriate moment.
3. A fixer makes the developed image permanent when it is followed by thorough washing.

This process is the same for films and for print materials; it can be carried out in tanks, trays, or mechanized equipment. Panchromatic emulsions must be handled in total darkness until fixing is complete, unless the processing tank has a lighttight cover. Other emulsions, including printing papers, can be handled under the safelight conditions given in the instructions for the material in use.

Equipment for Film Developing. The following items are commonly required for film developing:

Tank(s) and film hangers or reels
Opener for film cartridges
Thermometer
Timer
Scissors
Funnel
Processing solutions
Sponge—photographic quality
Film clips for drying

Tanks and reels, of plastic or stainless steel, such as these by Durst and Kindermann, come in various sizes to accommodate different film formats. Some tanks can hold a stack of several reels, as shown at center rear. Photo courtesy of Ehrenreich Photo-Optical Industries, Inc.

A plastic apron with dimpled edges can be coiled up with the film. Dimples keep the film layers separated and touch only the edges of the film; no reel is required.

Tanks and Film Hangers and Reels. Small-format films are commonly developed in cylindrical tanks that accommodate one to four films loaded into spiral reels. The tanks and reels are either stainless steel or plastic. The tanks usually have a light-tight lid with a provision for pouring solutions in and out while covered, so that only one tank is required for the entire process. Metal reels have a center clip or hook to hold one end of the film; the remaining length slips into the grooves created by the spiral (see the following section). Some plastic reels are loaded simply by pushing the film into the spiral from the outer end. Other reels have one flange that moves with a back-and-forth ratchet action; after the film has been engaged in the outside guide slots, the ratchet movement feeds it smoothly into the grooves. Most plastic reels can be adjusted to accommodate a number of different film sizes. Metal reels come in fixed sizes; a reel for 35 mm film also accepts 126-size film. An alternate method of

loading is a plastic "apron," the same width as the film, that has a continuous row of dimples along each edge; the dimples hold the film layers separated when the apron is coiled up along with the film. (See the accompanying illustrations.)

Some small-format tanks accept sheet films of various sizes, either loaded into a special compartmented insert, or in grooves in the tank walls that guide the film edges and keep the sheets separated.

Large-format sheet films are held in hangers of metal or plastic. The film is held either by edge channels or by corner clips. Multiple hangers hold two or four sheets of film, depending on the format size. Hangers are commonly loaded in batches of up to ten or twelve into individual rectangular tanks of solution. Because of the volume of solution required, it is not practical to empty and fill a single tank with the various solutions. (For more detailed information, see the article TANKS.) As explained in the next section, sheet films can also be developed in trays.

Openers. Some plastic cartridges can be snapped open by hand, but it is a good idea to have a pair of pliers available in case of difficulty. The end of a 35 mm cartridge can be removed with a bottle-cap opener or with pliers. Commercial openers for 110, 126, and 35 mm film cartridges are available. Paper-backed roll films are opened by tearing or cutting through the "exposed" tab that seals them when they are removed from the camera.

Thermometer. The thermometer must be clearly readable under safelight illumination in the 18 to 24 C (65 to 75 F) range used for black-and-white processing. It must slip easily into the neck of storage bottles or into the tanks used. The thermom-

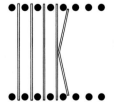

Cross-section of a loaded spiral reel. The film must fit without buckling in the spiral grooves or space; a buckled layer will touch an adjacent one, thus preventing development at that point.

Developers and Developing

eters built into the turning/agitation handles of some tanks are too small to read easily in the darkroom and are of doubtful accuracy.

Timer. Although any clock can be used, it is more convenient to have a timer that can be set to the required number of minutes for a process and that runs down to zero, so the time remaining can be quickly noted. The timer must be easy to start in the dark, and should be clearly visible in the dark or under safelight illumination.

Scissors. The tongue of 35 mm film must be trimmed to a square end before it can be loaded into most reels. Often it is preferable to cut the backing paper away from roll film rather than to tear off the tape. Blunt-end scissors will prevent accidental injury or damage in the dark.

Funnel. Some tanks have wide-mouth tops that act as funnels when solutions are poured; others require a funnel. In either case, a funnel is required to pour solutions back into their storage bottles when the tank is emptied. Funnels with plastic-screen filters help keep solutions free of dust.

Solutions. The developer, stop bath, and fixer can be mixed and stored in dark-brown glass or plastic containers. A wide mouth helps in pouring, mixing, and refilling. Developer should be kept in full containers with tight-fitting caps; excess contact with the air causes aerial oxidation that weakens the developer. Kodak hypo clearing agent, often used to shorten wash times, is another solution commonly employed.

Sponge. A photographic-quality viscose sponge is used to wipe excess water from a film when it is hung to dry. Household sponges are too coarse, and can easily damage the wet emulsion. (The use of a wetting agent such as Kodak Photo-Flo solution eliminates the need for a sponge.)

Clips. Stainless steel spring clips grip the film by an end or a corner so it can be hung to dry. One or more clips at the lower end prevent a roll film from curling up or swaying excessively. Many photographers use wooden or plastic spring-type clothespins as film clips.

Film Developing Procedures. (Many of the procedures mentioned here are fully described in separate articles; see list at the end of this article.)

1. Mix developer, stop bath, and fixer according to instructions, and bring them to temperature. The optimum temperature for most black-and-white

processing is 20 to 21 C (68 to 70 F). If the developer is not to be used full strength, dilute it as required and either pour the proper amount into the tank, or into a container from which the tank can be easily and quickly filled when required.

2. In a dry area, lay out the film, opener, scissors, reels, tank, and lid so they can be easily located in the dark. Check the developer temperature, and set the timer accordingly. Developer instructions usually include time-temperature data, as do film instruction sheets. See the article on CONTRAST for a method of finding developing times that produce consistent negative density ranges.

3. *In complete darkness,* open the film cartridge or roll, and load the reel or hanger. To open 110 and 126 cartridges, grasp them by the ends and bend them back, toward the label, until the plastic breaks. With 110-size film, draw the film out so that the backing paper, not the film surface, touches the edge of the cartridge. Locate the tape that holds the film

Solutions such as fixer, developer, and stop bath should be mixed and stored in wide-mouthed brown jars.

end to the paper and cut through it or carefully peel it off.

To open 35 mm cartridges, pry off the cap *opposite* the end where the long spool core protrudes. (Some reusable cartridges have snap-off or screw-type ends; do not damage them by improper opening.) Locate the tongue-shaped end of the film, and trim it off square at the point where the full film width begins.

With a roll film, break the sealing tab and separate the paper from the film until you locate the tape that connects them. Cut through the tape or carefully peel it from the film; peeling it too fast in dry conditions may cause a flash of static electricity that could mark the film.

To load a metal spiral reel, hold the film (rolled with the emulsion side in) loosely in one hand. Engage the film end in the center clip or onto the hook of the reel. Slightly squeeze the film width passing between your thumb and forefinger so that it narrows just enough to fit into the reel. Turn the reel with the other hand to pull the film onto the reel. Do not apply excessive pressure with the hand holding and squeezing the film; let the film pass freely. It will straighten out to full width in the spiral spaces of the reel. It is essential to practice loading this kind of reel with an unwanted roll of film, several times, first in the light, then with your eyes closed or in the dark, in order to make sure the film will not buckle and cause one layer to touch another in the reel. In such a case, the portion of the image where the two layers touch will not be developed because the solutions cannot get to it.

4. If the developer is already in the tank, start the timer and immediately put the loaded reel or holders into the tank and cover it. If the tank has not been filled with developer, insert reel or holders, cover tank, start the timer, and pour in developer.

In multiple-reel tanks, insert empty reels to fill up the tank if you are not developing the maximum number of films. The empty reels will keep the loaded reels from sliding during agitation, which would cause uneven development or overdevelopment. If the tank has a lighttight cover, turn on a working light as soon as the cover is in place. In any case, agitate the film continuously during the first 30 seconds of development. Rap small tanks firmly against a hard surface, or rap the handles of sheet-film hangers against the tank edge, to dislodge air bubbles that may have formed on the film surface. An alternative method is to tap the tank to release air bells as soon as the cover is on and the developer is in the tank, but to give no agitation for the first 30 seconds or 1 minute.

5. Agitate according to the recommended pattern throughout the development time. Some film-developer combinations require agitation every 30 seconds, others once a minute; a few may require constant agitation. The agitation given controls contrast to some degree. (*See:* AGITATION.)

Metal reels have a center clip or hook which engages the film. The reel is turned to pull the film into the spiral grooves. Slight finger and thumb pressure buckles the film just enough so that it will pass between the flanges of the reel.

Developers and Developing

(Left) A daylight-loading lid permits filling and emptying a tank in white light after the film reel has been placed inside in total darkness. (Right) Ideally, film should be washed in continuously running water. Use of a washing aid such as Kodak hypo clearing agent will significantly reduce washing time.

6. At the end of the developing time, pour out the developer or remove the film. Drain the film or tank for 10 seconds, then pour in the stop bath (or transfer the film to the next tank). After 15 to 30 seconds, drain the film or the tank, and cover the film with fresh fixer. Follow the fixer instructions for time and agitation.

NOTE: Used stop bath and fixer can be poured back into their containers for reuse. A diluted developer should be discarded; full-strength developer can be saved and replenished for further use.

7. Wash the film in several changes of water or, preferably, in continuously running water. The wash water should be within about 5 degrees of the developer temperature to avoid possible damage to the emulsion. Plain water washing takes up to 30 minutes; use of a washing aid such as Kodak hypo clearing agent will significantly reduce washing time.

8. Remove the film from its reel or hanger, drain it thoroughly, and hang it in clips to dry. Wet the sponge to soften it, squeeze it out thoroughly, then slowly wipe the excess water off each side of the film just after it has been hung up. Move the sponge slowly so that it is not necessary to wipe either side more than once. If a wetting agent such as Kodak Photo-Flo solution is used after washing, *do not* wipe the film surface; the wetting agent will promote spot-free drying.

Other Procedures. Sometimes a water prebath is suggested before a film is placed in the developer. Unless specifically recommended by the film manufacturer, this is of doubtful value in conventional processing. It is sometimes argued that a prebath softens the emulsion and prepares it to absorb the developer more rapidly and evenly. However, this is offset by the fact that the water already absorbed by the emulsion must diffuse out, which actually slows the time in which the developer begins to work fully, and in a small tank it dilutes the developer somewhat. A water prebath is recommended for some large-format sheet films that have an excessive tendency to curl during wetting. The prebath is used to thoroughly wet the emulsion and to overcome the curling before the film is tray-developed.

Developers and Developing

A hardening prebath may be required to prevent excessive swelling and softening of the gelatin emulsion with some extremely active developers, or in high-temperature, tropical, or high-speed processing. Follow developer or processing instructions carefully in such cases. Some color processes use a hardening prebath to protect the film because processing is carried out at high temperatures in order to achieve reasonable developing times.

Tray Development of Films. It is possible to develop films up to about 36 inches in length by attaching a clip to each end and see-sawing the film back and forth through a tray of solution. This is not a recommended procedure because the film has such great contact with the air that aerial fog is hard to avoid.

Sheet films larger than 8″ × 10″ are often developed one sheet at a time in trays. The film is inserted into the solution emulsion-side up, and the tray is rocked to provide agitation.

Films up to 8″ × 10″ can also be tray-processed in batches, but there is great danger of emulsion damage, especially with inexperienced handling. A tray size about twice that of the format being processed is recommended (e.g., 8″ × 10″ tray for 4″ × 5″ film). To prevent sticking, the tray should have a bottom with smooth ridges (or depressions). A separate tray for each solution is required.

The sheets to be processed are collected in a stack, up to a maximum of ten for safe handling. It is convenient to mark the first film by clipping off one corner.

When the timer is started, the first sheet is slipped into the developer, emulsion-side up, and agitated for 10 seconds. The next film is slipped in on top of the first, taking care that its corners do not gouge the surface of the film already in the tray. The second film must be thoroughly wetted before being allowed to settle down on top of the first. The remaining sheets follow at 10-second intervals. When the last film has been in the developer for 10 seconds, the first film is drawn smoothly from the bottom of the stack and transferred to the top. This procedure continues, so that all the films are carefully shuffled from the bottom to the top of the stack continuously for the remaining development time. The films should be moved to keep emulsion contact with the air at a minimum.

At the end of the developing time, they are withdrawn and drained for 10 seconds—starting with the first one inserted, and continuing in order—as they are transferred to the stop bath. Similar agitation is used in the stop bath and the fixer, then the films are washed thoroughly and hung to dry.

Because developers contain ingredients that can cause skin difficulties in some people, it is advisable to wear rubber gloves when tray processing films.

Equipment for Developing Prints. Black-and-white prints are commonly processed in trays. Three trays are used containing developer, stop bath, and fixer. (An alternative method is to use a cylindrical tube of the type employed for small-scale color print processing.)

A thermometer may be required to check the solutions periodically if the room temperature is significantly higher or lower than about 21 C (70 F), but in most conditions, processing can be carried out satisfactorily at the ambient temperature.

Stainless steel or plastic tongs are necessary for handling prints if the photographer is sensitive to photographic solutions (some people have an allergic skin reaction to metol in developers). Tongs or rubber gloves are essential for handling prints in color processing solutions.

A clock or timer with a large sweep second hand, and an appropriate safelight are the only other equipment requirements.

Print Developing Procedures. Slip an exposed print into the developer and agitate it continuously either by moving the print or by rocking the tray. Fresh developer should wash over the face of the print throughout development. Dark portions of the image will begin to appear in about 15 seconds; most papers complete development in 60 to 180 seconds.

Drain the print into the developer tray for about 10 seconds, or until the liquid stops running off in a continuous stream. Place the print in the stop bath and agitate it for about 15 seconds. Drain it and transfer it to the fixer. Fixing takes 5 to 10 minutes in a conventional fixer, 1 to 3 minutes in a rapid fixer. A two-bath system with conventional fixer is highly recommended. (*See:* FIXERS AND FIXING.)

After thorough washing, preferably with the use of a washing aid, the print is dried.

Water-resistant papers are made with a resin coating on the paper surface that eliminates the absorption of the solutions (except for the wet edges) by the paper base. When processing prints made on such papers, the development and stop-bath times are the same as for regular fiber-base papers, but the fixing time is reduced to 2 minutes in a conventional fixer, and the wash time to 4 minutes. The use of washing aids is not recommended for water-resistant papers, nor can glossy-surface water-resistant papers be ferrotyped (they dry naturally to a glossy surface).

Developer Formulation

A black-and-white film developer is a complex solution. The components of a typical developer are solvent, developing agent, preservative, accelerator (or activator), and restrainer. Various chemicals can serve these functions. The chemicals chosen and their relative proportions determine whether a developer is slow- or fast-acting, produces high, normal, or low contrast, achieves maximum emulsion speed, creates fine grain, or acts in a number of other ways. A developer's characteristics, however, are always relative to the inherent characteristics of the emulsion being developed. A fine-grain developer may produce slightly reduced graininess in a coarse-grain film, but it will not turn it into a fine-grain film. Similarly, a high-contrast developer can raise the contrast produced by a low-contrast emulsion, but the results will not be the same as would result from normal development of a high-contrast film. Thus, photographers looking for the best results will first choose a film that has the speed, contrast, and grain characteristics they want, and then will test to see what developer brings out those qualities to the best advantage.

Solvent. Water is used in all common developer formulas to dissolve the other ingredients. Unless distilled, water is likely to contain many impurities, of a wide variety. These are usually present only in such minute quantities that they have no deleterious effect upon photographic solutions. The concentration of chlorine in water treated for drinking purposes is too small to cause trouble, and the same is true of the copper sulfate often added to water supplies to kill vegetable and bacterial growths. The impurities found in water may be dissolved salts; suspended particles of iron, sulfur, vegetable matter, or dirt; extracts from decayed vegetable matter or the bark of trees; or gases. If the water is boiled and then allowed to settle, the gases are thrown off during the boiling and the other matter precipitated. If boiled water is allowed to stand until the precipitated matter has settled, the pure, supernatant liquid can be decanted for use. With this precaution, it is very rare that impurities in water cause any trouble in photographic solutions. The actual test is to mix a developer with water so prepared and try it out by comparison with the same developer mixed with distilled water. Distilled water is inexpensive, and readily obtainable in most places, and its use, especially in stock solutions, is advisable if there is any doubt about the water.

Hydrogen sulfides and soluble metallic sulfides, if present only in very small quantities in developers, can cause fog, and these are the only impurities in water ever likely to give serious trouble. They can be removed by adding to the water 1 grain of lead acetate for every 2 ounces of developer, and allowing the developer to stand until the impurities settle out.

Developing Agent. The developing agent is the compound that reduces the exposed silver halide crystals in an emulsion to image-forming metallic silver.

Developing agents are organic compounds that oxidize in the process of reducing the exposed halides. They must be protected from oxidizing prematurely in solution, and most agents must be in an alkaline solution to function effectively. The most commonly used developing agents are: paraphenylenediamine, Dimezone, hydroquinone, glycin, paraminophenol, chlorhydroquinone, Phenidone, pyrocatechin, pyrogallol, metol (Kodak Elon developing agent), adurol, and amidol.

Often more than one developing agent is used in a formula. When two appropriate developing agents are combined, the resulting activity is greater than the simple sum or the average of their working speeds. This phenomenon is known as superadditivity. For example, because of its slow working speed, hydroquinone is usually combined either with metol, or with Phenidone, or Dimezone. The two major classes of black-and-white developers are *M-Q* (metol-plus-hydroquinone), and *P-Q* (Phenidone-plus-hydroquinone).

Compared with what either agent could produce individually, an M-Q combination, for example, produces some of the high contrast characteristic of hydroquinone, but at a working time more nearly that of metol. In addition, the metol seems to replenish or restore the working properties of the hydroquinone, so that M-Q developers have an extended life, increased capacity, and the right contrast and speed characteristics for many purposes. (*See* DEVELOPMENT; SUPERADDITIVITY.)

Preservative. As all organic developers oxidize rapidly, it is necessary to add a preservative to developing solutions to retard the rate of oxidation. Because of its cheapness and efficiency, *sodium sulfite* (Na_2SO_3) is the preservative most commonly used. This is the anhydrous, or desiccated form, 1 part of which is equal to 2 parts of the crystals ($Na_2SO_3 \cdot 7H_2O$). The advantage of this form is that it keeps better, and is not too heavy or bulky. The anhydrous and the crystal forms can be substituted for each other in any formula in the above ratio, first taking care that the crystals are pure. They oxidize rapidly, and after storage, are likely to be covered with a fine powder of sulfate or carbonate that should be rinsed off and the crystals dried again before weighing out for use. The anhydrous form is readily soluble in cold water, and doubly so in water of about 38 C (100 F), but there is no advantage in using water hotter than this, as the sulfite will not dissolve until it has cooled. If used at greater than recommended concentration, sodium sulfite retards development because of its solvent action upon silver halide, and tends to increase fog.

Sodium bisulfite ($NaHSO_3$) is often used, wholly or in part, to replace sodium sulfite in a developer because it has less tendency to fog the emulsion. Sodium bisulfite can be substituted weight for weight in any formula for *potassium metabisulfite,* to which it is practically identical, for considerably less cost.

In addition to retarding the rate of oxidation of the developing agents, sodium sulfite reacts with oxidized developer, which has a brown color, and helps keep the developer from staining the material being developed. Sodium sulfite is also slightly alkaline, so it acts as a mild activator; in some fine-grain film developers it is the only activator. It is also a weak silver halide solvent, so it helps to keep graininess low.

Accelerator (or Activator). Most developing agents will not develop an emulsion, or at least not

in any practical length of time, except in an alkaline solution. The alkalis and alkaline salts most commonly used are the carbonates, the caustics, the basic phosphates, and the borates. The alkali softens the gelatin of the emulsion, allowing the developer to penetrate it more readily, so that a deficiency of alkali retards development. An excess of alkali results in chemical fog and an overswelling of the gelatin, which causes frilling and blisters.

Sodium carbonate is furnished in three forms—crystal ($Na_2CO_3 \cdot 10H_2O$), monohydrated ($Na_2CO_3 \cdot H_2O$), and anhydrous (desiccated) (Na_2CO_3). When stored, the crystals lose water and the anhydrous, if exposed to the air, tends to take up water; both tend to approach the strength of the monohydrated, which remains very constant. For that reason, the monohydrated is preferred; however, if the anhydrous is stored with reasonable care in a closed bottle or can, the quantity of water absorbed rarely has any appreciable photographic effect.

Potassium carbonate (K_2CO_3) is more soluble than sodium carbonate, and so is sometimes preferred for highly concentrated solutions. The two salts may be used interchangeably, weight for weight, the error caused by the difference in molecular weight being negligible for photographic purposes. Potassium carbonate readily takes up water from the air and must be kept in tight containers. It is more expensive than sodium carbonate and offers no advantages except in the matter of solubility.

Caustic alkalis like *sodium hydroxide* (NaOH) and *potassium hydroxide* (KOH) are used with developing agents of low energy to produce great density and high contrast. They must be kept protected from the air, as they absorb moisture and carbon dioxide. They should be dissolved in cold water because they generate considerable heat. Both are very corrosive and the hands should be rinsed after handling them. Caustic alkalis are avoided in fine-grain development because they soften and swell the gelatin more than other alkalis do.

Ammonia (NH_4OH) is a gas in a solution of water from which it is constantly escaping, so that the strength of the solution is always uncertain, and its action consequently not dependable. The saturated solution, of 0.880 density, contains about 35 percent of the gas, but is much less stable than a solution of 0.923 density containing 19 percent of the gas. Ammonia is rarely used in developers.

Tribasic sodium phosphate ($Na_3PO_4 \cdot 12H_2O$) is used principally in fine-grain developer formulas because it supplies a permanent reserve of caustic soda without causing excessive swelling and softening of the gelatin.

Acetone ($CH_3CO \cdot CH_3$) is sometimes used with the phenolic developing agents in place of an alkali. It dissociates the sodium sulfite into sodium bisulfite and caustic soda. It gives negatives notably free from fog and stain, and for that reason was once much used when developing plates with pyro. It should not be used with films, as it has a tendency to detach the emulsion from the film base.

Borax ($Na_2B_4O_7 \cdot 10H_2O$) is much used with low-contrast developers for fine grain. It is sometimes called a "buffer" alkali (developers in which it is used are often called "buffered" formulas) because in solution it slowly and constantly forms an alkali, keeping the alkaline strength of the solution constant, with at no time an undue concentration of alkali that would cause excessive swelling of the gelatin.

Kodalk is a proprietary alkali of Eastman Kodak Company with an alkalinity intermediate between borax and sodium carbonate. It has the valuable property of producing developer activities in proportion to the amount used in the formula, within limits, and so adjustment of development rate is accomplished merely by varying the amount of Kodalk used. A similar alkali, *sodium metaborate* ($Na_2B_2O_4 \cdot 4H_2O$), is used in much the same way.

Restrainer. *Potassium bromide* (KBr) is added to a developer to restrain fog and to minimize the effects of overexposure. In developing a negative, there is always a slight over-all reduction of silver, regardless of the action of light. This slight deposit is known as fog, and potassium bromide has a greater restraining action upon it than it has upon the latent image. Fog was once a considerable factor in development, and bromide had to be added to the developer to get a clean negative, but improvements in manufacturing processes have reduced the tendency to fog to such an extent that many formulas do not call for bromide.

The extreme latitude of most emulsions now makes it seldom necessary to use bromide to overcome the effects of overexposure. Bromide does have a restraining effect on development, especially noticeable in shadow details, so that in effect it reduces the speed of an emulsion. By delaying the appearance of fog, bromide makes it possible to develop films to a higher gamma than would otherwise be possible.

A different type of restrainer is in use for certain purposes. This is a group of organic antifoggants, of which the most popular are benzotriazole and 6-nitrobenzimidazole nitrate. These are used in very small amounts, and have a powerful antifoggant action. Like bromide, they also tend to reduce emulsion speed, though to a lesser extent. In paper developers, they have the same effect as bromide, except that they do not affect image color in the same way; bromide shifts image color toward green or brown, whereas the organic antifoggants tend to make the tone bluish or blue-black. Developers containing phenidone as developing agent always require the use of one of the organic antifoggants to eliminate a certain type of fog that is not affected by bromide.

Proprietary and Formula Developers. Developers manufactured and sold with trade names are proprietary developers; developers mixed from ingredients according to published formulas are formula developers.

Formula developers may be slightly less costly if only the cost of the ingredients is considered. But if the time taken to weigh out the chemicals and the cost of keeping a stock of ingredient chemicals is considered, the cost difference is little. For the experimental-minded, mixing from ingredients provides variations that are not obtainable with proprietary developers.

Generally speaking, the proprietary developers are outgrowths from original formulas, but contain ingredients (kept secret by the manufacturer) that provide certain advantages over solutions mixed from formulas. For example, Kodak Dektol developer is similar to the D-72 formula developer and produces practically identical results. However, the print capability of Dektol developer has been increased beyond that of the D-72 product. Kodak Microdol-X developer produces similar results to those provided by the DK-20 formula developer. DK-20, however, contains a silver halide solvent that produces dichroic fog on many films, while Microdol-X developer has been formulated to produce just as fine-grain results as the DK-20 developer, but without danger of dichroic fog.

Most proprietary developers are packaged in one or more of the following three forms:

1. Powder
2. Solution
3. Viscous solution

The powdered form may be in an airtight can or sealed, air-proof package. The ingredients are treated so that they do not react with each other (such as the activator oxidizing the developing agent) within the package. The powder is simply poured slowly into the right amount of water of the correct temperature and stirred until the powder has dissolved, creating the stock solution.

In the solution form, developer is available in glass or plastic bottles as a stock solution, ready to use or to dilute for use.

The viscous form is a highly concentrated solution, made viscous so that the ingredients do not crystalize out of solution. Kodak HC-110 developer is an example of this form. The viscous solution is mixed with water to form a stock solution, which is diluted again to form a working solution. Various dilutions are used for various purposes, making HC-110 developer an extremely versatile developer.

Dilution of Developer. Slight dilution of the developer gives identical images if the time of development has been properly compensated. The time is not directly proportional to the dilution except when using glycin, which does not oxidize in air. With all other developers, the reducing agent is oxidized by the air in the greater amount of water to such an extent that development takes longer than would be calculated by direct proportion to the amount of dilution. With very great dilution, the character of the image is changed. Shadows are fully developed before highlights attain their greatest density, so that a degree of dilution that necessitates development for an hour or more is often used to develop underexposed negatives, or to obtain soft gradation in negatives of contrasty subjects. The tendency to fog increases with the amount of dilution of the developer. In general, developers such as Kodak D-76 and Microdol-X produce slightly finer grain when used undiluted, while they produce slightly greater sharpness when used diluted.

In preparing a developer, it is important to note whether the formula produces a solution that is to be used at full strength, or whether it produces a *stock solution.* A stock solution must be diluted with a specified quantity of water for use, otherwise the developer would be too strong and would work too rapidly, producing uncontrollable contrast, density, and graininess. The required dilution is usually given as a proportion or a sum, such as 1:1 or 1 + 1. The developer quantity is given first; 1:2 means that one part (or quantity) of developer stock solution is to be mixed with two parts (twice as much) water. The amount represented by "a part" depends on the total quantity to be prepared; it might be a few ounces for a small tank, or more than a gallon for bulk work. Developers diluted from stock solutions are usually intended for one-time usage—that is, they are to be discarded after a single use because the amount of developing agent contained in the diluted solution will have been exhausted beyond further effectiveness.

Temperature Coefficient

In order to develop negatives to a constant contrast at different temperatures, it is necessary to know the rate at which changes of temperature affect the performance of the developer. The temperature (or thermal) coefficient of a developer is the factor by which the time of development at a given temperature must be multiplied to give identical development at 10 C (18 F) lower. This ratio varies with different developers, but is practically constant for different emulsions. It is found by developing two identical exposures in the same developer at different temperatures and timing the first appearance of the image on each. The total developing time will be proportionate to the time of image appearance. The temperature coefficient is then found by the following equation:

$$\text{Log of temperature coefficient} = \frac{(\log T_1 - \log T_2) \times 10}{t_1 - t_2}$$

where T_1 and T_2 are the times of appearance of the image, and t_1 and t_2 the temperatures used.

The temperature coefficients of some of the commonly used developers are:

1. Metol	1.3	4. Pyro	1.9
2. Paraminophenol	1.5	5. Hydroquinone	2.5
3. Ferrous oxalate	1.7		

Developers and Developing

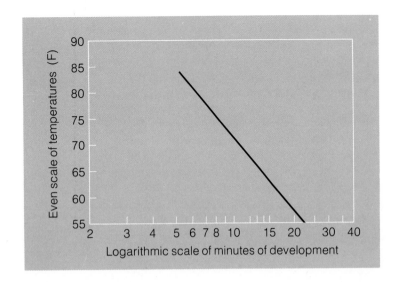

Most manufacturers supply developing times at several different temperatures for each film-developer combination; time - temperature curves can be drawn using these given times.

If the times of development for a constant gamma at two temperatures for a given emulsion have been found, the time of development at any other temperature can be found by plotting these points on a log scale of development time against an evenly-spaced scale of temperatures. The projection of a straight line through these two points will indicate the developing time at any temperature.

A method for converting development data for large tanks to data that apply to small tanks is given in the article CONTRAST INDEX.

With a developer containing two developing agents, the temperature coefficient operates only through a limited range of temperature, as each part of the developer in effect retains its own coefficient and the proportion of the developing done by each varies at different temperatures. But with metol-hydroquinone, the variation at ordinary working temperatures is negligible. However, hydroquinone becomes relatively inactive at lower temperatures so that it is unwise to use most developers at temperatures lower than 18 C (65 F).

High Emulsion Speed Developer

A vigorous developer will bring out more shadow detail in a negative, and from time to time, various formulas have made sensational claims of increasing emulsion speed. Most had such a tendency to produce fog and contrast in the negative that they were not very practical, and none of them ever attained any great popularity. However, by adding hydrazine dihydrochloride and an anti-fog agent to D-19 developer, Kodak devised the following formula that increases the emulsion speed as much as four times without producing fog in troublesome quantities.

High Emulsion-Speed Developer (Kodak SD-19a)

Solution A

0.2% solution of 6-nitro-benzimidazole nitrate*	20.0 ml
Hydrazine dihydrochloride**	1.6 g
Water to make	30.0 ml

Solution B (Kodak D-19 developer)

Water (about 125 F)	500.0 ml
Kodak Elon developing agent	2.2 g
Sodium sulfite	96.0 g
Hydroquinone	8.8 g
Sodium carbonate	48.0 g
Potassium bromide	5.0 g
Cold water to make	1.0 litre

---

*To prepare a 0.2 percent solution of 6-nitrobenzimidazole nitrate, dissolve 2g (30 gr.) in 1 litre (32 oz.) of hot distilled water. The compound 6-nitrobenzimidazole nitrate is available as Kodak anti-fog No. 2.

**Obtainable as Eastman Organic Chemical No. 1117, from the Chemical Sales Division, Eastman Kodak Company.

Dissolve chemicals in the order given. To prepare a working solution, add 30 ml (1 oz) of solution A to 1 litre (32 oz) of solution B (D-19 developer) and mix thoroughly. The working solution should be prepared just before using.

Use this high emulsion-speed developer like any conventional single-solution developer, with normal agitation in a tank, tray, or other apparatus. The best speed increase is obtained by developing for the time required to give a fog density of about 0.40, although fogs up to 0.60 can be tolerated. The major shortcoming with higher fog is an increase in printing time required for such negatives. The developing time will depend upon the temperature, processing equipment, and agitation. In general, with intermittent agitation in a tray or tank, the correct time of development at 20 C with conventional high speed negative materials is between 12 and 20 minutes. The optimum time can be determined for a particular emulsion by cutting a trial underexposure into three or more pieces, and developing the pieces for a series of times ranging from 10 to 20 minutes. By this means, the time of development can be selected that yields the lowest fog density at which a satisfactory increase in speed is obtained.

When extreme speed in developing normally exposed negatives is necessary, it can be secured without undue loss of quality by using the following developer for about 2 minutes at 18 C. The time can be shortened to 1 minute by using the developer at 30 C; or to ½ minute at that temperature for use in continuous developing machines only by adding 25 ml per 1 litre (12 minims per ounce) of strong ammonia. In a tray, development will not be uniform unless it lasts at least 1 minute. Tank developing times of less than 5 minutes are not recommended because poor uniformity may result.

Ultra rapid developer

Metol	14 g
Sodium sulfite	50 g
Hydroquinone	14 g
Caustic soda	19 g
Potassium bromide	9 g
Water to make	1 litre

Fine-Grain Developers

In any discussion of fine-grain processing, the nature of the film in use must be taken into account. The grain characteristics of the final negative image are primarily determined by the characteristics of the emulsion rather than those of the developer. Because grain size generally increases as emulsion speed increases, the finest-grain photographic results are obtained with thin, single-layer emulsions of the type used on slow-speed, fine-grain films.

There are developers that provide true fine-grain development, either by means of low activity and compensating action—which prevent the buildup of excessive density—or by means of a solvent that physically reduces the size of the developed silver grains. A few developers combine methods.

Kodak developer D-23 is a slow-working, compensating developer that will not produce high contrast even with extended developing times. When modified by the addition of sodium bisulfite, it becomes Kodak developer D-25, which has true fine-grain solvent action; however, it may produce dichroic fog on some modern films. Kodak Microdol-X developer is a proprietary formula especially designed to produce outstanding fine-grain development of modern films without fog or staining.

Elon developing agent sulfite developer (Kodak D-23)
(Low contrast developer for roll film, sheet film, and plates)

Water, about 50 C (125 F)	750.0 ml
Kodak Elon developing agent	7.5 g
Sodium sulfite	100.0 g
Cold water to make	1.0 litre

Dissolve chemicals in the order given. Average development time is about 19 minutes in a tank, or 15 minutes in a tray at 20 C (68 F).

The life of the developer can be extended by using Kodak replenisher DK-25R. Add the replenisher at the rate of 22 ml (¾ oz) for each 36-exposure 135 film processed, or the equivalent. The developer should be discarded after about 100 rolls (8000 sq. in.) of film have been developed per gallon.

Elon developing agent sulfite-bisulfite developer (Kodak D-25)
(Fine-grain developer for roll film, sheet film, and plates)

Water, about 50 C (125 F)	750.0 ml
Kodak Elon developing agent	7.5 g
Sodium sulfite	100.0 g
Sodium bisulfite	15.0 g
Cold water to make	1.0 litre

Developers and Developing

Dissolve chemicals in the order given. Average development time for Kodak roll films is about 35 minutes in a tank at 20 C (68 F). At 25 C (77 F), the average development time is about 18 minutes in a tank.

Grain is comparable to that obtained with the popular paraphenylenediamine type of developer, but Kodak D-25 is non-toxic and non-staining. If it is not essential to obtain minimum graininess, or if it is not convenient to work at the higher temperature, use half the specified quantity of sodium bisulfite. The development time will then be approximately 24 minutes at 20 C (68 F). Graininess is then intermediate between that for Kodak D-23 and that for Kodak D-25.

For replenishment, add Kodak replenisher DK-25R at the rate of 38 ml (1¼ oz) per roll for the first 50 rolls per gallon of developer, and 22 ml (¾ oz) per roll for the second 50 rolls per gallon. The developer should then be replaced with a fresh solution.

Kodak replenisher DK-25R
(For use with Kodak developers D-23 and D-25)

Water, about 50 C (125 F)	750 ml
Kodak Elon developing agent	10 g
Sodium sulfite	100 g
Kodalk balanced alkali	20 g
Cold water to make	1000 ml

Dissolve chemicals in the order given.

Accurate measurement of processing solutions is facilitated by the use of graduates, such as these by Kindermann, marked in ounces and millilitres. A set such as this, ranging in capacity from 50 to 1000 millilitres, should cover most darkroom requirements. Photo courtesy Ehrenreich Photo-Optical Industries, Inc.

Kodak Microdol-X Developer

Kodak Microdol-X developer is an excellent fine-grain developer which is designed to produce low graininess coupled with high sharpness of image detail. The stock solution can be diluted 1:3, in which case greater sharpness can be attained, with a slight sacrifice of quality in grain characteristics. Microdol-X has very little tendency to sludge with use, is free from sludge when dissolved in hard water, and has no tendency to form scum on exhaustion, aeration, or replenishment. It is available as powder, and as a ready-to-use liquid solution. As with nearly all fine-grain developers, some film-speed loss results from the use of Microdol-X developer. An increase in exposure of from ⅔ stop to 1 stop is usually required to compensate for this speed loss.

Capacity. Without replenishment, Microdol-X has a capacity of four rolls of 620-size film or 36-exposure 35 mm film, or the equivalent (2,060 square cm, or 320 square inches) per 946 millilitres (32 oz) of full-strength developer. After the first roll has been developed, the development time must be increased by about 15 percent for each succeeding roll developed per litre (or quart). With replenishment, capacity is increased to 15 rolls per litre, and development time remains constant.

When diluted 1:3, Microdol-X has a capacity of two rolls (1,030 square cm, or 160 square inches) per 946 millilitres. When developing a roll of 36-exposure 35 mm film in a 236-millilitre (8-oz) tank of Microdol-X diluted 1:3, increase the recommended

developing time by about 10 percent. Developer diluted 1:3 cannot be replenished; discard after use. See the accompanying table for developing times.

Replenishment. Use Microdol-X Replenisher. In large tanks, add replenisher to replace the amount of developer carried out by processing, about 22 ml (¾ oz) per roll. For small tank use, add 30 ml (1 oz) of replenisher for each 516 square cm (80 square inches, equivalent to one 36-exposure roll of 35 mm film) processed.

Kodak Developer *D-76*

Kodak developer D-76 is a classic. Its ability to produce full emulsion speed and maximum shadow detail with normal contrast has made it well known for superior performance. It produces images with high definition and moderately fine grain. Kodak developer D-76 is recommended for tray or tank use. Its excellent development latitude permits forced development with very little fog. However, forced de-

Kodak D-76 Developer

Water, 50C (125F)	750 ml
Kodak Elon developing agent .	2 g
Sodium sulfite (anhydrous) . . .	100 g
Hydroquinone	5 g
Borax (granular)	2 g
Water to make	1 litre

DEVELOPMENT TIMES (IN MINUTES) IN *KODAK MICRODOL-X* DEVELOPER

Kodak Films	Small Tank—Agitation at 30-Second Intervals							
	Stock Solution					Diluted 1:3*		
	18C 65F	20C 68F	21C 70F	22C 72F	24C 75F	21C 70F	22C 72F	24C 75F
Verichrome pan (rolls and cartridges)	10	9	8	7	6	13	12	11
Plus-X pan (135)	8	7	6½	6	5½	11	10	9½
Plus-X pan professional 4147 (sheets)†	11	10	9½	9	8	NR	NR	NR
Plus-X pan professional (rolls and packs)	8	7	6½	6	5	11	10	9½
Plus-X portrait 5068 (35 mm and 70 mm)	8	7	6½	6	5	11	10	9½
Royal pan 4141 (sheet)†	12	11	10½	10	9	NR	NR	NR
Panatomic-X (135 and roll)	8	7	6½	6	5	11	10	8½
Tri-X pan (135 and roll)	11	10	9½	9	8	15	14	13
Tri-X pan professional (rolls and packs)	11	10	9	8½	7½	NR	NR	NR
Tri-X pan professional 4164 (sheet)†	12	11	10	9	8	NR	NR	NR
Tri-X ortho 4163 (sheet)†	12	11	10	9	8	NR	NR	NR
High-speed infrared 4143 (sheet)†	16	14	12	10	9	NR	NR	NR
Ektapan 4162 (sheet)†	16	13	12	10	9	NR	NR	NR

*When developing a 135-size 36-exposure roll in a single-roll (236 ml or 8 oz) tank, increase recommended time by 10 percent.
†Large tank, agitation at 1-minute intervals
NR—Not Recommended

DEVELOPMENT TIMES (IN MINUTES) IN *KODAK* DEVELOPER *D-76*

Kodak Films	Dilution	SMALL TANK Agitation at 30-second intervals throughout development*					LARGE TANK Agitation at 1-minute intervals throughout development*				
		18C 65F	20C 68F	21C 70F	22C 72F	24C 75F	18C 65F	20C 68F	21C 70F	22C 72F	24C 75F
Verichrome pan (rolls and cartridges)	Full Strength	8	7	5	5	4½	9	8	7	6	5
	1:1	11	9	8	7	6	12½	10	9	8	7
Plus-X pan (135 and long rolls)	Full Strength	6½	5½	5	4½	3¾	7½	6½	6	5½	4½
	1:1	8	7	6½	6	5	10	9	8	7½	7
Plus-X pan professional (rolls and packs)	Full Strength	6½	5½	5	4½	3¾	7½	6½	6	5½	4½
	1:1	8	7	6½	6	5	10	9	8	7½	7
Panatomic-X (rolls, 135, and long rolls)	Full Strength	6	5	4½	4¼	3¾	6½	5½	5	4¾	4
	1:1	8	7	6½	6	5	9	7½	7	6½	5½
Tri-X pan (rolls, 135, and long rolls)	Full Strength	9	8	7½	6½	5½	10	9	8	7	6
	1:1	11	10	9½	9	8	13	12	11	10	9
Tri-X pan professional (rolls and packs)	Full Strength	9	8	7½	7	6	10	9	8½	8	7
High speed infrared 2481 (*Estar* base long rolls)	Full Strength	13	11	10	9½	8	14	12	11	10	9

*The complete agitation procedure is described in the Kodak data book, *Processing Chemicals and Formulas* (Kodak Publication No. J-1).

DEVELOPMENT TIMES (IN MINUTES) IN *KODAK* DEVELOPER *D-76* FULL STRENGTH

Kodak Sheet Films	Tray (Continuous agitation)*					Large Tank Agitation at 1-minute intervals throughout development*				
	18C 65F	20C 68F	21C 70F	22C 72F	24C 75F	18C 65F	20C 68F	21C 70F	22C 72F	24C 75F
Royal Pan 4141 (*Estar* thick base)	9	8	7½	7	6	11	10	9½	9	8
Tri-X pan professional 4164 (*Estar* thick base)	6	5½	5	5	4½	7½	7	6½	6	5½
Plus-X pan professional 4147 (*Estar* thick base)	7	6	5½	5	4½	9	8	7½	7	6
Ektapan 4162 *(Estar* thick base)	9	8	7	6½	5½	11	10	9	8½	7½
High speed infrared 4143 (*Estar* thick base)	11	9½	8½	7½	6½	14	12	11	10	9
Tri-X ortho 4163 (*Estar* thick base)	6	5½	5	4¾	4½	8	7½	7	6½	6

*The complete agitation procedure is described in the Kodak data book, *Processing Chemicals and Formulas* (Kodak publication No. J-1).

velopment increases graininess with any developer. (*See:* PUSH PROCESSING.)

Follow the development times in the accompanying tables. The times given in these tables can be expected to produce negatives with a contrast index of about 0.56, with negative density ranges of full-scale subjects suitable for printing with diffusion enlargers. For finding developing times for other purposes, see the article CONTRAST.

Life and Capacity. Mix the entire contents of the developer (or replenisher) package at one time. The keeping qualities of D-76 developer stored in a

Developers and Developing

REPLENISHMENT TABLE FOR FULL-STRENGTH *KODAK* REPLENISHER *D-76R*

Film Size	Area (square inches)	*Kodak* Replenisher *D-76R* Needed
126	25	7 ml ¼ oz
135 (20-exposure)	49	15 ml ½ oz
135 (36-exposure)	87	22 ml ¾ oz
828	25	7 ml ¼ oz
127	43	15 ml ½ oz
120, 620	80	22 ml ¾ oz
116, 616	105	30 ml 1 oz
4″ × 5″ sheets	20	7 ml ¼ oz
8″ × 10″ sheets	80	22 ml ¾ oz

*Kodak replenisher *D-76R* extends the capacity of Kodak developer *D-76* to 120 8 × 10-inch sheets, or equivalent, per gallon.

full, tightly stoppered bottle are excellent. You may want to keep the developer in several smaller bottles rather than one large bottle. It will keep for 6 months in a full, tightly stoppered bottle and for 2 months in a tightly stoppered bottle that is half full.

The capacity of D-76 developer is 16* rolls of 135-size film (36-exposure), or their equivalent, per gallon when used full strength without replenishment. When you use D-76 developer at the 1:1 dilution, dilute it just before use. No reuse or replenishment is recommended. The capacity of the 1:1 dilution in a single use is about 8 rolls of 135-size film (36-exposure, 87 square inches per roll), or equivalent, per gallon (4 litres) of diluted developer.† Do not store the diluted developer for future use or leave it in processing equipment for extended periods of time.

Replenishment. Proper replenishment of D-76 developer with Kodak replenisher D-76R will maintain a constant rate of development, film speed, and moderately fine-grain characteristics without the necessity of increasing the development time. Replenish only full-strength solutions of the developer. Discard D-76 developer diluted 1:1 after each use and do not replenish it.

---

*Increase the development time by 15 percent after each four rolls of film are processed.

†If only 8 ounces of solution (1:1) is used for each 36-exposure roll of 135-size film, the recommended development times should be increased by approximately 10 percent. The capacity for each gallon of 1:1 solution will then be increased to 16 rolls of film.

To replenish developer in small tanks, use 22 ml (¾ ounce) of replenisher D-76R for each 36-exposure roll of 135 film (87 square inches) developed. Add the replenisher to the developer bottle before returning the used developer from the tank.

In large tanks, add replenisher as needed to replace the developer carried out by the films and to keep the liquid level constant in the tank. Ordinarily, you can do this by adding 22 ml (¾ ounce) of replenisher D-76R for each 8″ × 10″ sheet of film, or its equivalent, that you process. Add the replenisher and stir it in thoroughly after each batch of film, or after not more than four 8″ × 10″ sheets of film, or their equivalent, have been processed per 3.8 litres (1 gallon) of developer. Refer to the accompanying replenishment table.

Kodak HC-110 Developer

Kodak HC-110 developer is a general-purpose developer for black-and-white films. It is a highly concentrated developer, a thick, syrupy liquid, to be diluted with water to give several different working-strength solutions.

Kodak HC-110 developer produces sharp images with a low fog level, takes full advantage of film speed, yields moderately fine grain, and is clean-working.

Because of the very high concentration of the developer as supplied, it is diluted in two steps. First, the developer concentrate is diluted with water to produce a stock solution; this is further diluted with water to yield the working-strength developer. It is not practical to mix the working solution directly from the concentrate because it is difficult to measure out small quantities of the thick, syrupy liquid. However, if you need large quantities of working solution, it is possible to mix the whole bottle of concentrate with enough water to produce the final concentration in one step.

Kodak HC-110 developer can be replenished, and a replenisher concentrate is packaged in the same form as the developer. The bottle of replenisher makes 3.8 litres (1 gallon) of stock solution, which is then diluted to match the working concentration in use before being added to the tank.

Kodak HC-110 developer has excellent keeping qualities; it keeps indefinitely in the unopened original bottle.

How to Mix the Stock Solution. To make a stock solution from the smaller size (473 ml or 16 oz) bottle of concentrate:

1. Pour the entire contents of the original plastic bottle into a container that holds at least 1.9 litres (2 quarts).
2. Rinse the plastic bottle thoroughly with water and pour the rinse water into the container.
3. Add enough water to bring the total volume to 1.9 litres (2 quarts).
4. Stir or shake thoroughly until the solution is uniform.

To make a stock solution from the larger (828 ml or 28 oz) bottle of concentrate:

1. Pour the entire contents of the original plastic bottle into a container that holds at least 3.4 litres (3½ quarts).
2. Rinse the plastic bottle thoroughly with water and pour the rinse water into the container.
3. Add enough water to bring the total volume to 3.4 litres (3½ quarts).
4. Stir or shake well until the solution is uniform.

To make the replenisher stock solution:

1. Pour the entire contents of the plastic bottle of replenisher concentrate into a container that holds at least 3.8 litres (1 gallon).
2. Rinse the plastic bottle thoroughly with water and pour the rinse water into the container.
3. Add enough water to bring the total volume to 3.8 litres (1 gallon).
4. Stir or shake thoroughly until the solution is uniform.

To mix working dilutions A,B,C,D,E, and F from the stock solution, see the accompanying table.

TO MIX WORKING DILUTIONS FROM *HC-110* STOCK SOLUTION

Working Dilution	Developer to Water Ratio	To Mix All Quantities		To Mix 500 ml	1 Pint	To Mix 1 Litre	1 Quart	To Mix 4 Litres	1 Gallon	To Mix 10 Litres	3½ Gallons
A	1:15	Stock	1 Part	125 ml	4 oz	250 ml	8 oz	1 litre	1 qt	2.5 litre	3 qt 16 oz
		Water	3 Parts	375 ml	12 oz	750 ml	24 oz	3 litre	3 qt	7.5 litre	10 qt 16 oz
B	1:31	Stock	1 Part	63 ml	2 oz	125 ml	4 oz	500 ml	16 oz	1.25 litre	1 qt 24 oz
		Water	7 Parts	437 ml	14 oz	875 ml	28 oz	3.51 litre	3 qt 16 oz	8.75 litre	12 qt 8 oz
C	1:19	Stock	1 Part	100 ml	3¼ oz	200 ml	6½ oz	800 ml	26 oz	2.0 litre	2 qt 26 oz
		Water	4 Parts	400 ml	28¾ oz	800 ml	25½ oz	3.2 litre	3 qt 6 oz	8.0 litre	11 qt 6 oz
D	1:39	Stock	1 Part	50 ml	—	100 ml	3¾ oz	400 ml	13 oz	1.0 litre	1 qt 13 oz
		Water	9 Parts	450 ml	—	900 ml	28¾ oz	3.6 litre	3 qt 19 oz	9.0 litre	12 qt 19 oz
E	1:47	Stock	1 Part	42 ml	—	84 ml	2½ oz	333 ml	11 oz	835 ml	1 qt 6 oz
		Water	11 Parts	458 ml	—	916 ml	29½ oz	3.667 litre	3 qt 21 oz	9.2 litre	12 qt 26 oz
F	1:79	Stock	1 Part	25 ml	—	50 ml	1½ oz	200 ml	6 oz	500 ml	22 oz
		Water	19 Parts	475 ml		950 ml	30½ oz	3.8 litre	3 qt 26 oz	9.5 litre	13 qt 10 oz

NOTE: Some quantities of stock solutions are too small for convenient measurement. Where quantities are specified for mixing 1 pint or 1 quart, they are rounded to the nearest ¼ fluidounce. Quantities for mixing larger volumes are rounded to the nearest fluidounce.

MIXING SOLUTIONS FROM *HC-110* CONCENTRATE

To Make this Working Dilution	Developer to Water Ratio	Use this amount of concentrate		With this amount of water		Use this amount of concentrate		With this amount of water	
		Millilitres	Fluidoz.	Litres	Quarts	Millilitres	Fluidounces	Litres	Quarts/Fluidounces
A	1:15	473	16	7.1	7½	828	28	12.50	13/4
B	1:31	473	16	14.7	15½	828	28	25.75	27/4
C	1:19	473	16	9.0	9½	828	28	15.75	16/20
D	1:39	473	16	18.4	19½	828	28	32.50	34/4
E	1:47	473	16	22.2	23½	828	28	39.00	41/4
F	1:79	473	16	37.4	39½	828	28	65.50	69/4

Uses of Working-Strength Dilutions

Dilution A is the most active of the dilutions. It is especially useful for tray development and gives short developing times for sheet and roll films.

Dilution B permits longer development time. It is recommended for most Kodak sheet and roll films. Developing times for these materials are given in the following section.

Dilutions C, D, and E are generally used for Kodak continuous-tone sheet films used in graphic arts reproduction. Recommended developing times are given in the next section.

Dilution F is for use with Kodak pan masking film in certain masking procedures used in color printing and some allied processes. Developing times are given in the instruction sheet that accompanies the film.

To Mix Working-Strength Dilutions from the

DEVELOPING TIMES FOR *KODAK* SHEET FILMS AND FILM PACKS

Kodak HC-110 Developer Dilution A Kodak Sheet Films	Tray* 18 C 65 F	20 C 68 F	21 C 70 F	22 C 72 F	24 C 75 F	Large Tank** 18 C 65 F	20 C 68 F	21 C 70 F	22 C 72 F	24 C 75 F
Ektapan 4162 (*Estar* thick base)	3¼	3	2¾	2½	2¼	4	3¼	3¼	3	2¾
Royal pan 4141 (*Estar* thick base)	3½	3	2¾	2½	2¼	4	3¼	3¼	3	2¾
Royal-X pan 4166 (*Estar* thick base)	5	4½	4¼	4	3½	7	6	5½	5	4½
Super-XX pan 4142 (*Estar* thick base)	4½	4	3¾	3½	3	6	5	4½	4¼	3½
Kodak Film Packs Tri-X pan professional	4½	4¼	4	3½	3	6	5½	5	4½	4
Dilution B Kodak Sheet Films	Tray* 18 C 65 F	20 C 68 F	21 C 70 F	22 C 72 F	24 C 75 F	Large Tank** 18 C 65 F	20 C 68 F	21 C 70 F	22 C 72 F	24 C 75 F
Commercial 6127 and 4127 (*Estar* thick base)	2¾	2¼	2¼	2	1¾	NR	NR	NR	NR	NR
Ektapan 4162 (*Estar* thick base)	5	4½	4¼	4	3½	7	5	5½	5	4¼
Plus-X pan professional 4147 (*Estar* thick base)	6	5	4¾	4½	4	8	7	6½	6	5½
Royal pan 4141 (*Estar* thick base)	7	6	5½	5	4½	9	8	7½	7	6
Royal-X pan 4166 (*Estar* thick base)	8½	8	7½	7	6½	11	10	9	8½	7½
Super-XX pan 4142 (*Estar* thick base)	8	7	6½	6	5	11	9	8	7	6
Tri-X pan professional 4164 (*Estar* thick base)	6	5½	5	4½	4	8	7½	7	6	5
Tri-X ortho 4163 (*Estar* thick base)	4½	4	3¾	3½	3	5½	5	4¾	4½	4
Kodak Film Packs Tri-X pan professional	9	8	7	6	5	11	10	9	8	7

*Development in a tray with continuous agitation
**Development on a hanger in a large tank with agitation at 1-minute intervals. NR=Not recommended.

NOTE: Development times shorter than 5 min in a tank cause poor uniformity.

Developers and Developing

Concentrate. Because small amounts of the concentrate are difficult to measure accurately, the working dilutions of Kodak HC-110 developer should not be prepared directly from the concentrate. However, if a relatively large quantity of developer is needed for immediate use, you can mix a *whole bottle* of concentrate with a given amount of water. For example, a 16-ounce bottle of concentrate makes 15.1 litres (4 gallons) of dilution B. The table at top left shows how the various dilutions can be mixed directly from whole bottles of concentrate.

Developing Times. The developing times given in the accompanying table assume exposure with camera lenses of moderate flare. They are aimed at giving negatives of full-scale subjects that will match the contrast of normal-grade papers when printed with diffusion-type enlargers. For printing with condenser enlargers, shorter development times are required (usually 25 to 50 percent less). The best developing time depends on a number of conditions, including the flare level of the camera lens. A method for finding a time for your conditions is given in the article CONTRAST. Another method is trial-and-error. Start with the time given in the tables and adjust it according to your results. If your negatives are consistently too high in contrast, decrease the developing time; if too low in contrast, increase the time.

The dilutions of Kodak HC-110 developer can be replenished with appropriate dilutions made from the replenisher stock solution as given in the table.

To maintain constant developer activity, replenish the working dilutions, with properly diluted replenisher, at the rate of 22 millilitres per 516 square centimetres (¾ fluidounce per 80 square inches) of film. However, if the negatives start to get too thin and low in contrast, or too dense and high in contrast, increase or decrease the replenishment rate.

DEVELOPING TIMES FOR *KODAK* ROLL FILMS

Kodak HC-110 Developer Dilution A *Kodak* Roll Films	Small Tank*					Large Tank**				
	18 C 65 F	20 C 68 F	21 C 70 F	22 C 72 F	24 C 75 F	18 C 65 F	20 C 68 F	21 C 70 F	22 C 72 F	24 C 75 F
Royal-X pan	6	5	4¾	4½	4¼	7	6	5½	5	4½
Tri-X pan	4¼	3¾	3¼	3	2½	4¾	4¼	4	3¾	3¼
Tri-X pan professional	NR	NR	NR	NR	NR	6	5½	5	4½	4
135 Films *Tri-X* pan	4¼	3¾	3¼	3	2½	4¾	4¼	4	3¾	3¼

Dilution B *Kodak* Roll Films	Small Tank*					Large Tank**				
	18 C 65 F	20 C 68 F	21 C 70 F	22 C 72 F	24 C 75 F	18 C 65 F	20 C 68 F	21 C 70 F	22 C 72 F	24 C 75 F
Panatomic-X professional	4¾	4¼	4	3¾	3¼	5½	4¾	4¼	4	3½
Plus-X pan professional	6	5	4½	4	3½	6½	5½	5	4¾	4
Royal-X pan	10	9	8	7½	6½	11	10	9	8½	7½
Tri-X pan	8½	7½	6½	6	5	9½	8¼	8	7½	6½
Tri-X pan professional	10	9	8	7	6	11	10	9	8	7
Verichrome pan	6	5	4½	4	2	8	6½	6	5½	4½
135 Films *Panatomic-X*	4¾	4¼	4	3¾	3¼	5½	4¾	4¼	4	3½
Plus-X pan	6	5	4½	4	3½	6½	5½	5	4¾	4
Tri-X pan	8½	7½	6½	6	5	9½	8½	8	7½	6½

*Development on a spiral reel in a small roll film tank, with agitation at 30-second intervals.
**Development of several reels in a basket, with agitation at 1-minute intervals.
NR = Not recommended.
NOTE: Development times shorter than 5 minutes in a tank may cause poor uniformity.

DEVELOPING TIMES FOR *KODAK* CONTINUOUS-TONE GRAPHIC ARTS FILMS

Kodak Films	Applications Graphic Arts	*Kodak* HC-110 Developer Dilutions	Tray Development Times (Minutes) at 20 C (68 F) with Continuous Agitation		
Commercial 4127 (*Estar* thick base)	Gravure	C	3		
Gravure positive 4135	Continuous-tone positives for photogravure and photoengraving	C	4		
Blue-sensitive masking 2136	Premasks for two-stage masking	C	3		
	Positive masks	E	2½		
	Premasks for two-stage masking	C	3½		
	Principal masks for two-stage masking	C	3½		
	Continuous-tone positives	C	4		
			When exposed through color-separation filters:		
			Red	**Green**	**Blue**
Separation negative, 4131 type 1	Color-separation negatives from masked color transparencies	C	4	3½	4
	Color-separation negatives from reflection copy (two-stage masking)	D	4½	4½	5½
	Color-separation negatives from unmasked color transparencies	E	4	3½	4½
	Principal masks for color transparencies	E	2½	2½	—
	Color Prints	E	4	4	5
	Color-separation negatives from original subjects or from masked color transparencies	D	3	3	4
	Color-separation negatives from unmasked color transparencies	E	2½	2½	3
Super-XX pan 4142 (*Estar* thick base)	Color-separation negatives made directly from the subject or from masked color transparencies	A	4½	4½	7
	Color-separation negatives made from unmasked transparencies	B	4½	4½	7
	Graphic Arts		**Cyan Printer Mask**	**Magenta Printer Mask**	**Yellow Printer Mask**
Pan masking 4570	Camera-back masking	E	4	4	4
	Masks on transparencies (for cyan, magenta, yellow, and black printers)	D	3¼	3¼	3¼
			Tray (continuous agitation)		Tank (intermittent agitation)
Professional copy 4125 (*Estar* thick base)	Photomechanical reproduction (for 1.70 highlight aim-density)	C	5½		8

With an average drain period between the developer and the stop bath, the stated replenishment rate will usually be sufficient to match the carry-out of developer. However, if much more of the solution is lost in the process than is replaced by replenishment, make up the loss by adding fresh HC-110 developer of the appropriate dilution.

When dilutions A, B, C, D, and E are used for tank development with the replenishment procedure just described, the developer activity should be monitored by Kodak control strips, 10-step (for professional film). The solution can be kept in service for at least 1 month if these strips indicate proper developer activity.

If control strips are not used, dilutions A, B, C, D, and E can be replenished until fifty 20.3×25.4 cm films per litre (two-hundred $8'' \times 10''$ films per gallon), or the equivalent area in other sizes, have been processed; or when the volume of added replenisher equals the original volume of solution in the tank; or after the developer has been replenished for 1 month.

Kodak HC-110 REPLENISHER DILUTIONS

To replenish working dilution	Replenisher stock solution*		Water
A	use	1 part	none
B	use	2 parts	1 part
C	use	1 part	none
D	use	1 part	1 part
E	use	8 parts	11 parts
F	Do not replenish		—

*For mixing instructions, see section on how to mix the stock solution.

Dilution F is generally used in a tray for developing masks; therefore, it should not be replenished, but used and discarded immediately.

Kodak Polydol Developer

Kodak Polydol developer has been formulated to meet the needs of portrait, commercial, industrial, school, and amateur photographers for a developer that yields high negative quality as well as long life and high capacity. Although Kodak Polydol developer is primarily a tank developer for sheet and roll films, it performs equally well as a tray developer for sheet films or as a developer for spiral-reel and machine processing of films in long rolls.

With the recommended replenishment procedure, this developer maintains uniform activity throughout a long period of use. Furthermore, Polydol developer is free from the high peak of activity characteristic of most developers when they are freshly mixed.

Kodak HC-110 Developer CAPACITY OF WORKING DILUTIONS

Dilution	Tray		Tank Without Replenishment		Tank With Replenishment*	
	20.3×25.4 cm Sheets per Litre	$8'' \times 10''$ Sheets per Gallon	20.3×25.4 cm Sheets per Litre	$8'' \times 10''$ Sheets per Gallon	20.3×25.4 cm Sheets per Litre	$8'' \times 10''$ Sheets per Gallon
A	5.0	20	10	40	50	200
B	2.5	10	5	20	50	200
C	4.0	15	8	30	50	200
D	2.0	8	4	15	50	200
E	1.5	5	3	10	50	200
F	1.0	2	Not recommended	Not recommended	50	200

*Use and replenish for 1 month only.

Kodak HC-110 Developer STORAGE LIFE OF UNUSED SOLUTIONS

Dilutions	Full stoppered glass bottle	½ Full stoppered glass bottle	Tank with floating lid
Stock solution	6 months	2 months	—
Stock replenisher	6 months	2 months	—
A	6 months	2 months	2 months
B	3 months	1 month	1 month
C	6 months	2 months	2 months
D	3 months	1 month	1 month
E	2 months	1 month	1 month
F	Do not store	—	—

Developers and Developing

Kodak Polydol developer is available in packages to make 3.8 and 13.2 litres (1 and 3 ½ gallons) of working solution. Kodak Polydol replenisher is supplied in packages to make 3.8 and 19 litres (1 and 5 gallons) of replenisher.

Developing Sheet Films. For developing sheet films with Kodak Polydol developer, see the accompanying table.

Agitation. The times recommended for tray development are for continuous agitation, either by tilting the tray for single films or by leafing through the stack when several films are developed together. The times recommended for tank development are for the development of films in hangers, with agitation by lifting and tilting hangers at 1-minute intervals. Details of these procedures are given in the article AGITATION.

As noted, times for continuous agitation in a tray also apply to the recommended conditions for nitrogen-burst agitation in tank processing. Polydol developer is particularly well suited by its activity level to the nitrogen-burst method of agitation. Developers of high activity in many cases require times appreciably shorter than 5 minutes and are not recommended because such short immersion times lead to nonuniformity. Further details can be found in the article GASEOUS-BURST AGITATION.

Developing Roll and 135 Films. For developing roll and 135 mm films with Kodak Polydol developer, see the accompanying table.

Agitation. The times recommended for a small tank apply when the film is developed on a spiral reel with agitation at 30-second intervals. The times given for a large tank are for development of several reels in a basket with agitation at 1-minute intervals.

Developing times given for Kodak films are aimed at yielding negatives that print well on normal-contrast paper. However, if negatives are consistently too low in contrast, increase the developing time. If they are consistently too high in contrast, decrease the developing time. For further details, see the article CONTRAST.

Developing Long Rolls. For developing long rolls of film with Kodak Polydol developer, see the accompanying table. Films in long rolls, such as 35 mm or 70 mm by 100 feet or 3 ½ inches by 75 feet, can be developed in spiral reels or in continuous-processing machines.

Development in Spiral Reels. Films on spiral reels should be agitated once each minute by the lifting-and-turning technique described in detail in the film instruction sheets.

NOTE: In certain situations, about 15.2 litres (4 gallons) of solution is required to cover the films adequately. To obtain the required quantity of developer, the 13.2-litre (3 ½-gallon) size of Kodak Polydol developer can be used with the addition of 1 litre (1 quart) of Kodak Polydol replenisher and 1 litre (1 quart) of water. The times of development in the long roll film developing table will still apply.

Replenishment. After developing sheet films or films in rolls, add Kodak Polydol replenisher as required to maintain a constant level of developer in

KODAK POLYDOL DEVELOPER

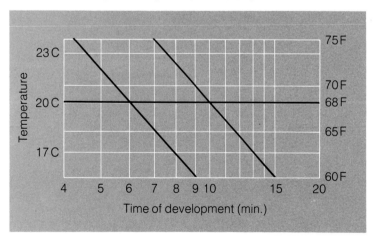

The time-temperature chart shows the development time at various temperatures corresponding to certain recommended times at 20 C (68 F). For other times at 20 C, additional lines can be drawn parallel to those shown.

DEVELOPING SHEET FILMS WITH *KODAK POLYDOL* DEVELOPER

Kodak Films in Sheets	Recommended Developing Time in Minutes									
	Tray (Continuous Agitation)*					Tank (Agitation at 1-Minute Intervals)				
	18 C 65 F	20 C 68 F	21 C 70 F	22 C 72 F	24 C 75 F	18 C 65 F	20 C 68 F	21 C 70 F	22 C 72 F	24 C 75 F
Ektapan 4162 (Estar thick base)	9 ½	8	7	6	5	12	10	9	8	7
Plus-X pan professional 4147 (Estar thick base)	7	6	5 ½	5	4 ½	9	8	7 ½	7	6
Royal pan 4141 (Estar thick base)	7	6	5 ½	5	4 ½	9	8	7 ½	7	6
Royal-X pan 4166 (Estar thick base)	7 ½	6 ½	6	5 ½	4 ½	9 ½	8 ½	8	7 ½	6 ½
Super-XX pan 4142 (Estar thick base)	11	9	8	7	6	13	11	10	9	8
Tri-X ortho 4163 (Estar thick base)	6	4 ¾	4 ½	4 ¼	3 ¾	8	6 ½	6	5 ½	4 ½†
Tri-X pan professional 4164 (Estar thick base)	7	6	5	5	4 ½	9	8	7	6 ½	5 ½

*Times also apply for nitrogen-burst agitation: 1-second burst duration; 10-second burst interval; pressure adjusted to raise the solution level about 16 mm (5.5 in.).
†Not recommended because tank development times of less than 5 minutes may produce poor uniformity.

DEVELOPING ROLL AND 135 FILMS WITH *KODAK POLYDOL* DEVELOPER

Kodak Films in Rolls	Recommended Developing Time in Minutes									
	Small Tank (Agitation at 30-Second Intervals)					Large Tank (Agitation at 1-Minute Intervals)				
	18 C 65 F	20 C 68 F	21 C 70 F	22 C 72 F	24 C 75 F	18 C 65 F	20 C 68 F	21 C 70 F	22 C 72 F	24 C 75 F
Panatomic-X	6 ½	5 ½	5	4 ½†	3 ½†	7	6	5 ½	5	4†
Plus-X pan	6 ½	5 ½	4 ¼†	4 ¼†	3 ½†	7 ½	6	5 ½	4 ¾†	3 ¼†
Plus-X pan professional	6 ½	5 ½	4 ¼†	4 ¼†	3†	7 ½	6	5 ½	4 ¾†	3 ¾†
Royal-X pan	8	7	6 ½	6	5	9 ½	8 ½	8	7 ½	6 ½
Tri-X pan	8	7	6 ½	6	5	9	8	7 ½	7	6
Tri-X pan professional	10	9	8	7 ½	6 ½	11	10	9	8	7
Verichrome pan	8	6	5	4 ½†	4†	9	7 ½	6	5	4 ½†

†Not recommended because tank development times of less than 5 minutes may produce poor uniformity.

DEVELOPING LONG ROLL FILMS WITH *KODAK POLYDOL* DEVELOPER

Kodak Films in Long Rolls	Recommended Developing Time in Minutes				
	18 C 65 F	20 C 68 F	21 C 70 F	22 C 72 F	24 C 75 F
Ektapan 4162 (Estar thick base)	13	11	10	9	7 ½
Panatomic-X	—	6 ½	—	—	4 ¼
Plus-X pan	—	6 ½	—	—	4
Plus-X portrait 5068	—	6 ½	—	—	4
Plus-X pan professional 2147 (Estar base) Plus-X pan professional 4147 (*Estar* thick base)	—	9	—	—	5 ½
Royal pan 4141 (Estar thick base)	—	9	—	—	6
Tri-X pan	—	8 ½	—	—	6
Tri-X pan professional 4164 (Estar thick base)	—	10	—	—	7

the tank, or at a rate of approximately 22 ml (¾ fl oz) per 516 square centimetres (80 square inches) of film. If the carryout rate should vary, or if the average negatives are unusually dense or thin, it may be necessary to adjust the replenishment rate to keep the activity constant.

For films in long rolls, after each roll is developed, Kodak Polydol replenisher should be added to the developer tank as follows:

Size of film	Replenisher
35 mm by 100 ft	450 ml (15 fl oz)
46 mm by 100 ft	600 ml (20 fl oz)
70 mm by 100 ft	900 ml (30 fl oz)
3½ in by 75 ft	900 ml (30 fl oz)

Useful Capacity. Without replenishment, about 40 sheets of 8″ × 10″ film can be developed per 3.8 litres (1 gallon) of Kodak Polydol developer.

With replenishment, Kodak Polydol developer and Kodak Polydol replenisher have been designed to maintain constant developing characteristics for an indefinite period when the replenishment rate is properly adjusted. The replenishment rate should be checked by periodic monitoring of the developer activity. For this purpose, the use of Kodak control strips, 10-step (for professional black-and-white film), is suggested.

Although some sludge may appear, the working solution remains free from massive sludge formation as well as from staining tendency. Therefore, it should not need replacement for several months. However, it should be replaced if the activity increases or decreases markedly (which indicates that the replenishment rate needs revision); if the bath shows excessive sludging or develops staining or scumming tendency (usually the result of contamination, as with hypo); or if the bath has been exposed excessively to the air (which can be minimized by the use of a floating cover).

Storage Life. Unused Kodak Polydol developer and Polydol replenisher can be stored in a full, tightly stoppered glass bottle for 6 months; in a partially full, tightly stoppered glass bottle for 2 months; in a tank with a floating cover for 1 month; or in an open tray for 24 hours.

Paper Developers

Although practically any developing agent that can be used for negatives will develop papers, most of them are not suitable because of their tendency to stain, and because they give a colored image. In practice, the developing agents most commonly used in paper developers are amidol, paraminophenol, glycin, and the various combinations of metol and hydroquinone.

The great majority of photographic prints are developed in some combination of metol and hydroquinone. Such a developer is generally conceded to be the most economical, versatile, and convenient. By varying the proportion of its chemicals and using different amounts of bromide with compensating times of exposure and development, an M-Q developer can be made to yield a variety of contrasts and different tones ranging from blue-black to brown.

Fast, coarse-grained enlarging papers normally produce cold black to blue-black tones. For such papers, the proper developer is one containing metol and hydroquinone, with a large proportion of alkali and only sufficient bromide to prevent fog. When the true bromide papers were popular, developers containing diaminophenol, amidol, Acrol, and so on were used in order to secure richer blacks than these papers normally produced. When chlorobromide papers came into use, it was found that they did not react well to amidol; the results were usually greenish in overall color, with muddy shadow tones. For a while, amidol was considered obsolete, as a result. But in recent years some of the improved chlorobromide papers have been found to react well to amidol, producing very rich, deep blacks. Those who wish to use this developer, therefore, will simply have to try it on the paper they prefer, to see how it reacts.

Even with metol-hydroquinone paper developers, some papers tend to produce greenish blacks, especially if development time is shortened to compensate for slight overexposure. This effect can be countered by the use of one of the synthetic antifoggants, such as Benzotriazole (Kodak anti-fog No. 1) 6-nitrobenzimidazole nitrate, or a blue-black agent such as potassium thiocyanate. Full development in a full strength developer is the best guarantee of good image tone with fast chlorobromide papers. Shortened development may produce not only inferior blacks but also streaks, mottle, and other image defects.

Developers and Developing

Warm-toned papers contain a higher proportion of silver chloride and thus have finer grain. Such papers react best to developers having a lower alkali content and a higher proportion of potassium bromide. Still warmer tones can be produced by increased exposure and shortened development; however, underdevelopment must be avoided since it produces poor image quality and streaks. One way to secure the benefits of shortened development without image defects is simply to dilute the developer with two to three parts of water or to increase the potassium bromide content or both. Developers containing less active developing agents also tend to produce warmer tones; these include glycin and adurol (chlorhydroquinone). In all cases, though, a warm-toned paper must be employed to begin with; most of these development expedients produce little or no effect on fast, cold-toned papers.

Many attempts have been made to design developers that can expand or contract the exposure scale of a paper, in a rather false analogy to the contrast or gamma control of development in negatives. Few of these variable-contrast paper developers have had any success, and the best of them produce little more increase or decrease in print scale than the distance between two adjacent grades of paper. Mainly, such developers are useful for the making of minor adjustments of scale on portrait-style papers, which are often available only in a single normal grade. For example, on Kodak Ektalure paper, Kodak Selectol-Soft developer produces results that are about one contrast grade softer than those produced by Kodak Selectol developer.

Except for the production of certain very warm tones, dilution of a developer should be kept within the limits outlined by the manufacturer.

A popular paper developer is the well-known Kodak D-72 developer (a similar developer is sold in packaged form under the trademark Dektol). Almost every manufacturer has a developer of this type, and while there may be minor discrepancies in the various formulas, they are close enough so they may be considered the same for all practical purposes. These include GAF 125, DuPont 53D, Gevaert G.251, and Ilford ID-36. Note, though, that in the case of the Ilford ID-36 formula, only the published formula corresponds to D-72 developer; the packaged version of this formula contains phenidone instead of metol and is a different formulation.

Elon developing agent hydroquinone universal paper developer (Kodak D-72)

Stock solution

Water 52 C (about 125 F)	500.0 ml
Kodak Elon developing agent	3.1 g
Sodium sulfite	45.0 g
Hydroquinone	12.0 g
Sodium carbonate	67.5 g
Potassium bromide	1.0 g
Water to make	1.0 litres

Take 1 part stock solution, 2 parts water. Develop about 45 seconds at 21 C (70 F). For colder, blue-black tones, the developer is somewhat modified, and less bromide is used.

Cold-Tone Developers. Commercial photographers often prefer a colder, blue-black tone on prints of certain subject matter. In general, since print color is related to grain size, large grains producing a colder tone, small ones a warmer image, it is not as easy to secure cold tones by manipulation of the developer. Whereas diluted developers with a high concentration of bromide will produce warm tones on nearly any paper, attempting to use a concentrated developer with little bromide to secure blue-black tones often results only in fog and poor image tone. In general, you must use a paper that has a naturally cold tone, and if even colder results are desired, try the following formula (this developer is not available in packaged form).

Cold-tone developer
(For contact papers [Kodak D-73])

Stock solution

Water 52 C (about 125 F)	500.0 ml
Kodak Elon developing agent	2.8 g
Sodium sulfite	40.0 g
Hydroquinone	10.8 g
Sodium carbonate	75.0 g
Potassium bromide	0.8 g
Water to make	1.0 litre

For use take stock solution 1 part, water 2 parts. Develop for 45 seconds at 21 C (70 F).

Low-Contrast Developers. Portrait photographers often desire a developer that will produce somewhat softer prints on standard portrait papers, which are frequently available only in a single contrast grade. Only a very small reduction of contrast can be obtained in this way. Where this limited amount of control will suffice, a developer such as Kodak Selectol-Soft can be used. It is available in packaged form; the formula has not been published. This produces results similar to the D-52 developer, but with lower contrast. The formula for D-52 developer is given below.

Warm-Tone Developers. A wide variety of tones ranging from warm black to rich browns and sepias is possible by variation of developer formula. It is important to remember, though, that the tone is also affected by the type of paper in use. The faster neutral-tone papers will produce only warm blacks and brown-blacks, while the naturally warm-tone papers will, in the same developers, produce tones from brown-black to very warm browns. It is necessary, therefore, to try the developer and paper of your choice together to determine whether the combination will produce the desired tone.

Elon developing agent hydroquinone developer (Kodak D-52)

Stock solution

Water 52 C (125 F)	500.0 cc
Kodak Elon developing agent	1.5 g
Sodium sulfite, desiccated	22.5 g
Hydroquinone	6.3 g
Sodium carbonate, monohydrated	15.0 g
Potassium bromide	1.5 g
Add cold water to make	1.0 litre

Dissolve chemicals in the order given. For Kodak studio proof, Kodabromide, Azo, Kodabrome RC, Ektalure, Panalure, Panalure portrait, and Portralure papers, use stock solution one part, water one part. Develop about 2 minutes at 20 C (68 F). More bromide can be added if warmer tones are desired. This developer produces results similar to those provided by Kodak Selectol developer.

Developing Data

The specific developing times given in this article are valid at the time of printing. Since recommendations are changed as product changes occur, it is wise to check for current recommendations given in instruction sheets packaged with film, or in recent literature published by the manufacturer.

• *See also:* ACTIVATOR; AGITATION; ALKALI; ANTIFOGGANT; BLACK-AND-WHITE PRINTING; CHEMISTRY OF PHOTOGRAPHY; COLOR FILM PROCESSING; COMPENSATING DEVELOPER; CONTRAST; DESENSITIZING; DEVELOPMENT; DIRECT POSITIVE PROCESSING; DRUM AND TUBE PROCESSING; DRYING FILMS AND PRINTS; FIXERS AND FIXING; FORMULAS FOR BLACK-AND-WHITE PROCESSING; MIXING PHOTOGRAPHIC SOLUTIONS; REPLENISHMENT; RESTRAINERS; TANKS.

Further Reading: Eastman Kodak Co. *How to Use* KODAK *Developer D-76,* pub. No. AJ-16. Rochester, NY: Eastman Kodak Co., 1976; ———. KODAK HC-110 *Developer,* pub. No. J-13. Rochester, NY: Eastman Kodak Co., 1976; ———. KODAK POLYDOL *Developer,* pub. No. J-23. Rochester, NY: Eastman Kodak Co., 1974; ———. *Processing Chemicals and Formulas,* pub. No. J-1. Rochester, NY: Eastman Kodak Co., 1977; Feininger, Andreas. *Darkroom Techniques,* Vol. 2. Englewood Cliffs, NJ: Prentice-Hall, Inc., 1974; Hertzberg, Robert. *Elementary Developing and Printing.* Garden City, NY: Amphoto, 1973; Jacobson, C.I., and L.A. Mannheim. *Developing: The Technique of the Negative,* 18th ed. Garden City, NY: Amphoto, 1972; Litzel, Otto. *Darkroom Magic,* 2nd ed. Garden City, NY: Amphoto, 1975; Mason, L.F. *Photographic Processing Chemistry,* 2nd ed. New York, NY: Halsted Press, 1976.

 **Development**

In photography, development is the process by which an invisible latent image in an emulsion is made visible. In black-and-white emulsions, the image is composed of grains of black metallic silver; in color emulsions, the developed silver is replaced by cyan, magenta, and yellow dyes.

Almost all development today is *chemical development:* A developing agent chemically breaks down, or reduces, exposed silver halide crystals to form grains of silver. However, a latent image can also be made visible by *physical development.* In this process, silver carried in the developing solution is deposited onto exposed halide crystals to form the image. Although it produces a very fine-grain image, physical development is seldom used today because it requires a long time—typically 25 to 30 minutes—and because many modern materials do not respond well to it.

The developed image, although visible, is not usable or permanent until the undeveloped silver halide is removed by fixation, and the soluble chemicals are removed by washing.

Developing Agents

Chemical compounds that can efficiently reduce exposed silver halides are called developing agents. Every developing solution must contain one or more such agents. Various agents differ in activity. That is, at the same time and temperature, an active agent will reduce more halide crystals than a less active agent; or, at a constant temperature, the more active agent will reduce the same number of halide crystals in a shorter time. Thus, activity is an expression of developing rate. It can be increased by raising the temperature or, with some agents, by increasing the alkalinity of the solution.

The characteristics of a developing solution are determined by the developing agents it contains, as well as by other ingredients and their concentration. As shown in the accompanying table, developing agents differ in the degree of grain and contrast they produce in images, as well as in the speed at which they work. "Graininess" is a visual impression of statistical clumps of silver grains in the image, and is primarily determined by emulsion characteristics. It becomes visible only when the image is magnified. Contrast is the difference in the density of silver grains in one area of a developed image as compared with another area.

Developing Solutions

Developers are solutions of one or more developing agents in water, along with other chemicals that help provide the desired keeping and working properties.

In addition to a solvent (water) and developing agents, the other ingredients of a typical black-and-white developer formula include:

1. *Preservative,* which keeps the oxygen of the air and that released during the chemical reactions of development from attacking the developing agents and reducing their effectiveness.
2. *Accelerator,* an alkali (most developing agents will not act, or will act only slightly on halide in a neutral solution; the degree of alkalinity is an important factor in developer activity).

CHARACTERISTICS OF DEVELOPING AGENTS IN MODERATELY ALKALINE SOLUTION*

Agent	Activity	Contrast	Grain
Amidol	Very high	Normal	Medium
Phenidone, Dimezone	High	Low	Medium
Metol (*Kodak Elon;* Photol; Pictol)	High	Very low	Medium
Pyrocatechin	Moderate	Normal to high	Medium
Rodinal (*Kodelon*)	Moderate	Low	Medium
Glycin	Slow	Moderately low	Medium
Hydroquinone	Slow	High	Moderately coarse
Paraphenylene-diamine	Very slow	Low	Fine

*Most agents are commonly used in highly alkaline solutions, which increase their activity significantly. Chemical formulas and other characteristics are given in the individual entries for each of the developing agents.

3. *Restrainer,* which holds down the tendency of developing agents to reduce unexposed as well as exposed halide crystals, an action that would produce non-image-forming density called chemical fog (some formulas—particularly those using powerful agents such as Phenidone—also require the addition of an antifoggant such as Benzotriazole to suppress the formation of fog density).

The article DEVELOPERS AND DEVELOPING explains further the functions of these ingredients and gives formulas for a number of developers.

Silver Halide Exposure and Development

Silver halide crystals—predominantly silver bromide*—are present in equal numbers in all parts of an emulsion. (See the accompanying illustration.) The number of crystals affected by exposure depends on the intensity of the light and the duration of the exposure. The crystals are of different sizes. In a typical film emulsion, the larger crystals may be about 15 times as large as the smallest ones. The larger ones are more light sensitive. It is this variation in size, with variations in sensitivity, that makes continuous-tone images possible.

In crystals struck by sufficient exposure, some silver ions are released from their bonds with bromine ions. They are trapped around sensitivity specks of silver sulfide in or on the surface of the crystals, forming potential development centers. In heavily exposed areas, many crystals are affected; in less exposed areas, only a few are affected.

The affected (exposed) crystals make up a latent image that must be amplified (increased in strength) to become visible. Development is the amplifying process.

If exposure is too weak, any of these things can occur:

1. No crystals are affected.
2. Some silver ions are released, but recombine with free bromine ions before

they become trapped at a sensitivity speck.
3. Not enough silver ions are trapped to make a development center of sufficient size; although exposed, the crystal is not developable.

As a result, no visible image will be produced.

The Development Process

The process of silver halide image development is the same for negative and positive films and papers, in both black-and-white and color. When an exposed emulsion is placed in a developer, the developing agent attacks the crystals at their development centers. These centers are specks of silver sulfide that have trapped the silver ions released by the action of the exposing energy (light, ultraviolet rays, infrared rays, x-rays, etc., depending on the sensitivity of the emulsion). The predominant halide in most emulsions is silver bromide. The developing agent rapidly reduces exposed crystals to black metallic silver and bromine. Part of the bromine is absorbed by the gelatin of the emulsion and is removed by the final washing; most of the bromine combines with chemicals in the solution to form by-products that are left in the used developer when the film or paper is removed.

If the developer activity is high enough, or if development time is extended long enough, every exposed halide grain will be completely reduced to metallic silver. This is called *infinity development.* However, development is seldom carried this far because the densities of the most heavily exposed portions (the highlights of a negative) would become so great that printing light could not pass through. Consequently, it is common to stop development at a point when the highlights have reached suitable densities that remain printable.

Densities in the least exposed areas of the negative (those light sections that represent the dark or shadow areas of the photographed scene) build up more slowly, because there are fewer exposed crystals for the developer to work on, and their development centers are smaller and therefore less easily attacked. In some cases, such areas will not have reached printable densities by the time the highlights are suitably developed. This can sometimes be avoided by using a formula that provides *compensating development,* in which the action of the devel-

---

*Most films have silver bromide, with slight amounts of silver iodide, that makes imperfections in the silver bromide crystals. These imperfections provide locations for the sensitivity specks. Contact papers usually contain mostly silver chloride crystals, while enlarging papers are mixtures of silver bromide and chloride crystals.

Silver Halide Exposure and Development

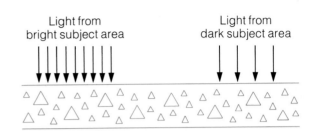

Light from bright subject area   Light from dark subject area

Silver halide crystals—predominantly silver bromide—are present in equal numbers in all parts of an emulsion. The number of crystals affected by exposure depends upon the intensity of the light and the duration of the exposure.

In heavily exposed areas, many crystals are affected; in less exposed areas, only a few are affected.

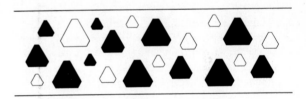

When the developer penetrates the emulsion, the developing agent attacks at the development centers and reduces exposed crystals to metallic silver. Virtually no unexposed crystals are reduced if the formula includes sufficient restrainer or antifoggant.

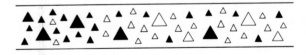

Exposure is the primary determinant of density in the shadow areas of the negative. With proper exposure, only sufficient silver will be formed there by the time development is stopped to keep highlight densities within a printable range.

Fixing and washing remove all remaining halides. Only metallic silver remains in the gelatin to form the image.

Development

oper slows progressively in the highlights as more and more silver is developed there, but proceeds without change in the shadow areas. Thus, the slightly exposed areas can build up to printable densities while the highlights are kept below the point where they begin to block up.

Films are usually developed to the point at which the density range is suitable for making prints. Prints are developed to a point that approaches infinity development, so that the blacks of the image will have maximum density. Variations in contrast are achieved by choosing different paper grades. Overdevelopment of prints leads to chemical fog of the highlights.

Subsequent Steps

Once development has progressed to a desired point, it must be stopped. If the emulsion is simply removed from the developer, solution absorbed by the gelatin will continue to act, with uneven results. If a water rinse is used, residual developer will be flushed out of the emulsion (or diluted to ineffectiveness) in a minute or so, but that may be a significant percentage of the total developing time, and again the results may be uneven. Because a developer is an alkaline solution, it can be neutralized by an acid solution. A one- to three-percent solution of acetic acid in water is the most common stop bath used. It completely halts developer action in 10 to 15 seconds, and thus is particularly useful in accurately controlling the short development times used with modern films and papers.

All silver halides that are not developed must be removed from the emulsion. Otherwise they would eventually be reduced by the cumulative effects of light, thus obscuring the developed image. The halides are insoluble in water. A fixing solution of sodium or ammonium thiosulfate converts the halides to soluble compounds that are removed by a final wash. Treatment in a washing aid such as Kodak hypo clearing agent increases the solubility of the compounds and significantly reduces the time required to wash emulsions, and especially paper bases, clean.

Fine-Grain Development

While there is considerable difference in the size of the silver grains in different emulsions, none of them individually is large enough to cause trouble in photographic work. The mottled effect at great enlargement, noticeable especially in the lighter tones of a photograph, is caused by the statistical clumping of grains during development. In an ordinary photographic emulsion, there are about six to ten layers of these grains, and while they are very evenly distributed in the emulsion during manufacture, the random distribution of various size grains in a processed film causes variations in micro density that give the appearance of clumps of grains. When enlarged sufficiently, this shows up in the print as the salt and pepper effect called graininess. Individual grain size varies quite generally with the speed of the emulsion, the faster emulsions having larger grains. Naturally the effect of clumping is more noticeable proportionately as the grains are larger, so the trouble is greater with fast emulsions than with slow, and "fine-grain" emulsions gain their immunity at a sacrifice of speed.

The first interest in fine grain was manifested between 1904 and 1920 by astronomers and other scientists who were interested in getting the utmost resolving power out of photographic emulsions. During the 1920s, the motion-picture industry became greatly concerned with the problem; and after 1930, the enormous increase in the use of miniature cameras and high-speed films, and the need of gigantic enlargements for photo-murals, made it acute.

In 1927, Eastman Kodak Company, as a result of the researches of Capstaff and Purdy, announced its famous fine-grain formula developer, D-76 which was the prototype of many other developers working on the same principle of low alkalinity and a very high concentration of sodium sulfite that has a solvent action on the silver grains, reducing their size and minimizing graininess. During development, the image is also probably somewhat augmented by a form of physical development, the silver bromide dissolved by the great amount of sulfite being converted into a silver salt from which silver is liberated by the developer and deposited upon the image. This type of developer gives negatives that are sufficiently fine-grained for many purposes. It is clean-working, long-lived, utilizes the maximum film speed, and even with coarse-grained, high-speed emulsions gives enlargements up to about ten diameters without troublesome grain.

As early as 1904, attention had been called to the fine-grained image produced by paraphenylenediamine, but in any formulas known at the time it resulted in great loss of emulsion speed, excessive development time, and at best a thin, flat negative. In 1928, workers applied the principle of a high concentration of sodium sulfite to paraphenylenediamine, producing very fine-grained negatives with a 1-hour development, but with a prohibitive loss of emulsion speed. In 1933, with the addition of trisodium phosphate, to which attention had been called by the Lumière brothers and Seyewetz in 1895, and metol, the developing time was reduced to 7 minutes. In the same year, Purdon announced a formula combining paraphenylenediamine with glycin, which was the first of many formulas along that line.

In 1934, Dr. Sease of the DuPont Film Laboratories announced a group of four formulas, all of which contained the same proportions of paraphenylenediamine and sodium sulfite, but with glycin varying from none at all to 12 grams per 1000 cc. The fineness of grain is in indirect ratio to the amount of glycin. With no glycin, or with amounts up to 2 grams per litre, three to four times normal exposure is required for fast films, although little or no increase in exposure is needed with the slower, fine-grained films. With 2 or more grams of glycin per litre, the exposure is cut to about two times normal, but with graininess increasing with the amount of glycin used. While these developers immediately became very popular, the loss of speed in the emulsion was a great handicap to their use.

All of this work on "fine-grain" processing was done with the intention of making big enlargements possible from small negatives. There was a tacit assumption that reducing grain size would also produce an image that was sharper and contained finer detail. Later investigations on the subject of fine-grain developers, and especially those of the solvent type, showed that the latter assumption was not true; the solvent developers not only removed silver from the image, they also redeposited it. The result often was a noticeable image diffusion that made "fine-grain" images actually less sharp than those processed in conventional developers, even though the latter had demonstrably coarser, and in some cases, obtrusive, grain.

It was becoming evident that for both fine-grain and maximum image detail, it would be necessary to design new film types, having, among other things,

thinner coatings. New sensitizers made it possible to increase the speed of fine-grain emulsions without losing the graininess advantage. Here, though, a new problem arose. The solvent-type developers reacted badly with the new films; the dissolved silver was redeposited as dichroic fog, stain, and other defects. Today, developers like Kodak DK-20 have been completely abandoned for this reason, and, in fact, instructions supplied with modern fine-grain films distinctly warn against the use of DK-20 developer or any other solvent-type developer.

About 1944, Kodak introduced two new developers to replace DK-20; they are D-23 and D-25, respectively. D-23 is a simple metol-sulfite developer, with some slight compensating action. D-25 was considered a true fine-grain developer at the time, depending upon the solvent action of the sulfite, rather than on the addition of a separate solvent such as thiocyanate. D-23 developer is still used to some extent, but D-25 developer may also react with modern fine-grain films to produce stain or dichroic fog. (For formulas and use, *see* DEVELOPERS AND DEVELOPING.)

Special Development

There are two modifications of normal developer formulation or developing procedure that are useful in reducing contrast, especially in cases of overexposure. They are split, or two-bath, development and water-bath development. Both methods appear to work satisfactorily with older films, such as Kodak Super-XX pan film 4142, but not with many films introduced in recent years. Both are procedures to be experimented with before processing films with valuable exposures.

Split Development. Virtually any developer formula can be divided into two separate solutions. The first consists of the solvent, the developing agents, and the preservative. The second consists of the solvent, the activator (accelerator), and the restrainer. When a film is immersed in the first solution, virtually no development takes place because there is no activator to provide the alkalinity that most developing agents require to become active. The film simply absorbs the developing-agent solution; the maximum necessary time is about 3 minutes. When the film is transferred to the second solution, the developing agents are immediately activated. The amount of development is limited, however, by how much the emulsion can absorb in the first bath. In the heavily exposed, highlight areas, the developer is quickly exhausted because there is such a large amount of halide for it to work on. In less exposed areas, there is the same quantity of developing agent available, but less halide to be developed, so the action continues longer than in the highlights. This is a self-limiting procedure. Developer in the highlights is exhausted before excess density can be formed, while shadow areas build to greater density and local contrast until the developer there is also exhausted. Again, the practical time limit is about 3 minutes. This procedure restricts overall contrast, and it eliminates the need for controlling time and temperature precisely. The emulsion can absorb only so much in the first bath, and after a certain period of time, exhaustion stops development in the second bath. As long as the temperature is within the normal working range, around 21 C (70 F), only overly long soaking times—which would cause the gelatin emulsion to swell and soften excessively—could cause a problem. It is essential that none of the second bath ever be mixed or splashed into the first bath; that would add activator, and development would begin in the first bath, making the results unpredictable.

As an example of split developer formulation, here is the formula for Kodak D-76 developer, probably the most widely used film developer in the world.

Kodak D-76 Developer
Water, 50 C (125 F)	750 ml (solvent)
Kodak Elon developing agent	2 g (developing agent)
Sodium Sulfite (Anhydrous)	100 g (preservative)
Hydroquinone	5 g (developing agent)
Borax (granular)	2 g (activator)
Water to make	1 litre

(D-76 developer does not require a restrainer.)

"Split D-76 developer" can be made up this way:

Solution A, split *D-76 developer*
Water, 50 C (125 F)	750 ml
Kodak Elon developing agent	2 g
Sodium sulfite (anhydrous)	100 g
Hydroquinone	5 g
Water to make	1 litre

Solution B,* Split *D-76 Developer*
Water, 50 C (125 F)	750 ml
Borax (granular)	60 g
Water to make	1 litre

For use at normal temperatures, immerse film in Solution A for 3 minutes; drain; immerse in Solution B for 3 minutes; rinse in stop bath; fix, wash, and dry in usual manner.

Water Bath Development. A two-bath procedure for controlling contrast and building shadow detail can use plain water as the second bath and a normally compounded developer as the first bath. The film is immersed in the developer for about half the usual time then transferred to the water bath. The developer is more quickly diluted to ineffectiveness in the highlight areas than in the shadow areas. Therefore, development continues there, building density, without further buildup in the highlights. This technique is effective primarily with sheet films and with prints. The emulsion must lie absolutely still in the water; any agitation will wash the developer out of the shadow areas and diffuse it over the whole image area, eliminating the differential action. Also, the emulsion must lie flat in a tray of water; if it is vertical, gravity will cause development by-products and developer diffusing out of the emulsion to flow down across the face of the image, causing streaking or uneven development. The film may be transferred back to the developer and returned to the water bath any number of times, although four or five times is a practical limit. Fresh water should be used each time to prevent buildup of by-products that would restrain or otherwise affect subsequent development.

Color Development
Color materials have silver halide emulsions that also contain color couplers. (There are a few exceptions, notably Kodachrome film. *See:* COLOR FILM PROCESSING.) As the exposed halides are reduced by developing agents, the used developing agents combine with the color couplers to form dyes.

---

*If a formula includes a restrainer or antifoggant, it is included in the B solution. Note that a greatly increased quantity of activator is called for; this insures long term usability of the solution.

Development

The three basic color dyes—cyan, magenta and yellow—result from three different couplers located in the three respective film layers. The dye densities are in direct proportion to the silver image densities. This silver image and dye-forming process occurs simultaneously as a negative film is developed. In color reversal materials, the first developer produces a negative silver image. The remaining halides are then sensitized chemically or by reexposure to white light and developed. The second development produces a positive silver image and a corresponding dye image. (Also, the second developer may contain a fogging agent that makes exposure to light or a separate sensitization unnecessary.) All the silver is then bleached, or converted into silver halide, and removed by a fixing bath, leaving only color dye images.

Other Methods of Development

Although the most common procedure is to immerse an emulsion in a liquid solution for development, other methods may be used. Some automatic processing machines spray developer on continuous lengths of film or paper as they move past. An exposed emulsion may be covered with a thick paste or jellylike coating of developing substance. Or it may be pressed in contact with a material soaked in a developer. (*See:* BIMAT PROCESS; DIFFUSION TRANSFER PROCESS.)

Tanning Development. This type of development toughens (tans) the gelatin of an emulsion in proportion to the amount of silver developed in each area of the image. When the unhardened gelatin is removed, a gelatin relief image remains. It may be used for dye transfer, photo-silkscreen, lithographic, and other methods of reproduction.

Stain Development. This produces a color in the gelatin in proportion to the amount of silver developed there. Although the silver densities may be slight, the stain is opaque to printing light, and therefore increases the effective densities in the image.

Whatever method of development is used, the action of reducing exposed halides to metallic silver is essentially the same, and is basic to nearly all photographic processes.

• *See also:* ACTIVATOR; ACUTANCE; ADJACENCY EFFECTS; BIMAT PROCESS; BLOCKED HIGHLIGHTS; CHEMISTRY OF PHOTOGRAPHY; COLOR FILM PROCESSING; DENSITOMETRY; DEVELOPERS AND DEVELOPING; DIFFUSION TRANSFER PROCESS; DIRECTIONAL EFFECTS; DIRECT POSITIVE PROCESSING; DYE DESTRUCTION COLOR PROCESS; EDGE EFFECT; EMULSIONS; FIXERS AND FIXING; HALIDE; LATENT IMAGE; REDUCTION; SILVER BROMIDE; SILVER HALIDES; STABILIZATION PROCESS; STOP BATH; SUPERADDITIVITY; TANNING DEVELOPER.

Further Reading: Eastman Kodak Co. *Creative Darkroom Techniques.* Rochester, NY: Eastman Kodak Co., 1973; Litzel, Otto. *Darkroom Magic,* 2nd ed. Garden City, NY: Amphoto, 1975; Mason, L. F. *Photographic Processing Chemistry,* 2nd ed. London, England: Focal Press, 1976; Mortensen, William. *Mortensen on the Negative.* New York, NY: Simon and Schuster, 1940; Vickers, John. *Making and Printing Color Negatives.* Hastings-on-the-Hudson, NY: Morgan and Morgan, 1971.

Diaminophenol

2,4-Diaminophenol Dihydrochloride; Acrol; Amidol; Diamol

A very rapid working developing agent requiring only sodium sulfite as both preservative and alkali. Even with sulfite it oxidizes rapidly, and cannot be kept as a stock solution. It was formerly very popular in developers for bromide papers, but produces inferior tones with modern enlarging papers that contain both silver bromide and silver chloride.
Formula: $(NH_2)_2C_6H_3OH \cdot 2HCl$
Molecular Weight: 197.07

Fine white or bluish-gray crystals, soluble in water, slightly soluble in alcohol. Reduction potential 35.0.

Diaphragm

A diaphragm, or stop, is a device used to limit the diameter of the bundle of light rays that passes through a lens. It is used to control the brightness of the image formed and the sharpness of the image by partially correcting many of the lens aberrations.

Types of Diaphragms

Depending on its design, a diaphragm may provide fixed or adjustable stops. Fixed stops are limited to one or, at most, a few openings of predetermined size; adjustable stops can be changed continuously from the minimum opening through which a useful image can be formed to the maximum clear diameter of the lens.

Waterhouse Stops. The simplest fixed stop—so-called because its function is to stop a certain portion of the light—is a hole in a metal plate that is inserted in front of, behind, or between the elements of a lens. Invented in 1858 by John Waterhouse, sets of such stops were used with most photographic lenses in the second half of the 19th century. Today, Waterhouse stops are used with some process lenses in photomechanical reproduction, and with some fisheye lenses.

Rotating and Strip Stops. The idea of a single device with a series of fixed-diameter openings has been used in two major ways. One is a disc that rotates in front of or within the lens barrel to bring the desired opening into position. The other is a rectangular strip that slides left to right or up and down to change from one size to another. The strip was once widely used on simple box cameras. Neither device is used in modern equipment to any significant extent.

Slotted Blades. An opening of variable size can be formed by two overlapping blades with tapering slots. As the blades move, the tapers cause the size of the opening between them to change. This is a common device in simple adjustable cameras. It has the disadvantage that the opening is not necessarily circular, which can have some effect on image sharpness. In practice, this is not a serious drawback because of the simple lenses commonly used in such cameras and the fact that the pictures are seldom enlarged to any great degree. A single rotating blade with a curved slot over a dumbbell-shaped opening, in a fixed plate, and controlled by the output from a photocell, has been used in some simple, automatic-exposure cameras.

Iris Diaphragm. Virtually all lenses of good quality today have built-in iris diaphragms that provide continuous control over the diameter of the

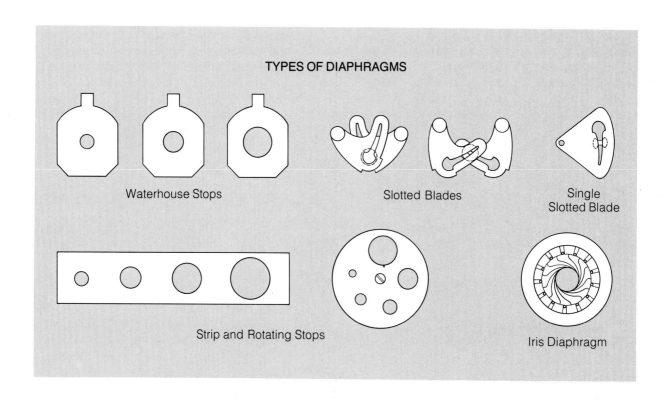

TYPES OF DIAPHRAGMS

Waterhouse Stops

Slotted Blades

Single Slotted Blade

Strip and Rotating Stops

Iris Diaphragm

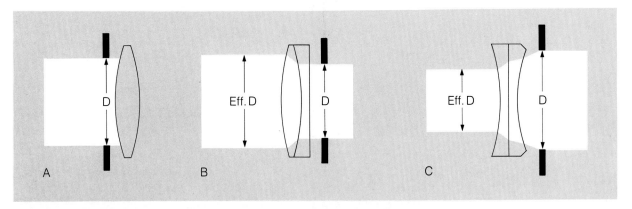

(Left) When the diaphragm in in front of the lens, the real and effective diameters are equal. (Center) In a converging lens system, the effective diameter is larger; the lens refracts a bundle of parallel incident light rays to the smaller, real diameter of the diaphragm. (Right) A diverging lens expands a bundle with a smaller effective diameter to fill the real diameter of the diaphragm.

aperture. The iris consists of a series of overlapping curved blades that move in unison as a setting ring or lever is moved, forming a circle of any desired diameter. Usually the setting ring is marked with *f*-numbers that show the series of positions that result in the amount of light passed being doubled or halved. Often the full *f*-stop and half *f*-stop positions have notches or detents so the setting ring clicks into place.

Automatic Diaphragms. Many lenses have automatic diaphragms that couple to camera shutter and metering systems. They remain fully open to provide the brightest image for viewing and focusing in cameras that have through-the-lens viewing systems, then automatically close down to the required aperture when the shutter is released. The aperture may have been selected by the photographer and set on the lens aperture ring or on a corresponding coupled camera control. In shutter-preferred automatic exposure control systems, the photographer selects a shutter speed and the camera's metering system closes the diaphragm to the aperture required for proper exposure at a given film speed.

Brightness Control

The amount of light a lens passes depends primarily on the area of the diaphragm opening or aperture and the way in which the lens refracts light. Because a diaphragm opening is usually circular, it is easier to measure the diameter than the area of the

aperture. At any given diaphragm setting, the brightness of the image is related to how far behind the lens the image is formed. The marked series of aperture settings—the *f*-numbers or *f*-stops—is determined by the relationship between the lens focal length and the effective diameter of the diaphragm opening.

Real and Effective Diameters. The *real diameter* of an aperture is the actual physical size of the opening (see the accompanying illustration). If the opening is not circular, the real diameter is the diameter of a circle that has the same area as the opening.

The *effective diameter* is the diameter of the bundle of light rays that, as they strike the lens, parallel to the axis, are refracted to just fill the real diameter of the diaphragm opening. When the diaphragm is in front of the lens, the real and effective diameters are equal. In conventional normal-focal-length or telephoto lenses, the diaphragm is usually behind a converging lens element or group. In that case, the real diameter is smaller than the effective diameter because the bundle of light rays is made smaller by diffraction. When the diaphragm is behind a diverging lens element or group—as in an inverted telephoto type of wide-angle lens—the light rays are spread by refraction, and the real diameter is larger than the effective diameter.

To measure the effective diameter of a between-the-lens diaphragm setting, sight through the front of the lens and measure the diameter of the image of the opening. A light background behind the lens

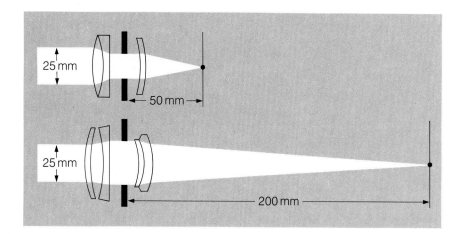

When focused on an object at infinity, lenses form images at distances equal to their focal lengths. Although both lenses are adjusted to apertures of the same effective diameter, the image formed by the 200 mm lens will be 1/16th as bright as that formed by the 50 mm lens.

makes it easier to see the size of the opening. The image will be larger or smaller than the actual diameter in the same degree that light rays entering the lens are converged or diverged. This measurement is also called the entrance pupil of the lens at a given aperture; it is sometimes used to determine exposure compensation in very close-up photography. (*See:* PHOTOMACROGRAPHY.) It is seldom necessary to measure the effective diameter directly; as explained in the section on *f*-numbers, it can be determined from the focal length and the *f*-number.

Image Brightness. If two lenses that form images of a subject at the same distance from the lens at different lens-to-film distances (and thus have different focal lengths) are set to apertures that have the same effective diameters, the images will differ in brightness. The degree of difference can be determined from the ratio of the squares of the lens-to-film distances. Using the accompanying illustration of a 50 mm lens and a 200 mm lens, the difference can be determined in various ways:

1. From the inverse square law:

$$\frac{50^2}{200^2} = \frac{2500}{40,000} = \frac{1}{16}$$

2. From the ratio of the *f*-values of the two apertures:

$$\frac{50}{25} = f/2; \frac{200}{25} = f/8;$$
$$\frac{2^2}{8^2} = \frac{4}{64} = \frac{1}{16}$$

3. By counting full stops between the two *f*-values, with a brightness change of ½ × at each stop:

Stop:	$f/2$	$f/2.8$	$f/4$	$f/5.6$	$f/8$
Relative brightness:	1	½	¼	⅛	1/16

If the effective diameter of the 200 mm lens aperture is increased to 100 mm, then it will have the same *f*-value as the 50 mm lens, and the images will be equally bright.

$$\frac{200}{100} = f/2; \frac{50}{25} = f/2$$

The difference in the image brightness can be determined by the ratios of the square of the lens-to-film distances because each image point is effectively illuminated by a corresponding point source at the optical center of the lens. (*See:* INVERSE SQUARE LAW.) For the more distant image to have the same brightness as the near image, the effective diameter of that lens would have to be larger. In other words, the light-passing capability of any lens is a function of the ratio between the lens focal length and the effective diameter of the diaphragm aperture. From this relationship it is possible to derive a series of numbered diaphragm openings that will change the amount of light passing through the lens by 2× or ½× at each step. In addition, the series can apply to all lenses so that when a variety of lenses are all set to the same numbered aperture, they will all pass almost the same amount of light regardless of differences in focal length. (There are second-order differences depending on the amount of light absorbed by the glass lens elements and on the amount of light lost by reflection from the glass-air surfaces of the lens elements.)

f-Numbers. The diaphragm settings are called *f*-stops, and are designated by *f*-numbers. The numbers are obtained by the formula:

$$f\text{-number} = \frac{\text{Lens focal length}}{\text{Effective diameter of diaphragm}}$$

As explained more fully in the article *f*-NUMBER, the standard series is: 1, 1.4, 2, 2.8, 4, 5.6, 8, 11, 16, 22, 32, 45, 64, 90. In lens manufacture, the markings on the aperture-setting ring are determined by adjusting the diaphragm until its effective diameter, when divided into the lens focal length, produces one of the above numbers. That position is marked and numbered accordingly. The lowest *f*-number setting represents the maximum light-passing power of the lens. (It may not be one of the above series, depending on the maximum effective diameter obtainable with that lens. But all succeeding positions as the diaphragm is closed will correspond to numbers in the standard series.)

Each time the aperture setting is changed from one *f*-number to the next higher number, the amount of light transmitted is reduced by one-half because the *area* (not the effective diameter) of the diaphragm opening is cut in half; as a result, the image is also reduced to half its previous brightness. Changing from one *f*-number to the next lower numbered setting doubles the aperture area, the amount of light passed, and the image brightness.

When it is necessary to know the effective diameter of any aperture setting of a lens, the above formula can be used in this way:

$$\text{Effective diameter} = \frac{\text{Focal length}}{f\text{-number}}$$

Image Sharpness

With a simple single-element lens, a diaphragm can improve image sharpness by cutting off light rays that pass through the outer edges of the lens. (See the accompanying illustration.) That is the region where the lens is least likely to be well-corrected, so light rays passing through there may not be bent (refracted) to come to focus at the same point as rays passing through the central portion of the lens. The diaphragm can be placed either in front of or behind the lens, but is always placed on the concave side of the lens.

A more important aspect of image sharpness is to use the diaphragm aperture to control depth of field. As the diaphragm is stopped down, the depth of field increases, with the result that the range of sharpness of the image also increases. (See the accompanying diagram.) This is because the extreme rays from points not exactly at the focused distance form increasingly smaller angles at the focal plane as the diaphragm is stopped down. Thus, those points are imaged as smaller, more distinct circles and appear sharper. At a certain size, the circles are no longer distinguishable from the points imaged exactly at the focal plane and therefore appear equally as sharp. The critical size of this "circle of confusion" depends on the degree to which the image will be enlarged.

The rays shown are axial, but stopping down the lens improves rays coming from off-axis angles as well; in the outer field this reduces the effects of some other aberrations such as field curvature, which does not actually flatten the field, but gives increased sharpness due to increased depth-of-field.

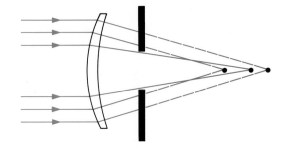
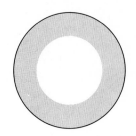

Limits of Stopping Down for Increased Sharpness. Although smaller openings give greater depth of field—which increases the range of reasonable sharpness when photographing three-dimensional subjects—critical examination of details in the plane of accurate focus will show that they are less sharply recorded when the aperture becomes very small. This is caused by diffraction of light rays that strike the edge of the diaphragm opening. (See the accompanying illustration.) The smallest opening on camera lenses is usually determined by the diffraction effect. For example, 50 mm lenses on 35 mm cameras will usually not stop down farther than $f/16$. Diffraction is usually only a problem with large-format and process lenses that close to $f/45$ and smaller. The resulting loss of sharpness is especially noticeable in copying and reproduction work where the subject is flat and two-dimensional.

The Best Opening. The particular lens opening that produces the sharpest image varies somewhat from one lens to another, but almost always neither the smallest nor the largest lens opening produces the best image sharpness. Wide open, the sharpness is reduced by undercorrected lens aberrations; stopped down, the sharpness of the image is reduced by diffraction.

Maximum sharpness with most lenses is obtainable at apertures somewhere between the maximum and minimum openings, where the aberrations have been minimized by stopping down, but not stopping down so far that diffraction has become a major factor. The results of resolving power tests of various lenses, which are frequently printed in photographic magazines, show which apertures are best for each lens tested. In photographing subjects that have depth, you may not be able to use the aperture that produces optimum sharpness because the required depth of field necessitates a smaller aperture.

The illustration of $13\times$ enlargements from four test negatives shows how changing the aperture affects the resolving power of a lens. The lens used was an $f/11$ 18-inch process lens. The four series at different apertures were enlarged 13 times from the original $\frac{5}{16}$-inch negative strips. Stopping down from $f/11$ to $f/16$ produced improved resolving power—the best results were obtained from $f/16$ to $f/22$. From $f/22$ on down to $f/90$, the definition became poorer due to diffraction.

With fast lenses used on 35 mm cameras, the best definition is usually achieved at about $f/8$. The accompanying table shows the resolving power of a 50 mm $f/1.4$ normal-focal-length lens for a 35 mm camera.

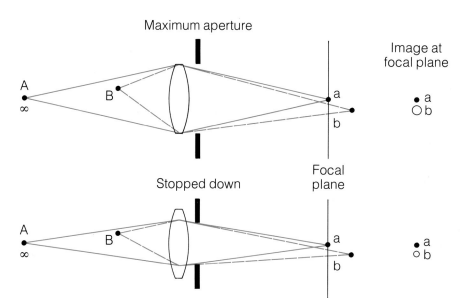

Maximum aperture

Stopped down

Image at focal plane

Focal plane

(Above) At the focal plane, extreme rays forming the image of a near point (B) create a large cirlce (b). Focused point (A) is imaged sharply (a). (Below) Reducing the diaphragm diameter also reduces the angle of image-forming rays. The circle at (b) is much smaller than that above, so the image of (B) appears more distinct. If this "circle of confusion" is small enough, the eye cannot detect it in the final image, and (b) looks as sharp as (a). When the lens is focused on a point closer than infinity, points both nearer and farther away will be imaged more sharply as the diaphragm is closed.

Diaphragm

Light rays striking the edges of very small apertures are diffracted, causing some light to scatter outward. The result is a soft-edged circle (a) rather than a sharp image (b) of a subject point. This effect counteracts the sharpness gained from increased depth-of-field at small openings. Further stopping down would only decrease sharpness more.

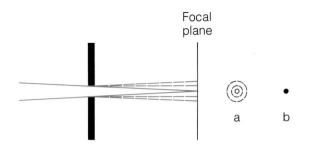

RESOLVING POWER OF A 50 mm *f*/1.4 LENS FOR A 35 mm CAMERA		
	Lines/millimetre	
f-number	Center	Corner
f/1.4	50	40*
f/2	56	45*
f/2.8	63	50*
f/4	63	56*
f/5.6	63	63*
f/8	70	63**
f/11	63	56†
f/16	56	50†

*Lowered by incompletely corrected lens aberrations.
**Best resolving power.
†Lowered by diffraction.

Lenses designed for larger format cameras generally have lower resolving-power capabilities. Typical is the following table of a test made on an *f*/2.8 75 mm lens for a 6 × 6 cm (2 ¼″ × 2 ¼″) camera.

RESOLVING POWER OF A 75 mm *f*/2.8 LENS FOR A 6 × 6 cm CAMERA		
	Lines/millimetre	
f-number	Center	Corner
f/2.8	37	33*
f/4	42	30*
f/5.6	47	33*
f/8	52	33*
f/11	52	42**
f/16	52	42**
f/22	47	37†

*Lowered by incompletely corrected lens aberrations.
**Best resolving power.
†Lowered by diffraction

The longer focal-length lenses used on large-format cameras can be stopped down farther than can short-focal-length lenses on smaller cameras be-

cause the apparent loss of definition caused by diffraction is less. The definition in the final print is dependent both on the sharpness of the negative and the degree of enlargement, and large-format negatives do not require as much enlargement as do small-format negatives. Because of these interacting factors, the amount of diffraction is inversely related to the diameter of the effective aperture. With a 16-inch lens, the effective aperture is 1 inch at *f*/16. With a 50 mm (2-inch) lens, when the effective aperture is 1 inch, the *f*-number is *f*/2. For these reasons, longer focal-length lenses will often stop down to *f*/32 or *f*/64, while shorter focal-length lenses for small-format cameras will only stop down to *f*/16 or *f*/22 at the most. This is fortunate because the longer focal-length lenses often need to be stopped down to very small apertures to obtain adequate depth of field.

• *See also:* APERTURE; DEPTH OF FIELD; DIFFRACTION; *f*-NUMBER; *f*-STOP; INVERSE SQUARE LAW; IRIS DIAPHRAGM; LENSES; OPTICS; PHOTOMACROGRAPHY.

 Diapositive

The word (in various spellings) in several European languages means a positive image on film, a transparency. In the European languages, "dia" is commonly used in the same way as "slide" is used in American English: to mean a small format (usually 35 mm) transparency mounted for projection.

"Diapositive" is also sometimes used to mean an interpositive—a positive image on film or a translucent support, made from a master negative and used for the production of duplicate negatives.

Diazotype

Diazotype is a general term for a number of printing processes utilizing dye couplers that are sensitive to light. Usually, the action of light destroys the coupler, so that only unexposed couplers can be transformed into the dye image; the result is a positive image from a positive, or a negative from a negative. Other diazo processes are known, which are negative-working, but none of these has come into general use. The commercially available diazotype papers, sold under the Ozalid and other trademarks, are of high contrast, and are used mainly for reproduction of line material, such as architects' drawings. A film-based material, called Ozophane, was proposed for motion pictures but never became commercially accepted.

Dichroic Filters

Most light filters for photographic use contain dyes or similar substances that absorb certain wavelengths of energy and permit others to pass. They are relatively inexpensive to produce in a variety of media (glass, gelatin, plastic) and serve the majority of filtration needs in photography. However, it is difficult to give such filters high selectivity—that is, to make filters that begin and end transmission at precise wavelengths and that may include only a small group of wavelengths between those two points.

(Top) Light ray (A) striking dichroic layer will reflect particular wavelength at the upper boundary and, at the lower boundary (a, c), other wavelengths will pass. The lower-boundary reflection (b) of the same wavelength from another light ray (B) will coincide with the path of (a). Reflections from other rays not shown would be interfered with by (c) or would interfere with (d), depending upon where they struck the layer boundaries. If the layer thickness is an odd number of half-wavelengths of the wavelength that is reflected, the interfering waves (a,b) will be out of phase, as in center. One will reach a maximum positive state at the same time the other reaches an equal maximum negative state; as a result, they cancel one another. If layer thickness is an even number of half-wavelengths, the reflected waves are in phase, as in bottom. They add together to produce a wave of greater intensity, but of the same frequency and wavelength.

It is possible to produce sharp-cutting, narrow-band filters by utilizing wavelength interference rather than wavelength absorption. Interference filters made by depositing very thin layers of metallic compounds on glass or plastic are called *dichroic* (two-color) filters because they change between two

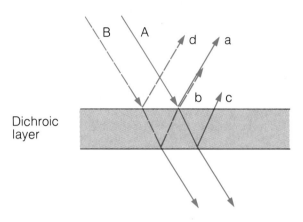

Out-of-phase relationship

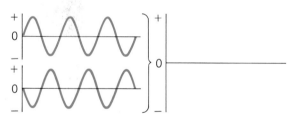

In-phase relationship

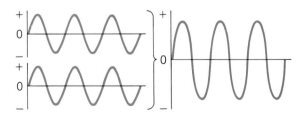

predominant colors when alternately viewed at different angles or by reflected and transmitted light.

The compounds used for dichroic filter coatings may be the same as those used for antireflection coatings on lenses—manganese fluoride, titanium oxide, zinc sulfide, and others—and they are similarly applied, by evaporation in a vacuum. Depending on the materials used, the number of layers and the thickness of each layer, and their refractive indices, a filter can be made to pass certain precise wavelengths and reflect all others.

If the thickness of a particular layer is equal to an odd number of half-wavelengths of the wavelength that the layer reflects, energy reflected from the lower boundary of the layer will be out of phase with energy reflected from the upper boundary, and they will cancel one another (see the accompanying illustration). The energy does not disappear; it is dispersed and apparently helps to increase the transmission of the wavelengths that can pass.

If the layer boundaries are an even number of half-wavelengths apart (that is, are equal to one or more full wavelengths), the reflected waves will be in phase and will reinforce one another. This effectively creates a dichroic mirror that acts like a very selective beamsplitter to separate certain wavelengths from the total energy striking the mirror. For example, such a mirror could be made to reflect only ultraviolet wavelengths and pass visible wavelengths. It could be used either as a source of ultraviolet illumination for special-purpose photography, or as a filter to provide ultraviolet-free illumination for conventional photography. A dichroic "cold mirror"—also called a diathermic mirror, or a heat filter—is used in some slide projectors with high-intensity lamps to reflect visible illumination to the slide and lens while passing infrared and other heat wavelengths on a separate path so they cannot damage the slide (see the accompanying diagram).

Dichroic filters and mirrors must be precisely positioned in the light beam they act on. If angled improperly, the effective thickness of each layer is changed and the required half-wavelength relationship between two reflected rays is lost, as shown in the illustration. For this reason, as well as their greater expense, dichroic filters are seldom used at the camera. They are, however, used in some forms of the most modern color enlargers. They can be properly positioned with great accuracy during manufacture, and can be designed to pivot in and out of position. This eliminates the need to repeatedly remove and replace the filters and they are consequently not likely to become misaligned.

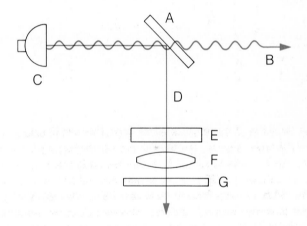

(Above) A "cold mirror" has a dichroic coating that passes infrared wavelengths (B) in energy from a high-intensity lamp (C), but reflects all visible wavelengths (D). Not all heat can be eliminated, so slide projectors using this system include a heat-absorbing glass (E) to further protect the condenser lens (F) and slide (G). (Left) Dichroic layers (A) and (B) have the same physical thickness. However, the effective thickness (a) for a ray passing through an angled layer is greater than the distance (b) through a layer perpendicular to the ray path. If a filter is meant to be used as in (B), even slight misalignment will increase the distance and thus change the phase relationship between reflections from both boundaries. Similarly, if a dichroic mirror or beam splitter is meant to be used at a 45-degree angle, as in (A), misalignment will reduce the effective layer thickness, which will change the reflected-wave phase relationships.

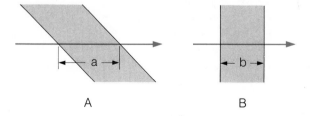

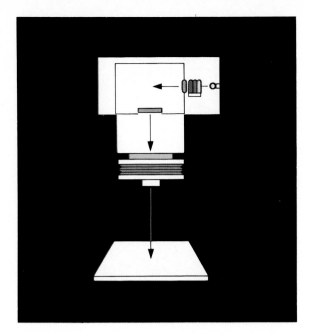

Dichroic filters in a color enlarger modify light as it enters the integrating chamber which produces totally diffuse illumination for making an exposure. Dial controls permit adjusting each filter to any desired degree of density independently of the others.

intensity light sources, they have a life thousands of hours longer than conventional filters.

3. Dichroic filters can be made to produce continuous density changes, whereas conventional filters for color printing are manufactured in density steps equivalent to one-third of a stop (0.10, 0.20, 0.30, and so forth). In addition, a single dichroic filter can achieve a maximum density that it would take three or more gelatin or acetate filters to match.

4. The sharp cut-off characteristics of dichroic filters allow them to transmit only the desired wavelengths, with no significant proportion of other colors. Conventional filters cannot be as precise, and typically pass some colors that must be removed by other filtration (see the accompanying illustrations).

There are a number of advantages to using dichroic filters in a color enlarger:

1. They are unaffected by heat and can be used in front of high-intensity light sources such as tungsten-halogen lamps. These lamps produce enough light for conveniently short exposures, even at relatively small lens apertures, but they also generate so much heat that acetate filters would be melted almost immediately if they were to be placed in the light beam.

2. Compared to gelatin and acetate filters, dichroic filters are virtually fadeless. Although they will eventually lose efficiency from being used close to high-

Schematic comparison shows the density of dichroic and gelatin magenta (minus green) color-printing filters. The area beneath the curves represents light not transmitted; an ideal filter would eliminate all green and pass all blue and red. The sharper cut-off of the dichroic filter, shown by the steeper rise of the curve, eliminates the green light (a,a) that the gelatin filter passes. The greater efficiency of the dichroic filter passes the blue (b) and red (c) light that the gelatin filter absorbs. These curves do not represent actual filters; the wavelength/color relationships shown are approximate.

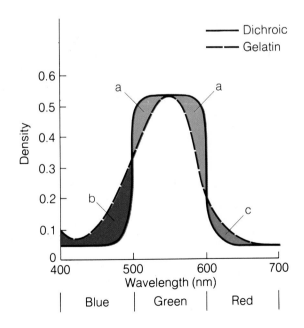

Dichroic Color Printing Filter

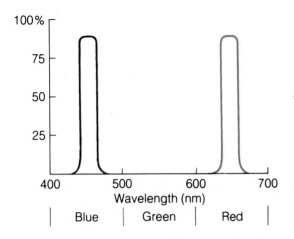

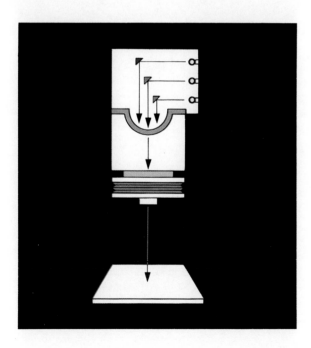

(Above) This transmission graph shows the characteristics of a typical dichroic magenta printing filter. The curves represent the amount of blue and red light transmitted. Although transmission curve widths are narrow, the efficiency is very high for the wavelengths that the various coating layers allow to pass. All green light is excluded, a selectivity not possible with conventional filters of equivalent efficiency. (Below) Three attenuated tungsten-halogen lamps, coupled with red, green, and blue dichroic glass mirrors, make an additive color enlarger that exposes prints with a single exposure.

5. Within its transmission band, a dichroic filter passes almost all wavelengths with equally high efficiency. Compared to a conventional filter, it passes more of exactly the desired color of light. As a result, major exposure adjustments due to changed filtration are much less of a problem with dichroic filters than with conventional filters.

• *See also:* BEAM SPLITTER; DIFFRACTION; DICHROIC FOG; DISPERSION; ENLARGERS AND ENLARGING; FILTERS; LIGHT; OPTICS; PRISMS; REFRACTION; SCIENTIFIC PHOTOGRAPHY.

Dichroic Fog

Portions of improperly processed black-and-white negatives and prints may have a stain that appears one color, usually yellowish or purplish, by transmitted light and another color, often greenish; by reflected light. This effect is created by dichroic fog, a thin layer of silver deposited over the surface of the developed image that interferes with various wavelengths of the viewing light. The fog raises the density and lowers local contrast in negatives; it obscures details and colors the image erratically in prints.

Causes of Dichroic Fog

Dichroic fog results when silver compounds in a processing solution are reduced so that fine particles of silver are released to attach themselves to the developed image. The action is basically unwanted physical development; it can occur in the developer or in the fixer.

A developer that is contaminated with hypo or ammonia, or that has an excess of sodium sulfite, will produce dichroic fog. A small amount of hypo contamination is all that is required; it can be caused by insufficient washing of mixing containers, tanks, or film reels and holders, or by careless handling and splashing of solutions. Ammonia contamination commonly arises from improperly mixing a compound containing ammonia into a solution, with the result that ammonia is released. An excess of sulfite may arise from improper measurement when mixing a formula, from adding too much sulfite in an effort to increase the fine-grain characteristics of a developer, or from exhaustion—as the developing agent is used up, the proportional strength of the sulfite in the solution increases. Some older fine-grain developers contained silver halide solvents such as sodium thiocyanate, which causes dichroic fog on most modern black-and-white films.

Dichroic fog in a fixer can result when the solution turns alkaline. This is most often caused by alkaline developer carried into the fixer in emulsions that have not been treated in an acid stop bath, or have been insufficiently rinsed (or not rinsed at all) in plain water. A more common cause of dichroic fog in a fixer is allowing prints to stick together so that a portion of the image receives little or no fixation. Some of the undeveloped silver in such an area may dissolve into the solution and immediately be redeposited on the developed image.

Prevention

The causes of dichroic fog suggest preventive measures.

1. Wash all containers, mixers, tanks, and film holders thoroughly after each use.
2. Mix and pour solutions accurately and carefully.
3. Do not use a developer to near-exhaustion; the expense of fresh solution at frequent intervals is slight. Also, the proper use of a replenisher to avoid exhaustion results in more consistent development as well avoidance of the hazard of dichroic fog.
4. Use an acid rinse stop bath to completely neutralize the alkalinity of developer in the emulsion before transferring a film or print to the fixer. To make a stop bath, stir 48 millilitres of 28 percent acetic acid into 1 litre of water. To neutralize highly alkaline developers such as those used for high-contrast and graphic-arts films, increase the acetic acid to 148 millilitres.
5. Use fresh acid fixer.
6. Be sure prints receive constant agitation for at least the first full minute in the fixer, and frequent agitation the time thereafter.

Removing Dichroic Fog

If noticed, dichroic fog can often be removed by gentle swabbing with cotton or a photographic sponge while the emulsion is still wet with solution. This is a delicate procedure because the softened gelatin is easily damaged.

Once an emulsion has dried, dichroic fog may resist removal. However, treating a thoroughly washed emulsion in either of the following solutions usually will remove the fog. Note: Treatment of very old images is not recommended. There is a risk of destroying part of the image along with the fog, and base materials—especially in the case of prints —may be damaged or may disintegrate upon being wetted. Do not treat prints with print cement on them; the cement may cause staining. It is better to try to make a duplicate image by photographing the original through a filter. (*See:* COPYING; FILTERS.)

Thiourea solution

Thiourea	3.0 g
Citric acid	3.0 g
Water to make	250.0 ml

Treat the image until the fog has dissolved, then wash it thoroughly before drying.

Farmer's reducer
Stock solution A

Potassium ferricyanide (anhydrous)	37.5 g
Water to make	500.0 ml

Stock solution B

Sodium thiosulfate (pentahydrated)	480.0 g
Water to make	2.0 litres

Mix 30 ml of stock solution A into 120 ml of stock solution B, then add water to make 1 litre. Use immediately. Bathe the image until the fog has disappeared; watch the action closely, for the reducer will attack the image as soon as the fog layer is gone. For slower action, use only 15 ml of stock solution A with the same quantities of B and water. Wash emulsion immediately and thoroughly before drying. • *See also:* COPYING; ERRORS IN PROCESSING; REDUCTION.

Dickson, William Kennedy Laurie

(1860–1935)
French-born inventor of Scottish ancestry

Dickson joined the Edison organization in 1881 and worked on electrical equipment until 1885, at which time he was transferred to Edison's Newark office to work on photographic experiments, and then to the East Orange plant where he designed and built motion-picture cameras, projectors, and a linked-up projector and phonograph for the earliest known talking films. He later worked with the Biograph Company, and others.

Diffraction

When radiant energy with wavelike properties, such as light, passes an obstruction with a cleanly defined thin edge, secondary waves are generated at the point of contact. The secondary waves spread outward, in the same overall direction of travel, into the shadow area behind the obstruction and into the path of the unobstructed energy. This phenomenon is called diffraction.

If the energy is light moving toward an observer, diffraction seems to bend the light around the

(Above) Secondary waves are generated at the point where light touches an edge in passing. The waves spread into the shadow area behind obstruction and into the path of unobstructed waves. To an observer at X, diffraction seems to bend the light nearest the edge around and behind it; other diffracted light adds brilliance in the unobstructed area beside the edge. Thus, the observer does not see a sharp edge and a single tone in the shadow area (left), rather (right), an indistinct edge with graduated tone. (Center) When the light source behind the subject is not concealed, diffracted light (a) is masked by the intensity of light reflected from the edge to the lens (b), and by even greater intensity of light directly from the source (c). (Below) When the source is on the axis of the lens but concealed light reflected from the rim or edge of the subject (a) does not travel to the lens, light passing the subject (b) will be visible only if it is diffused by particles in the air (mist, dust, smoke, etc.). As a result, diffracted light (c) will have maximum visibility. It can be washed out, however, by frontal light on the subject from the direction of the lens.

edges of obstructions, "eating" into them and causing an apparent soft halo of brightness. The effect is often seen in exterior subjects backlighted by the sun, and may be created in the studio with a single intense light source aimed at the camera lens. Diffraction is most visible when the light source is on

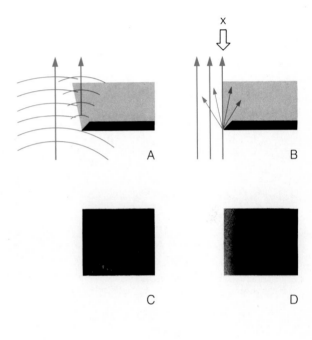

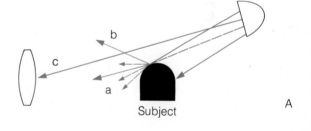

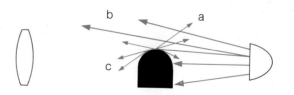

Diffraction, most often seen in exterior subjects backlighted by the sun, is most visible when the light source is on the optical axis of the lens, but concealed by the subject. In this photograph, the camera is facing in the direction of the sun, but the sun is hidden behind the building. What the camera sees are the secondary waves of radiant energy (light waves from the sun) which have been generated at the point of contact with the obstruction (the building). Photo by Bob Clemens.

the optical axis of the observer or lens, but is concealed by the obstruction or subject. Otherwise, light reflected off the subject edges, or the intensity of direct light from the source usually masks the diffraction effect.

Aside from creating a pictorial effect, diffraction affects the definition of images formed at very small apertures, and it can be deliberately used to separate energy into its constituent wavelengths for analysis, as in spectrography.

Image Definition

As the illustrations show, diffraction occurs at the edges of a diaphragm in a lens. When the aperture is large, so much light forms the image of a subject point that the very small amount of light diffracted is negligible. It cannot be seen by direct observation, and it is far too weak to affect an emulsion when the exposure is appropriate for the intensity of the focused point.

However, as the aperture size decreases, the amount of light forming the image is reduced. Consequently, the diffracted light decreases and becomes a larger percentage of light passed. The diffracted light becomes increasingly visible as alternating light and dark interference rings, which are successively feebler, move out from the center point. The amount of exposing light reduces by a square function as the aperture is made smaller, while the diffracting edge is reduced linearly.

The pattern of an image point and its surrounding diffraction rings is called an Airy disc, after G. B. Airy, who discovered the phenomenon in 1830. The effective size of the Airy disc increases as the aperture is made smaller because additional interference rings become visible or reach a significant level of comparative intensity. Thus, point images are spread and become less distinct, and overall sharpness deteriorates. When the radius of the Airy discs

Diffraction

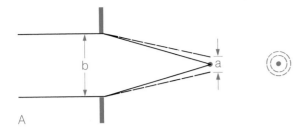

A

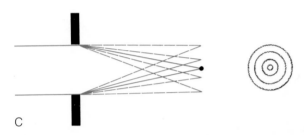

C

(Above left) At a wide aperture, light diffracted at the edges of the diaphragm makes up only a fraction (a) of the total amount (b) which forms the image of a subject point. Although diffraction effects are present around the point image, they are too faint to be seen when recorded under ordinary conditions. (Right) At a small aperture, diffracted light is a significant portion (a) of the greatly reduced total amount (b) which forms the image. The diffraction effects thus become visible and can be recorded by adequate exposure for image brightness. (Below left) A magnified view explains the formation of rings around the point image. Some light diffracted at each side of the small diaphragm opening crosses into the path of light from the other edge. Rings are brightest where interfering wavelengths are in phase and add together; they graduate into dark rings as waves are increasingly out of phase, canceling one another.

A transmission diffraction grating adds interest to pictures by revealing the colors contained in white light. Transmission diffraction gratings are made in acetate plastic with thousands of precisely spaced ridges on the surface. There is no exposure change with a diffraction grating, which is simply held in front of the camera while the picture is being taken. Photo by Norm Kerr.

Diffraction

becomes greater than the size of closely-spaced, fine details in the subject, the details can no longer be resolved. Their images merge indistinguishably because the Airy discs representing the points that make up the details overlap and interfere with one another.

Wavelength Analysis

A very narrow slit diffracts light. If the light is of a single color, the image of the diffracted light forms various brightnesses as interference causes reinforcement of some waves and partial or total cancellation of others. When white light — which contains wavelengths of all colors—is diffracted, a spectrum is formed because the degree of diffraction varies with wavelength. The wavelength spacing of a spectrum formed by diffraction is proportional to the change in wavelength.

A series of very finely spaced parallel lines—as many as 12,000 per centimetre (30,000 per inch)—forms a *diffraction grating* which can separate white light into a series of spectra that reinforce one another. A reflective grating consists of lines engraved on a polished metal or mirrorlike surface. Lines ruled on a transparent material form a transmission

(Above) Transmission diffraction grating consists of thousands of parallel lines per centimetre. Spaces between the opaque lines function as diffraction slits which disperse a narrow beam of white light into a spectrum of equal wavelength bands. (Below) A prism disperses white light by refraction, not diffraction. The spectrum produced does not have bands of equal width; shortest wavelengths (blue, violet) are spread the most, long wavelengths (red) are spread the least.

Diffraction

diffraction grating. The opaque lines are the obstacle edges and the spaces between are the slits that produce diffraction. Such gratings are used in spectrographs to produce distinct color bands to measure the spectral (color) sensitivity of photographic emulsions.

Most of the white light directed at a transmission grating passes directly through the slits; only a small portion is diffracted. Therefore, the resulting spectrum is less intense than that formed by a prism, which disperses all of the light which enters it. However, the diffraction grating is usually preferred for spectrography because it spreads all colors equally, and they can be graphed with equal spacing. In contrast, a prism produces greater spreading as the wavelength grows shorter; thus blue and violet are spread wider than equivalent bands of red and orange light. The result is a spectrograph that is difficult to interpret accurately because the horizontal spacing is constantly changing.

• *See also:* BEAM SPLITTER; DIAPHRAGM; DICHROIC FILTERS; DISPERSION; LIGHT; OPTICS; PRISMS; REFRACTION; RESOLVING POWER; SPECTROGRAPHY.

Diffusion

Diffusion means a random spreading out of energy or particles. In photography it is an important factor in chemical processes, lighting, and image control.

Chemical Diffusion

Chemically, diffusion is the movement of molecules, atoms, or ions from an area of high concentration into areas of lower concentration. If unaffected by other factors, diffusing particles will eventually achieve a uniform distribution throughout the medium in which they are contained. A properly mixed chemical solution, such as a developer, is one in which all the ingredients have diffused completely through the solvent (water) so that one sample will contain exactly the same proportion of each ingredient as any other sample. This kind of uniform distribution is promoted by:

1. using warm solvent to aid in dissolving the ingredients;

2. adding the ingredients one at a time in the order prescribed by the formula, to avoid the formation of unwanted compounds; and

3. stirring constantly in a random or irregular pattern so that particles do not become trapped in regular currents and eddies.

Diffusion is the mechanism by which processing solutions enter photographic emulsions. Agitation during the first part of each processing step helps the solution diffuse into the gelatin quickly and uniformly. Agitation continues to help fresh solution diffuse in, to replace chemically charged or exhausted solution, and to wash away by-products which slowly diffuse out of the emulsion as the processing reactions take place. If left undisturbed, such by-products can partially block the entry of fresh solution, and they can affect the image. For example, development streaks can result if there is not sufficient agitation to wash away the bromide that diffuses out of an emulsion as exposed silver bromide crystals are reduced to metallic silver.

Controlled diffusion is used in instant print and similar self-processing materials. The silver or dye compounds which will form a positive image diffuse out of the layer where a negative is being developed, into a receiving layer where they will be developed or combined. (*See:* DIFFUSION TRANSFER PROCESS.)

Diffusion in Lighting

Light which travels a well-defined path, with essentially parallel rays, is specular or "hard" illumination. It creates distinct highlights, harsh reflections, and shadows with sharp edges. Diffused light does not have parallel rays; the light follows many different paths in the overall direction of movement, and consequently spreads over a larger area. Diffused light is "soft" illumination. It does not produce glaring highlights; the shadows it creates have indistinct edges and are lighter in tone because some light gets into them. Each kind of light can be used to increase the expressive qualities of an image. For example, specular light emphasizes surface texture; diffused light from a discernible direction is suitable for modeling form without adding harshness, while overall diffused light acts to smooth out surface imperfections.

Diffusion in lighting for photography is controlled by choice of the types of light. A floodlight produces a more general illumination than a spotlight. Satin-finish and matte reflectors provide respectively greater diffusion than a polished metal reflector. However, for truly diffuse illumination it is necessary to diffuse the light even more.

Diffusing screens or diffusers can be placed in front of the light source; the light is diffused as it is transmitted by the translucent material. A diffuser can be a fine mesh such as stocking material, or layers of window screening; or it can be a sheet of spun-glass fibers, opal glass, or opal or matte plastic. The thicker the material and the more dense its structure, the greater the degree of diffusion—and the greater the reduction in intensity of the transmitted illumination.

Fabric and mesh materials are easily rolled up and transported for location work where diffusion of sunlight is often required. Diffusion materials for use with lighting instruments such as those commonly used in studios may be flexible or rigid. When used with continuous-burning lamps, they must be mounted with clamps or on separate stands

Photographs taken with diffused lighting are characterized by soft illumination, lack of glaring highlights, and light shadow areas with indistinct edges. Light from a discernible direction created the soft modeling of the children's faces and chests.

Diffusion

Diffused lighting is frequently used in por-traiture especially of women. While the result-ing softness is sufficient for gentle modeling, it reduces surface imperfections such as skin blemishes, poor hair texture, harsh makeup, and similar problems.

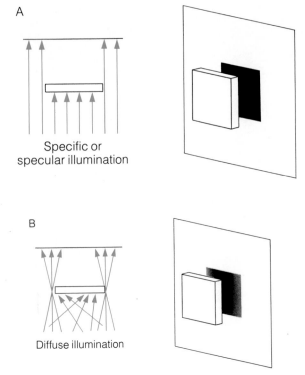

A

Specific or specular illumination

B

Diffuse illumination

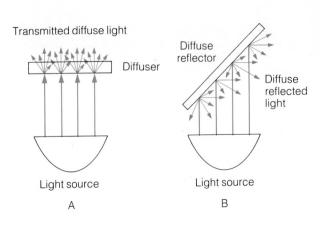

Transmitted diffuse light

Diffuser

Light source

A

Diffuse reflector

Diffuse reflected light

Light source

B

(Above left) Parallel paths of direct, specular light create sharply defined shadows of uniform darkness. (Below left) Diffuse light has many paths, some of which lead into the shadow area behind the subject. Indistinct shadows with vary-ing darkness result because light "wraps" around the subject. (Above Right) Translucent diffusing medium spreads out the light passing through. If the subject is in direct line with the light source, a significant amount of light will be diffused into paths which do not reach it. A reflector with a matte or irregu-lar surfaces diffuses light that it reflects, as at the right.

Diffusion

Several methods are available for diffusing light in photography. (Left) This photograph was taken using direct light from an 8″ reflector held 12 feet from the subject. Note the harsh shadows cast by the subject herself, her hat, and the crease in her slacks. (Center) Transmitted light from a 4′ × 4′ tissue flat placed 6 feet from the subject significantly reduces shadows and specular highlight on the ski goggles. (Right) Bounced, diffuse light obtained with a 40″ umbrella, 12 feet from the subject, gives an effect very similar to that produced by transmitted light. Differences in cast shadow and specular highlight between this and the center photo are solely due to the relative size of the light source. Photos by Norm Kerr.

so there is air space between them and the enclosed lamp. Otherwise, the screen may scorch or melt—the need for nonflammable materials is obvious—and the life of the lamp and the lighting instrument may be affected. Proper ventilation is especially important with heat-intensive sources such as tungsten-halogen lamps, and in large box-reflectors which have several lamps to provide evenly diffused illumination over a large area. In addition to the diffusion of the light by use of satin reflectors and diffusing screens, the size of the light source affects the softness or hardness of the illumination as well. Very small sources produce hard light with sharp-edged shadows, while broad, large area sources produce softer light.

Diffusers for electronic flash units do not need to be separated from the instrument housing because there is no significant heat build-up. However, they must not touch the flash tube, and they should be far enough away (at least twice the longest dimension of the tube) to avoid a central spot of excess intensity. It is easy to improvise diffusion for close-ups with a small flash unit by placing one or more layers of white handkerchief over the flash head. Each layer will reduce the intensity about the equivalent of one stop.

A useful technique to minimize the reflection of large dark areas by the shiny surfaces of such objects as silverware and glazed pieces, and glassware is to surround them with a "tent" of diffusing material. Lights shining onto the tent from outside provide almost totally diffuse illumination within, but with no glare or hot spots. The camera lens protrudes through a slit in the tent. Light can also be diffused by directing it onto a suitable surface from which it is reflected to the subject. Outdoors, folding matte-surface boards or large transluscent screens called scrims are commonly used to diffuse the sunlight to provide softer light. A white shirt or a sheet of newspaper makes an easily improvised diffusing reflector for small subjects. In the studio, movable painted flats or panels, and folding umbrella-type reflectors are the most common devices for creating diffuse reflected light. A translucent fabric umbrella can also produce diffuse transmitted light when it is placed between the source and the subject.

Umbrella reflectors are convenient for interior location work because they fold compactly and are lightweight. Many photographers find it even easier to reflect light off the walls, ceiling, or floor at the scene. "Bounce flash" is a common example of this technique. In color photography, the reflecting sur-

Diffusion

face must be white; otherwise, neutral and white subject areas will be tinged the same color as the reflector.

Whenever diffusion is employed, the subject illumination is reduced because some light is scattered into paths which do not reach the subject, and the remaining light is spread over a larger area. When a diffuser is placed in front of a direct light source, the illumination will be at least cut in half. If the same source is directed onto a diffusing reflector, the illumination will be one-fourth as bright, or even less.

Diffusion in Image Control

When image-forming light—rather than the illumination falling on the subject—is diffused, the apparent sharpness is reduced. The result can be a pleasing softness of detail and a spreading of light at the edges of contrasting areas. A diffuser placed in front of the camera lens will cause light to spread from bright areas into dark areas in the recorded image. A diffuser placed in front of an enlarger lens will spread the edges of dark areas into lighter areas. That is because the thinnest portions of a negative, representing the dark subject areas, transmit the greatest amount of printing light. There is a decided difference in the expressive character of images of the same subject produced by these two methods.

Some camera and enlarging lenses have built-in or insertable diffusion-control discs which provide a choice of various degrees of diffusion. An image which is sharp at the center and diffused in the outer areas can be created by cutting a hole in the center of a diffuser used over the lens.

Enlargers with diffused *light sources* do not produce diffused images. Rather, the light tends to eliminate scratches, dust spots and similar minor imperfections in negatives because it passes around them from many different directions. Diffused light is used in color enlargers to insure even illumination and complete color mixing of lamphouse filtration. Diffuse illumination also minimizes any grain char-

Unlike photographs made directly with a diffuser, prints made with a diffuser over the enlarger lens will spread the dark areas into lighter portions of the picture. (Left) This is a straight photograph, made with no diffuser over the camera lens and printed without a diffuser on the enlarger. (Right) The same photograph, printed with No. 2 and No. 3 Tiffin fog filters on the enlarger, gives a totally different effect. Highlights are eliminated because the thinnest portions of the negative, representing the dark subject areas, transmit the most light to be diffused into other print areas. Photos by Norm Kerr.

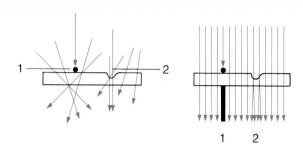

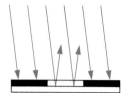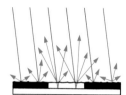

cause some light is lost due to scattering caused by the irregular surface. The image will also have less visual contrast because some light striking dark areas will be diffused across them, and because some light striking light areas will be scattered into dark areas as the image strikes the eye. Both effects make the areas look less dark, and thus to have less contrast in comparison with the light areas. Diffusion similarly affects the perception of mid-range tonalities to some degree. The tonal scale achievable on glossy papers is thus greater than can be achieved on lustre or matte-surface papers.

• *See also:* ADDITIVE COLOR SYNTHESIS; BOUNCE LIGHT; CALLIER EFFECT; DENSITOMETRY; DIFFUSION TRANSFER PROCESS; ENLARGERS and ENLARGING; LIGHTING; REFLECTORS; TENT LIGHTING; UMBRELLA LIGHTING.

Diffusion Transfer Process

(Above left) Diffuse enlarging light passes through the negative from many directions, washing out a potential shadow of dust (1) and increased brightness through scratch (2). (Above right) Parallel paths of light in the condenser-system enlarger pass through the negative in a single direction, creating a distinct shadow of dust (1), and increased brightness through scratch (2). (Below left) A glossy surface print emulsion allows light to penetrate the dark portions and be absorbed without being diffused and light striking white areas to be reflected cleanly. (Below right) A matte surface emulsion scatters light across dark areas, and spreads light that is reflected from white areas into the visual path of other parts of the image. Comparatively, this print would appear less brilliant, and have a lower contrast and shorter scale.

acteristics of a black-and-white negative. Negatives for diffuse-light enlarging must be developed to a higher contrast than negatives for condenser enlargers, if comparable prints are to be obtained. (See: CALLIER EFFECT; ENLARGERS and ENLARGING.)

Diffusion affects the contrast of prints on papers of various surfaces. A glossy print surface provides an essentially mirrorlike reflection of light striking the image. Because virtually no light is lost by scattering, the image seems brilliant and the maximum tonal difference is perceived between areas of different tonality. The same image printed on a matte-surface paper will appear to have less brilliance be-

Photographic instant print materials produce negative and positive images simultaneously during processing by means of diffusion transfer. In this process, as the negative develops, undeveloped compounds or released dyes diffuse into an adjacent receiving layer where they form a positive image. Development is extremely rapid; it typically requires only 10 to 60 seconds for systems that use separate negative and positive sheets, and only a few minutes for self-contained integral materials. Most final images do not require fixing. In addition to photography, diffusion transfer is used in some document copiers, and in the preparation of some kinds of metal or paper plates for printing by offset lithography.

While slow-speed emulsions are used for copying purposes, the diffusion-transfer films for ordinary photography have speeds up to an equivalent of ASA 3000; emulsions such as those used to record cathode ray tube displays have equivalent speeds of up to ASA 10,000. Very high emulsion speeds and very fast processing are possible because highly alkaline development is used, and because the process is so efficient that far less exposure and less silver are required to create a positive image than with conventional emulsions and processes. Fixation is usually not required because all silver halides in the

The progressive development of a photograph made on diffusion transfer film takes place over a matter of several minutes at most. This is made possible by a process so efficient that considerably less exposure and silver are required to create a positive image than with conventional emulsions and processes.

materials are either reduced to metallic silver or are removed and discarded.

Diffusion transfer can be used with still and motion picture films to produce images in black-and-white or in color. The images are virtually grainless and have resolution, contrast and other characteristics comparable to images made with conventional materials. Still pictures from in-camera materials are the same size as the negative, but some diffusion-transfer processes produce negatives from which enlargements can be made. Depending on the materials used, diffusion-transfer processes can produce: a positive image on paper (print); a print and a reusable film negative; a print and a paper negative with limited reusability (in some copying processes); a transparency on film; or an image on a lithographic plate.

Black-and-White Still Photography

Two separate diffusion transfer sheets are used in black-and-white still photography: a negative, and a receiving or print sheet where the positive image is formed. The negative material consists of a gelatin emulsion on either a paper or film base; the emulsion contains light-sensitive silver halide crystals and crystals of developing agent. The print material usually has a paper base coated with an emulsion that is not light sensitive, but contains silver sulfide or similar particles and crystals of developing agent. The silver sulfide particles serve as development nuclei. Sheets of negative and positive material are arranged in pairs in packs or rolls in such a way that the negative can be exposed, and then the two sheets can be pressed emulsion-to-emulsion when they are withdrawn from the camera.

As the sheets emerge from the camera or film holder, they pass between two pressure rollers which break a pod of viscous activating agent or developer reagent and spread it evenly between the two emulsions. The reagent is composed of a strong alkali and a silver halide solvent, usually sodium thiosulfate (hypo). The alkali immediately activates the developing agent in the negative emulsion, which proceeds to reduce the exposed halides to metallic silver, forming a negative image.

At the same time, the solvent in the reagent dissolves the unexposed halides which correspond to

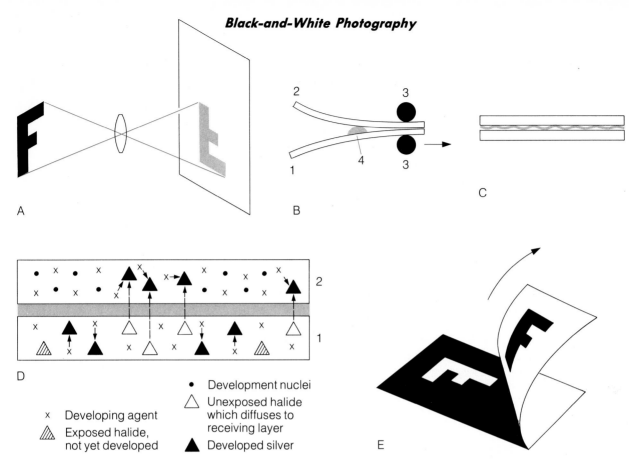

A

B

C

D

Development nuclei

x   Developing agent

△ Unexposed halide
which diffuses to
receiving layer

▧ Exposed halide,
not yet developed

▲ Developed silver

E

(A) Exposure creates a latent image in the negative of the diffusion-transfer material. The image is inverted and laterally reversed, just as in conventional films. In B, the exposed negative (1) and receiving sheet (2) are pulled between processing rollers (3) which rupture the pod (4) of jellylike activator. In the next illustration, (C), roller pressure spreads the activator in an even layer between the face-to-face negative and receiving sheet. In D, alkali in the activator causes the developing agent in the negative emulsion (1) to reduce exposed halide crystals to metallic silver. Solvent in the activator dissolves unexposed halides which diffuse to development nuclei in the receiving sheet emulsion (2). There, they are reduced to metallic silver by the activated developing agent in the receiving layer; the resulting image is positive. (E) When peeled away at completion of processing, the positive image is unreversed. If a negative is on film, it may be washed to remove activator and used for conventional contact printing or enlarging; if it is on a paper base, it is discarded.

the positive aspect of the image. Although halide crystals are normally held firmly in position in an emulsion, in liquid form they are able to move by diffusion out of the negative emulsion, through the reagent, into the positive-forming receiving layer. Because the two emulsions are pressed together, the dissolved halides move directly to corresponding positions with virtually no migration sideways; thus, image resolution is not affected to any significant degree.

The development nuclei in the receiving emulsion make the diffused halides developable. The developing agent in that layer—also activated by the alkali in the reagent—reduces the halides to grains of metallic silver, which build up around the development nuclei to form a positive image. Although some contrast control can be achieved by varying the development time, the process essentially carries itself to completion. As dissolved halides are developed, solvent is released to return to the negative emulsion to dissolve any remaining unexposed halides. In this way, a minimum amount of reagent is required to process all the halides. When the negative is peeled away from the positive, it takes the reagent layer with it. Paper-base negatives are discarded; film-base negatives can be saved for use by washing away the reagent, usually in a sodium sulfite solution which toughens the gelatin emulsion against damage.

Some prints must be coated with a wipe-on plasticizer solution which is slightly acid. This solution neutralizes any residual processing activator, and forms a moisture-proof coating when dry. Other print materials form self-neutralizing compounds during the final stages of processing and have emulsions that do not require coating. Transparencies are commonly dipped in a solution which dries to form a protective coating on both sides of the film.

Black-and-White Movies

One of the major uses of diffusion transfer in black-and-white motion pictures was in the Kodak Bimat transfer films. Bimat transfer film was soaked so that its emulsion absorbed processing chemicals, and was kept in a moist roll. As a conventional negative film was exposed in the camera, it was laminated emulsion-to-emulsion with the Bimat film. Within one to two minutes, diffusion transfer processing produced a negative image in the camera-exposed film, and a transfer positive transparency image in the Bimat film. The system was widely used to obtain immediate inspection of results in such applications as continuous operation aerial photography. In a still picture form, Bimat transfer film was used in the Lunar Orbiter. The pictures were exposed and processed as described above. The positive transparency was then scanned electronically and the scan information was transmitted by radio waves to earth stations, where it was recorded on magnetic tape. The tape was then used to recreate the photographs of the moon.

Copying and Photomechanical Reproduction

Diffusion transfer materials for copying and offset lithography utilize a high-contrast negative

A diffusion transfer processor such as this can make reproductions of continuous tone originals as well as line copies. To reproduce photographs, as shown here, a screen must be placed between the original and the negative during exposure to break the image into halftone dots.

emulsion on a paper base, and a positive emulsion on paper or metal. The emulsions do not usually include crystals of a developing agent, as do the emulsions of continuous-tone diffusion-transfer materials. Copying is effectively limited to reproductions of line originals because a very high contrast negative material is required to make reflex exposures.

Lithographic products such as Kodak photomechanical transfer materials can make reproductions of continuous tone originals if a screen is placed between the original and the negative during exposure to break the image into halftone dots. (*See:* PHOTOMECHANICAL REPRODUCTION METHODS.)

When the image-forming material has a paper base, it is fed into a processor along with the negative. The sheets are kept separated while both emulsions absorb processing solution, but are pressed face-to-face as they emerge from the processor; they are peeled apart after about one minute, when the transfer image has formed. If the receiving layer is on a metal plate, only the paper negative passes through the processing solution before the two materials are laminated together. Lithographic diffusion-transfer images usually must be fixed in a conventional hypo solution after the negative has been peeled away.

Color Still Photography

Diffusion-transfer materials for color photography with still cameras are of two types—peel-apart films, and self-contained integral films. Like conventional color films, both types have three emulsion layers in the negative section which are individually sensitive to blue, green, and red light. In the Polaroid films, each emulsion layer has an adjacent layer of dye-developer, a compound which is both a devel-

oping agent and a dye. Although the final image is formed by diffusion, it is dye compounds, not silver halides, that transfer to the receiving layer.

Two major methods are used for color diffusion transfer processing. In one, exposed halides are developed by dye-developers which are trapped in the negative layers; dye-developers in the unexposed portions are not trapped and diffuse into the receiving layer to form a positive image. This "exposed halide" method has primarily been used in Polaroid Land Polacolor and SX-70 materials. The second method is unique; it had never been applied to photography before the introduction of PR10 Kodak instant print film in 1976. In this process, *exposure* makes silver halide crystals undevelopable. The *unexposed* halides, which correspond to a positive image, can be developed, however. As this occurs, dyes are released by a series of chemical reactions and create a positive color image in the receiving layer of the film. The accompanying illustrations will help to clarify the following descriptions of materials using these two methods of processing.

Peel-Apart Color Materials

The negative and positive sections of peel-apart (Polacolor) films are on separate sheets in rolls or

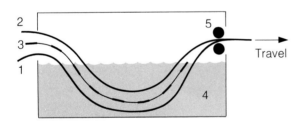

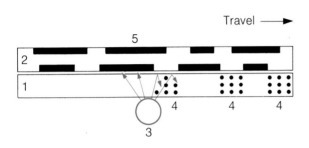

(Above) Graphic representation of reflex exposure. Negative sheet (1) and original to be copied (2) pass face-to-face over the light source (3). Illumination transmitted through the back of the negative is absorbed by dark portions of the original, reflected by light portions. A high-contrast negative emulsion has low sensitivity so that only areas affected by both transmitted and reflected light reach a developable level of exposure (4). Because light is not transmitted through the original, printing an image on the opposite side (5) does not affect the negative exposure. (Below) In processing, the exposed negative (1) is fed face-up into the processor along with the face-down positive receiving sheet (2). A divider (3) keeps the sheets separate as they pass through the processing liquid (4) (transporting rollers are not shown). As the sheets emerge, the pressure rollers (5) squeeze away excess liquid and insure contact over the entire face area of the sheets.

(Top) In processing, the development of the exposed portions of the negative (1) which began in the processor is carried to completion by the absorbed processing liquid. Solvent in the liquid dissolves halides in the unexposed portions (2) which diffuse into the receiving layer of the positive sheet; there they are developed (3), forming a positive image. (bottom) In image orientation, reflex exposure causes the negative to have a reversed image (1), thus, positive transfer image (2) is right-reading when the sheets are separated at completion of processing. The negative may have limited reusability in some processes; it is discarded when its unexposed halides have been exhausted.

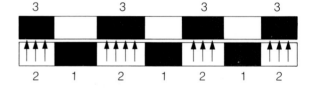

Peel-Apart Materials Exposure

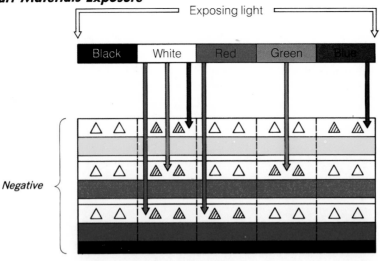

Blue-sensitive emulsion

Yellow dye developer
Spacer
Magenta dye developer

Green-sensitive emulsion
Spacer
Red-sensitive emulsion

Cyan dye developer

Black paper base

△ Unexposed halide crystal
▲ Exposed halide crystal (latent image)

Each emulsion layer of the diffusion transfer color negative is sensitive to one primary color of light. The adjacent layer below each emulsion contains molecules of a complementary color dye developer. Exposure creates a latent negative image in each emulsion according to the color composition of the subject.

Peel-Apart Materials Processing

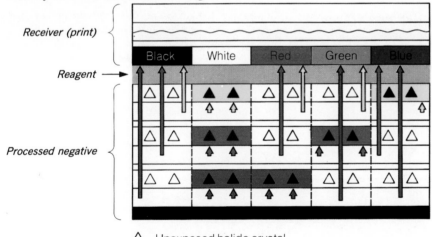

White paper base

Acid layer
Spacer
Mordant (image-forming) layer

△ Unexposed halide crystal
▲ Developed silver (visible negative image)

Alkali in the processing reagent causes dye-developer molecules to move into their associated emulsion layers. Exposed halides are developed to a negative silver image, trapping associated dye-developer molecules there. Unexposed halides and developed silver do not impede diffusion of dye developers into the mordant or receiving layer of the print sheet, where they form a positive image. Processing is terminated when alkali reagent is neutralized by the acid in the acid layer.

packs. Like black-and-white materials, they are laminated face-to-face with processing reagent as they are pulled between pressure rollers in the camera or film holder.

The negative image-forming layers contain silver halide emulsions sensitive to blue, green, and red light. Below each emulsion there is a layer consisting of dye-developer molecules; each dye is the complement of the color sensitivity of its associated emulsion (blue:yellow; green:magenta; red:cyan). Spacing layers make certain that dye-developer molecules from one emulsion section do not diffuse into another section before development is completed there. The negative layers are coated onto a black paper base which prevents light from affecting the emulsions from below when the film is withdrawn from the camera for processing.

During exposure the red, green, and blue components of light from the subject affect halide crystals in the various emulsion layers, forming a latent negative image. As with black-and-white films, a pod of alkali processing reagent is broken by rollers and the contents spread evenly between the negative and positive sheets. The paper base of the positive sheet protects the negative layers from additional exposure from the top, just as the negative base does at the bottom.

The alkali reagent diffuses into the negative and causes each dye-developer to move into its associated emulsion layer. Wherever the dye-developer encounters an exposed halide crystal, it reduces it to metallic silver, forming a negative image. Each dye-developer molecule oxidized in processing the negative is immobilized. Dye-developer molecules which do not encounter exposed halides diffuse into the mordant layer of the receiving sheet. The mordant locks the dyes in place

there. Dye-developer molecules in the negative also are not stopped by developed silver. Thus, cyan dye-developer can pass through developed green-magenta and blue-yellow negative areas, and magenta dye-developer can pass through developed blue-yellow areas. The spacing layers in the negative prevent dyes from reaching another emulsion layer before all development has been completed there.

After a period of time, a protective layer in the receiver sheet breaks down and the alkali reagent contacts and is neutralized by an acid layer. No washing is required after the print is peeled away from the negative, which is discarded. The dyes are seen against the white paper base of the receiving sheet; they act subtractively on white viewing light to produce a full-color positive image.

Integral Exposed Halide Materials

In integral diffusion transfer films, the receiving layers are in place along with the negative layers in a single unit. Materials such as Polaroid SX-70 film which use exposed-halide processing have receiving layers which are transparent before processing so that light can pass through them to expose the negative. When the film passes between the processing rollers, developing reagent is injected between the top negative layer and the image-receiving layer. The reagent has three major components: alkali to dissolve the dye-developers in the negative; opacifiers to prevent light from reaching the negative during processing; and white pigment.

Processing occurs as described for peel-apart color materials. Exposed silver halide is developed by dye-developer which becomes trapped. Untrapped dye-developers diffuse through the reagent to form a positive image in the receiving layer. When

Opaque reagent, injected between the negative and receiving sections, prevents further exposure and activates dye-developer molecules. Dye developer is trapped where exposed halide is developed in the negative; otherwise, it diffuses into the receiving layer to form a positive image. The image becomes visible as alkali in the processing reagent is neutralized by acid and opacifiers in the reagent become colorless and allow accompanying white pigment to become visible as a background for the image. The picture is viewed from the same direction as the exposure, so the exposing image must be made right-reading by the mirror reflection in the camera. ▶

Integral Exposed Halide Materials—Exposure

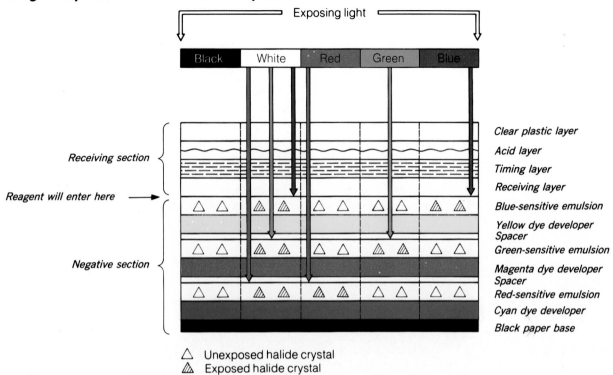

Transparent layers in the receiving section of the integral exposed halide material permit the light from the subject to expose the negative emulsion layers below.

Integral Exposed Halide Materials—Processing

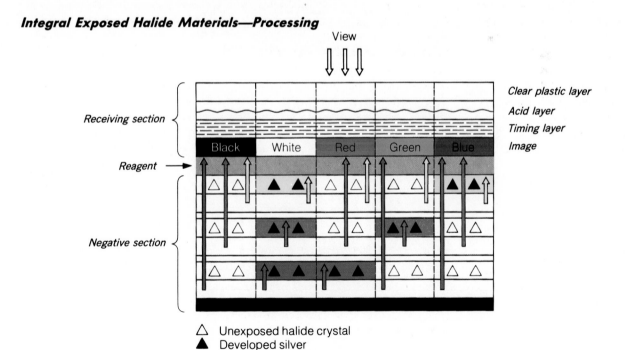

the protective layer breaks down,the alkali activator is neutralized by an acid layer which causes the protective opacifiers in the reagent to become colorless. This permits the white pigment in the reagent layer to become visible in full strength. The pigment provides the white component of the finished image and, along with the positive image dyes, it conceals the negative layers below. Nothing is peeled away or discarded, and no washing is necessary. Because the image is not transferred to a separate sheet, no final right-left reversal occurs. To obtain a right-reading image, cameras using this kind of material must use a mirror to reverse the image from the lens and reflect a right-reading image onto the film for correct exposure.

Integral Unexposed Halide Materials

The reversal emulsion and processing created for Kodak instant print film are complete changes in photography. Conventional emulsions form a latent image on the surface of exposed halide crystals, which makes them developable. The crystals, in the three color-sensitive emulsions of instant print film, trap exposing energy inside their structure; the resulting "interior" latent image cannot be reached by the developer, and therefore these crystals cannot be reduced. However, chemicals in the emulsion and the developer make the unexposed crystals in each layer developable, so that a direct positive silver image is produced by processing.

Kodak instant print film PR 10 is exposed through the back. As in other color films, emulsions sensitive to primary colors of light are exposed according to subject color composition. Exposure effect is locked inside the halide crystals instead of creating a latent image of crystal surfaces. Black-and-white opaque layers between print and negative sections prevent exposure from the front when the sheet emerges from the camera for processing.

Single-Sheet Unexposed Halide Materials—Exposure

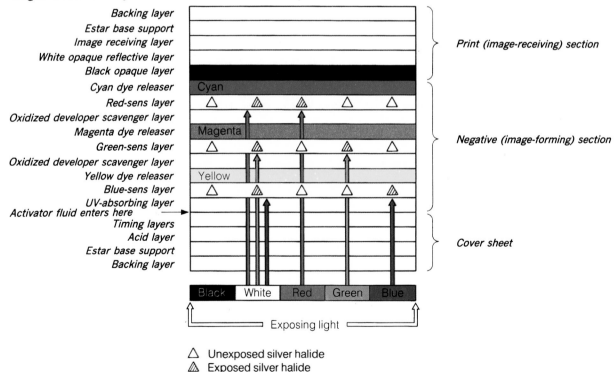

△ Unexposed silver halide
🔺 Exposed silver halide

Single-Sheet Unexposed Halide Materials—Processing

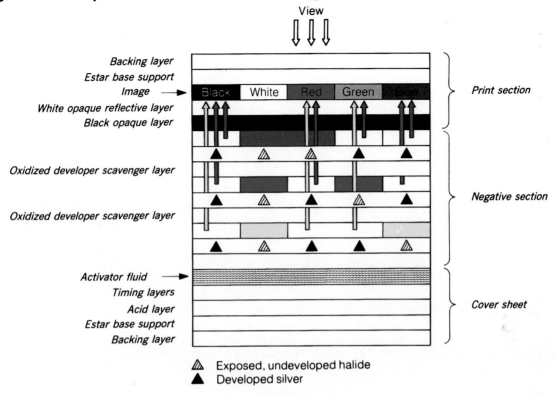

Backing layer
Estar base support
Image
White opaque reflective layer
Black opaque layer

Oxidized developer scavenger layer

Oxidized developer scavenger layer

Activator fluid
Timing layers
Acid layer
Estar base support
Backing layer

View

Black | White | Red | Green | Blue

Print section

Negative section

Cover sheet

⧄ Exposed, undeveloped halide
▲ Developed silver

Opaque processing activator fluid prevents additional exposure from the back during processing. The developer reduces unexposed halides to a positive silver image; the developer which is oxidized by this process, reacts with dye releasers which, by hydrolysis, release associated dyes which diffuse to the receiving layer in the print section. The acid layer in the bottom cover sheet breaks down to neutralize the activator and terminate the process when diffusion is complete. The image is viewed against the white opaque layer, from the side opposite that of exposure. Therefore, the image from the lens is not optically reversed in the camera and appears right-reading in print.

The film is exposed from one side, the "back," and is viewed from the other, the "front." Because of this, it is not necessary to optically reverse the image in the camera. The film may be exposed directly to the lens image, or the image may be reflected in two mirrors from lens to film. The mirror system is used to produce large images in cameras that are physically compact.

The red, green, and blue components of the exposing light affect their corresponding emulsion layers. As the exposed film passes through processing rollers, activator fluid is forced between layers at the face of the image-forming section. The activator is opaque in order to protect the emulsions from further exposure; opaque layers at the other side of the negative section provide light protection from that direction.

Developing agent in the activator causes the unexposed halide to be developed. As this takes place, oxidized developer is formed which diffuses into the adjacent layer which contains a dye releaser. (The oxidized developer reacts with the dye releaser to form oxidized dye releaser which then is hydrolyzed to release dye.) The released dyes correspond

This series demonstrates the progressive diffusion of dyes into the image-receiving section of a sheet of Kodak Instant Print Film.

to the developed positive silver image; they diffuse into the image-receiving section. Scavenger layers prevent the oxidized developer of one layer from reaching the dye of a different layer.

The diffusion path of the released dyes carries them through the black and white opaque layers in the image-receiving section, into the receiving layer where they form a full-color positive image. The white opaque layer provides the whites of the image and conceals the blackened negative layers below it. The image is viewed through the transparent backing and support layers of the receiving section. To complete processing, timing layers on the cover sheet of the film break down and permit acid to neutralize all alkali. As with other diffusion transfer films, no washing is necessary. Integral instant prints do not require coating.

Color Motion Pictures

Diffusion transfer processing has been combined in Polavision film with a method of additive color synthesis to produce color movies. Exposing light passes through the transparent film base and a three-color screen before striking a silver-halide emulsion. The screen is composed of sets of parallel red, green, and blue lines which cover the entire film area. These lines are transparent and act as color filters, passing only light of their own color. Because they are extremely fine—4500 to the inch—very fine details in the image are analyzed according to their composition in the three primary colors, and the emulsion receives corresponding exposures.

The film is contained in a cassette. After exposure, a processing reagent is spread over the emulsion as the film is rewound; only 14 drops of reagent are required for a 42-foot length of super-8 film. The reagent develops the exposed halides, creating a very low-density negative, and simultaneously dissolves the unexposed halides. These diffuse to development nuclei in a receiving layer where they develop to form a high-density positive image. The processing chemicals are completely absorbed into the emul-

Diffusion Transfer Process

Color Motion Pictures

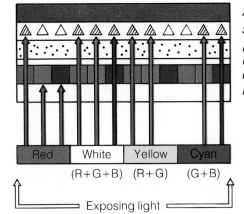

Anti-halation dye and stabilizer
Silver halide emulsion
Receiving layer
Guard layer
Color line screen
Polyester base

Red	White	Yellow	Cyan
	(R+G+B)	(R+G)	(G+B)

△ Unexposed halide
⧄ Exposed halide
∴ Development nuclei

⟶ Exposing light ⟵

(Left)   The color screen is composed of parallel transparent red, green, and blue lines which cover the entire area between the film base and emulsion layers. There are approximately 180 lines per millimetre (4500 per inch), so even light from very small details in the image is analyzed in terms of the three primary colors. (Right) Exposing light, reflected from the subject, is composed of various combinations of primary colors. Screen filters light, each line transmitting only the light of its own color. Light reaching the silver halide emulsion layer varies in proportion to the intensity and color of each subject area. The alkali guard layer prevents chemicals from affecting the lenticular screen during processing. Gray anti-halation dye prevents unwanted exposure from reflection in the outer emulsion layer; the dye bleaches out during processing.

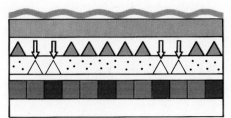

Processing reagent

Receiving layer

△ Unexposed halide
▲ Developed silver in negative
▲ Developed silver in positive
∴ Development nuclei

The processing reagent deposited on the emulsion penetrates to develop the exposed halides (negative image) and causes the unexposed halides to diffuse into the receiving layer. At the same time, the anti-halation dye begins to be bleached.

Diffused halides develop to a positive image in the receiving layer. Anti-halation dye becomes colorless, and stabilizer is released from that layer to neutralize chemicals in all layers. The low-density negative passes the projection light with only a moderate effect on intensity. Higher densities in the positive image primarily determine which proportions reach the color line screen. At this point, light represents a black-and-white positive image. Screen lines color the various intensities of light, which combine in the projected image to reproduce the original subject colors.

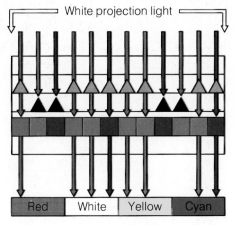

⟶ White projection light ⟵

Negative image
Positive image

Red	White	Yellow	Cyan

Projected image

Diffusion Transfer Process

sion; there is no residue to be removed. In the final stages of processing, a stabilizer is released from an upper layer to neutralize the chemical products and reagent in all layers.

The negative image remains in place in the film. Because of its low density, light can pass through it. The maximum density is 0.3, which reduces transmitted light by 50%; most areas of the negative image will reduce light transmission by much less. In comparison to the far greater density (maximum, 3.0) of the positive image, negative density is relatively insignificant and the negative is essentially invisible for viewing purposes.

In projection, light passes through the film from the side opposite that which the exposing light entered. In this way, light intensity is affected by the developed images before it passes through the color line screen. The positive image densities control how much light can pass through the screen to become colored in the same proportions as the composition of the original exposing light. When projected on a screen, the various amounts of red, green, and blue light combine additively to produce a full-color image.

The projected image is kept relatively small (approximately 8×10 inches) so that an extremely high wattage lamp is not required to achieve adequate image brightness, and so that the color screen line pattern is not enlarged to such a degree that it becomes noticeable or interferes with image resolution. At normal viewing distances the screen pattern in the small image is less apparent than the lines in a television image.

• *See also:* ADDITIVE COLOR SYNTHESIS; BIMAT PROCESS; COLOR FILMS; COLOR THEORY; DEVELOPMENT; DIFFUSION; DUFAYCOLOR; EMULSIONS; LENTICULAR SYSTEMS; LINE SCREEN SYSTEMS; LUMIERE COLOR PROCESSES; MOSAIC SYSTEMS; PHOTOMECHANICAL REPRODUCTION METHODS; PMT PROCESS; SUBTRACTIVE COLOR SYNTHESIS.

DIN Speeds

DIN is a German standard system for determining film emulsion speed, and was named from the initials of *Deutsche Industrie Norm,* the German standards association. The method of measurement is the same as that used by the American manufacturers for the ASA ratings, but a different scale of numbers is used to express the speed ratings. The DIN speed of a film can be derived from the ASA by the following formula:

$$DIN \ Speed = 10 \log_{10} ASA + 1$$

Example: Convert 100 ASA to DIN:

$$\log 100 = 2$$

$$Then \ 10 \times 2 = 20 + 1 = 21$$

$$Thus, \ ASA \ 100 = DIN \ 21$$

• *See also:* ASA, ASAP SPEEDS; BSI SPEEDS; GOST SPEEDS; SENSITOMETRY; SPEED SYSTEMS.

Directional Effects

Sometimes called "bromide drag" or "bromide streamers," directional effects are found in film images that have been developed without agitation, or occasionally in films that have been agitated in only one direction during processing. Essentially, they are the result of the release of soluble bromides from the silver emulsion when a heavily exposed area is developed. If not quickly dispersed into the developer solution by agitation, these released bromides spread over the surface of the film and cause adjacent areas to be developed slightly less than areas with the same exposure, but which are not next to highly exposed areas. Thus, they result in lighter streaks in areas of moderate density. Once formed, they cannot be removed, but they can be prevented by *non-uniform* agitation of the proper degree.

• *See also:* DEVELOPMENT; EDGE EFFECT; ERRORS IN PROCESSING.

Diffusion Transfer Process

Bromide drag, an effect caused by developing film without agitation, is characterized by streaked areas of less development than other areas of the same exposure. The darker, shadow-like bars extending from the bottom of the "H" demonstrate this effect.

Direct Positive Paper Photography

Photography with direct positive paper is a simple way to make paper prints without using an intermediate negative. By this method, the subject is photographed on Kodak direct positive paper instead of the usual film. When the exposure has been made, a simple chemical reversal process yields a positive print directly from the material exposed in the camera. The entire process takes very few minutes, and because the emulsion of this material is coated on a water-resistant paper base, drying is also rapid.

The following gives detailed information on exposing and processing Kodak direct positive paper, and on some of the equipment normally used with it. A table of common faults, with their probable causes and remedies, has been included to help trace any difficulties that may be encountered.

Applications

The most extensive application for the process is in coin-operated strip-picture machines and while-you-wait booths located in shopping centers, airline terminals, bus and railway stations, fairgrounds, and amusement parks.

However, direct positive paper may be loaded into sheet film holders and exposed in any press or view camera. The orthochromatic emulsion provides a changed gray-tone rendering of subject colors that may have special pictorial or graphic value for some kinds of images. Red areas in the subject will be somewhat darker gray, while blues and green will be somewhat lighter than the way they would be rendered by a panchromatic emulsion.

The direct-positive process positive is also a fast and economical method of obtaining prints from black-and-white transparencies, either by contact printing or by enlarging.

When a normal gray-tone rendering is unimportant, as with prints for file use or for layout work in printing production, the direct positive method can be utilized for making prints from color transparencies. Kodak direct positive paper has an orthochromatic emulsion that can be handled, both before and during processing, under the illumination of a Kodak safelight filter No. 2 (dark red) mounted in a suitable safelight lamp. As in direct photography, prints made from color transparencies render the red areas darker in tone, and the blue and green areas slightly lighter, than the normal color-brightness response of the eye.

A further application for the process is to determine the correct exposure for more expensive and less easily processed reversal materials such as color films. To use this method, a correctly exposed and

PHOTOS

ELECTRONIC LIGHTING   ALL PHOTOS ARE SHARP AND CLEAR

ever, the use of electronic flash units permit smaller apertures, and shutter speed is not critical because the duration and intensity of the flash determine the exposure. With inanimate subjects such as landscapes, architecture and still-life arrangements there is no problem in using small apertures and long exposure times.

As with all reversal processes, the image on direct positive paper is laterally reversed; that is, the picture appears as though viewed in a mirror. To obtain a true image, the camera must be equipped with a prism placed either behind or in front of the lens. Although mirror images are often quite acceptable to a portrait customer, true images are required if the pictures are intended for identification.

Lights. The exposing lights used in the studio or in a posing booth can be incandescent lamps, fluorescent tubes, or electronic flash units. The latter are popular because the short flash duration eliminates movement of the sitter—this is especially important when children are being photographed—and because the light intensity is great enough to give adequate exposure without the heat that is generated by large incandescent lamps.

The usual lighting in a direct positive booth is almost all frontal; one light is placed high enough to avoid reflections in eyeglasses, and another is placed low enough to fill the shadows cast by the nose and chin. To obtain some reflected sidelight, the sides of the booth are often painted white or draped with white curtains. Outdoors, natural daylight—with or without fill-in flash—provides excellent results.

carefully processed direct positive print is made, and then the exposure required for the other material is easily determined from the relative speeds of the two emulsions.

Equipment

Cameras and Lenses. A user-operated booth is usually leased or purchased as a commercially manufactured unit, although it is possible to construct one. For direct photography in the field or studio, portraiture, copying, and other applications on an individual level, any camera that accepts suitable film holders may be used.

Because of space limitations, a lens of short focal length is necessary for direct positive portraiture in a posing booth. Otherwise, normal or longer focal length lenses are quite suitable. If tungsten lighting is used, the lens aperture must be large so that the exposure time for portraits can be kept at a minimum. Lenses with maximum apertures of f/1.9 to f/4.5 are common for booth cameras. How-

Exposing and Processing

Correct exposure is essential to making good-quality direct positive prints. In this connection, it must be remembered that an exposure is correct only for a given developing time and temperature. When processing is done in trays, Kodak direct positive paper should be developed for 45 seconds at 20 C (68 F) in the first developer.

Daylight and tungsten exposure indexes for two processes are given in the accompanying chart.

To determine the correct exposure for tungsten or fluorescent lighting, make a series of test exposures at different shutter speeds and select the one that made the best print. To determine the correct exposure with electronic flash units, make a series of test exposures at different *lens apertures* and select the one that made the best print. The selected exposure can then be used as your standard if the lighting and the light-to-subject distance remain unaltered.

In direct positive photography, overexposure yields a light print, whereas underexposure yields a dark print. Make sure that the lens is clean and free from dust, because a dirty lens results in flat prints that lack contrast.

Chemicals. Kodak prepared chemicals for processing Kodak direct positive paper are supplied in convenient ready-to-mix form; they save time and reduce the possibility of error in chemical mixing. Kodak developer D–88, Kodak bleach, Kodak clearing bath, and Kodak direct positive paper redeveloper are available in units to make 1 gallon of working solution. Kodak direct positive toning redeveloper is available in units to make 2 gallons of working solution.

Processing Procedure. When correct exposure has been established, processing direct positive prints is both rapid and simple.

Step 1. Develop exposed prints in Kodak developer D–88 for 45 seconds at 20 C

(68 F). For uniform results, the developer must be kept at an even temperature. Remember that overdevelopment or too high temperature results in light prints, and that underdevelopment or too low temperature results in dark prints. Stale, overworked, or contaminated developer also causes dark prints, which may be stained as well.

Step 2. Rinse for at least 15 seconds in running water. Failure to rinse the prints properly results in stained prints and contaminated solution.

Step 3. Bleach in Kodak bleach or Kodak bleaching bath R-9 for 30 seconds, or until the image disappears.

Step 4. Rinse in running water for at least 15 seconds.

Step 5. Clear for 30 seconds in Kodak clearing bath or Kodak clearing bath CB-1.

Step 6. Rinse in running water for at least 15 seconds.

Step 7. (Process 1) Redevelop the prints in Kodak direct positive paper redeveloper or Kodak sulfide redeveloper T-19 for 60 seconds at 20 C (68 F). If a brown tone is desired, redevelop in Kodak direct positive toning redeveloper for 60 seconds at 20 C (68 F).

DATA: *KODAK* DIRECT POSITIVE PAPER											
Emulsion	Orthochromatic; has sufficient speed for camera exposure										
Paper base	White, medium-weight, water-resistant										
Image tone	Neutral black; can also be redeveloped to a brown tone										
Surface; sizes	Smooth; available in popular sheet sizes and narrow roll sizes.										
Darkroom safelighting	*Kodak* safelight filter No. 2 (dark red), in a suitable safelight lamp with a 15-watt bulb, kept at least 4 feet from the material										
Exposure indexes	Process 1—Daylight 25 Tungsten 12 • Process 2—Daylight 20 Tungsten 10 There is a difference in effective speed with different methods of redevelopment. When *Kodak* direct positive paper redeveloper, *Kodak* sulfide redeveloper T-19, or *Kodak* direct positive toning redeveloper is used, the speed numbers for process 1 apply. If *Kodak* developer D-88 is used for redevelopment, the speed numbers for Process 2 apply.										
Electronic flash guide numbers	Output of units (ECPS or BCPS)	350	500	700	1000	1400	2000	2800	4000	5600	8000
	Guide numbers—process 1	18	22	26	32	35	45	55	65	75	90
	Guide numbers—process 2	17	20	24	28	32	40	50	55	65	80

Step 7A. (Process 2) If Kodak developer D-88 is used for redevelopment, re-expose the prints either by the light of a 40-watt bulb for 3 seconds at a distance of 20 cm (8 in.) or by turning the white light on as soon as the prints are in the clearing bath. In either case, redevelop for 30 seconds at 20 C (68 F).

NOTE: Use either Step 7 or 7A; Step 7 makes re-exposure unnecessary.

Step 8. After Step 7 or Step 7A, wash the prints in running water for 30 seconds.

Step 9. For fast drying, remove surface water with blotters or a soft, wet viscose sponge or cloth. Do not ferrotype. Prints can be air-dried at room temperature or by circulated warm air. Double-belt drum driers can be used if the drum-surface temperature does not exceed 88 C (190 F).

Processing Formulas If you wish to mix your own chemicals, the formulas given below can be used to process Kodak direct positive paper.

Kodak developer D-88

Water, about 50 C (125 F).	750	ml	96	ounces
Sodium sulfite (anhydrous)	45.0	grams	6	ounces
Hydroquinone	22.5	grams	3	ounces
Boric acid, crystals*	5.5	grams	¾	ounce
Potassium bromide (anhydrous)	2.5	grams	145	grains
Sodium hydroxide† (caustic soda)	22.5	grams	3	ounces
Cold water to make	1.0	litre	1	gallon

*Crystalline boric acid should be used as specified. Powdered boric acid dissolves only with great difficulty, and its use should be avoided.

†CAUTION: Dissolve the caustic soda in a small volume of water in a separate container and then add it to the solution of the other constituents. Then dilute the whole to the required volume. If a glass container is employed in dissolving the caustic soda, the solution should be stirred constantly until the soda is dissolved, to prevent cracking the glass by the heat evolved. Dissolve chemicals in the order given.

Use full strength at 20 C (68 F). Develop 45 seconds.

Kodak bleaching bath R-9

Water	1.0	litre	1	gallon
Potassium dichromate	9.5	grams	1¼	ounces
Sulfuric acid* (concentrated)	12.0	ml	1½	ounces

*WARNING: Always add the sulfuric acid to the solution slowly, stirring constantly. Never add the solution to the acid; otherwise, the solution may boil and spatter the acid on the hands or face, causing serious burns.

Use full strength at 18 to 24 C (65 to 75 F) for about 30 seconds.

Kodak clearing bath CB-1

Sodium sulfite (anhydrous)	90.0	grams	12	ounces
Water to make	1.0	litre	1	gallon

Use full strength at 18 to 24 C (65 to 75 F) for about 30 seconds.

Kodak sulfide redeveloper T-19

Sodium sulfide (anhydrous)	20.0	grams	290	grains
Water to make	1.0	litre	32	ounces

Use full strength at 20 C (68 F) for about 1 minute.

How to avoid processing troubles:

1. Keep the developing time and temperature constant.
2. Avoid contaminating the processing solutions with one another.
3. Use clean rinse water.
4. Do not allow the solutions, particularly developer, to stand in the trays for long periods. Pour out only enough for your immediate needs.
5. Always use clean trays, and label each one so that it is always used for the same solution.
6. Agitate the prints thoroughly in the solutions and in the rinse water.
7. Use the recommended safelighting in the darkroom.

For specific faults and their remedies, see the accompanying chart.

PROBABLE CAUSES AND REMEDIES OF FAULTS IN DIRECT POSITIVE PHOTOGRAPHY

Fault	Probable Cause	Remedy
Prints too dark	1. Underexposure 2. Underdevelopment 3. Developer temperature too low 4. Exhausted developer 5. Contaminated developer 6. Light out in posing booth 7. Batteries of electronic flash running down, or insufficient time between exposures	1. Open lens stop or decrease shutter speed 2. Increase developing time to 45 seconds 3. Increase temperature to 68 F 4. Mix fresh developer 5. Wash tray, mix fresh developer 6. Replace lamp 7. Renew or recharge batteries; allow more time between exposures
Prints too light	1. Overexposure 2. Overdevelopment 3. Developer temperature too high 4. Unsafe darkroom illumination 5. White light entering darkroom 6. Stray light from enlarger	1. Reduce lens aperture or increase shutter speed 2. Reduce developing time to 45 seconds 3. Reduce temperature to 68 F 4. Check safelight. See data sheet 5. Cover all openings where light can enter 6. Check enlarger lamphouse for leakage
Prints flat and diffused	Dirty lens	Brush dust from lens or use lens cleaner to remove finger marks or grime
Solutions exhaust quickly—too frequent mixing needed	1. Insufficient rinsing 2. Dirty rinse water 3. Dirty trays 4. Chemicals on hands	1. Rinse for at least 15 seconds with agitation 2. Use separate tray for each rinse. Use running water 3. Clean the trays, and always use the same tray for the same solution 4. Rinse hands frequently in clean water
Streaks and mottle	1. Insufficient agitation 2. Developing time too short	1. Keep the prints moving and separated in all solutions 2. See section on processing procedure for correct developing and redeveloping times
Streaks and stains, especially in highlight areas	Contaminated solutions	Keep trays, hands, and rinse water clean. Rinse prints for at least 15 seconds in running water
Finger marks	1. Chemicals on fingers 2. Perspiration on fingers	1. Wash hands frequently 2. Wear cotton gloves to handle dry paper
Picture very light with double image	Double exposure	Take care to keep exposed and unexposed paper separate
No picture; paper blank or nearly blank	1. Fogged paper 2. Re-exposure omitted (Process 2 only) 3. Gross overexposure	1. Keep paper covered except under proper safelight conditions 2. Follow re-exposure instructions 3. Reduce exposure; check shutter for malfunction
No picture, paper black	1. Shutter not operating 2. Electronic flash not firing	1. Check shutter 2. Check batteries and connections

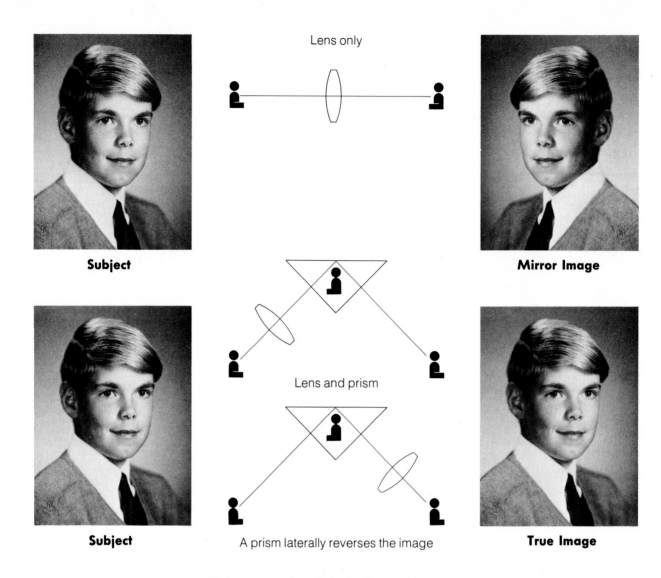

Subject — Lens only — **Mirror Image**

Subject — Lens and prism — A prism laterally reverses the image — **True Image**

The image normally made by the direct positive method is reversed, as if taken in a mirror. A prism placed either behind the lens (center drawing) or in front of the lens (bottom drawing) will reverse the image to produce a true left–right image in the print.

Enlarging

Direct positive pictures can be enlarged with a reflection-type enlarger. Enlarging is a darkroom operation, of course. When correct exposure has been found by trial, the larger size print is processed in the same way as the smaller sizes exposed in the camera. Unless the enlarger is fitted with a device for optical reversal, the enlargement has a laterally reversed image; however, direct positive enlargers, like direct positive cameras, can be fitted with a prism to give true images. Incidentally, a reflection-type enlarger can be used to make direct positive copies from almost any kind of picture if the original is not too big to fit the enlarger carrier.

Printing Transparencies

Direct positive prints can be made from either black-and-white or color transparencies by using a conventional photographic enlarger. Color transparencies are placed in the negative carrier with the base side toward the light source, whereas black-and-white transparencies that have been printed from camera negatives are placed in the carrier with the emulsion side toward the light source; in this way, lateral reversal of the direct positive image is avoided.

For a good-quality direct positive print from a transparency, the exposure must be correct for the developing time and temperature recommended for Kodak direct positive paper. Also, the density and contrast of the transparency should be normal, because too thin or too dense an original yields prints that lack contrast.

• *See also:* DIRECT POSITIVE (REVERSAL) PROCESSING

Further Reading: Burbank, W. H. *Photographic Printing Methods: A practical guide to the professional and amateur worker.* 3rd. ed. New York, NY: Arno; Carroll, John S. *Photographic Lab Handbook.* Garden City, NY: Amphoto, 1976. Croy, O. R. *The Complete Art of Printing and Enlarging.* 13th ed. Garden City, NY: Amphoto, 1976.

Direct Positive (Reversal) Processing

Some photographic emulsions may be processed to produce an image of the same brightness and tonal relationships as the original subject, without an intermediate printing or copying step. That is, the emulsion exposed to a subject (or to a positive image such as a slide) produces a positive image directly during processing. There is no separate negative from which positives may be printed; for each copy desired by this method, a separate frame or sheet of material must be exposed. (If a large number of copies is required, it is simpler to make a copy negative of the direct positive image, or to photograph the subject on negative film in the first place.)

One method by which a direct positive image is produced is called reversal processing. It has the following major steps:

1. Material is exposed to a subject or to a positive image.
2. First development produces a negative image in the emulsion.
3. The negative image is bleached in a bleach that removes metallic silver from the emulsion but which leaves the remaining silver halide in the emulsion.
4. The unexposed, undeveloped portion of the emulsion corresponds to a positive image of the subject. It is made developable either chemically or by exposure to white light.
5. The positive image is developed and fixed.

A number of materials are specifically designed for this kind of processing. They include color slide and transparency films, color reversal printing paper, direct positive black-and-white paper, and a number of black-and-white and color reversal motion picture films. In addition, some negative films may be reversal processed. Processing procedures for color materials and black-and-white direct positive paper are covered elsewhere (see list at the end of this article). The discussion here describes reversal processing to produce black-and-white slides on suitable 35 mm still films. The procedures are also applicable to some black-and-white reversal motion picture films. There are some films (usually called duplicating films) that develop directly to a positive image in a standard developer. Such films are discussed in the article entitled DUPLICATE COLOR NEGATIVES

Black-and-White Transparencies

There are occasions when limited production of black-and-white slides or filmstrips may be required.

While most films can be reversal processed, not all black-and-white films yield high-quality images with reversal processing. Two films that will produce satisfactory results are Kodak Panatomic-X film (FX135), available in the 135 size in 20- or 36-exposure cartridges, and Kodak direct positive panchromatic film 5246, available in 35 mm 100-foot rolls.

Although Kodak Panatomic-X film is normally intended for negative processing, it can be used in a reversal process. And, since both of these films can be easily exposed by artificial light, they are especially convenient for the preparation of slides or filmstrips of artwork, photographs, printed materials, color transparencies, and even radiographs or dental x-rays.

Both Panatomic-X and direct positive panchromatic film 5246 have a gray film base to control halation. However, the gray density in the film base will not affect the contrast or the sharpness of the projected image—the only effect is a slight reduction of image brightness. It is not possible to remove the gray dye from the film base.

The two films may be exposed at the same exposure index, and processed identically. Processing chemicals are available in prepared form in the Kodak direct positive film developing outfit, or they may be mixed from formulas.

Exposure

To expose either Panatomic-X film or direct positive panchromatic film for reversal processing, use an exposure index (ASA speed setting) of 80 for daylight, or 64 for tungsten illumination. These speeds are for trial exposures based on an incident light meter reading, or a reflected-light reading from an 18% gray card.

Exposures for reversal-processed films are more critical than exposures for films processed as negatives, because there are few opportunities to make corrections during processing.

Thus, until correct exposures for various subjects and conditions are established, it is advisable to bracket them to be certain of satisfactory results. For example, if the correct exposure is thought to be 1/125 sec. at $f/11$, set the shutter speed at 1/125 sec. and make a series of 5 exposures in half-stop increments from $f/8$ to $f/16$. As with all reversal materials, more exposure will produce lighter final results, less exposure will produce darker results, and exposure is more critical than with negative materials.

After exposing and processing procedures are established, it should be possible to reduce or to eliminate extra exposures except for unfamiliar subjects. Accurate records must be kept, and procedures must be consistent.

Processing

Whether the processing solutions are prepared from the Kodak direct positive film developing outfit or from formulas, the times, temperatures, and procedures for their use are the same.

Safelight. Carry out all operations in total darkness until the bleaching has been completed. You can use a Kodak safelight filter OA (greenish yellow) with a 15-watt bulb at least 4 feet from the film during the subsequent operations. Do not examine the film before an illuminator or otherwise expose it to strong light until fixing has been completed; otherwise veiled highlights may result.

Agitation. Agitate continuously during the first 30 seconds in each solution and for 5 seconds every minute thereafter.

The best method of agitation is to move the reel up and down while it is under solution, and at the same time turn the reel back and forth through approximately half a revolution. With some tanks, it is possible to obtain satisfactory results with the cover on, by using the agitation procedure recommended in the instructions for the tank, but it is preferable to use the cover-off method.

Processing Temperatures. The recommended processing temperature for this reversal process is 20 C (68 F). However, when it is more convenient to

SUMMARY OF PROCESSING STEPS (SMALL TANKS)				
Step	Treatment	Kodak Outfit Solution	Kodak Formula Solution	Time at 20 C (68 F)*
1	First development	First developer	Developer D-67	8 min
2	Rinse	Water	Water	2 to 5 min†
3	Bleach	Bleach	Bleaching bath R-9	1 min
4	Clear	Clearing bath	Clearing bath CB-1	2 min‡
5	Redevelopment	Redeveloper	Fogging developer FD-70a	8 min
6	Rinse	Water or stop bath SB-1	Water or stop bath SB-1	1 min
7	Fix	*Kodak* fixer or fixing bath F-5 or F-6	Fixing bath F-5 or F-6	5 min
8	Wash	Water	Water	20 min

*Including drain time of 10 to 15 seconds at the end of each step.
†2 minutes is sufficient with adequate running-water wash and agitation.
‡No more than 2 minutes or a density loss in the final positive image may result.

Direct Positive (Reversal) Processing

operate at some other temperature, satisfactory results will be obtained from 18 C (65 F) to at least 29 C (85 F) provided the processing times are adjusted accordingly.

For first development temperatures higher than the recommended 20 C (68 F), the development time should be decreased about 1 minute for every 3 C (5.5 F) rise in temperature. Decreasing the temperature below 20 C (68 F) will necessitate a similar increase in the development times.

When the developer temperature is changed, the temperature of all other solutions should be changed as well, so that all are within a reasonable range of each other. Note that this instruction applies equally to normal black-and-white negative processing, and that this reversal process is no more likely to cause film damage by temperature changes between solutions than the negative processes. At 29 C (85 F) the time in the baths following the first developer should be about one-half that at 20 C (68 F). Optimum times should be determined by trial, because they will be affected by the type of processing equipment used, and by the time, rate, and duration of the agitation.

Capacity of Solutions.

First Developer (Outfit). Kodak developer D-67 (made from formula). About 4 square feet of film (eight 36-exposure rolls of 35 mm film or one 100-foot roll of 16 mm film) can be processed per quart (litre) of solution without replenishment. With use* of Kodak replenisher D-67R (see formula), up to 12 square feet (twenty 36-exposure rolls of 35 mm or two 100-foot rolls of 16 mm film) can be processed per quart (litre) if care is taken to protect the solution from aerial oxidation. The use of floating lids on tanks or replacement of the solution in a full, stoppered bottle between usages will help minimize oxidation.

For any volume loss greater than this, replace with first developer or Kodak developer D-67.

For any volume loss less than this, discard enough of the solution to permit the addition of the correct volume of replenisher.

---

*Replenishment rate: 31 ml per square foot.
17 ml per 36-exposure roll of 35 mm film.
170 ml per 100-foot roll of 16 mm film.

Bleach, Clearing Bath (Outfit). Kodak bleach bath R-9, Kodak clearing bath CB-1; Kodak fixer, Kodak fixing baths F-5 and F-6. Up to 12 square feet of film (twenty rolls of 36-exposure 35 mm film or two 100-foot rolls of 16 mm film) can be processed per quart (litre) of each of the above solutions.

Redeveloper Solution (Outfit). Kodak fogging developer FD-70a. The redeveloper solution must be mixed immediately before use, because it will keep for only 1 to 2 hours. For this reason, two 35 mm rolls should be redeveloped together or in quick succession, in 1 pint (half-litre) of redeveloper, with the time 1 minute longer for the second roll. If the solution gets more than 2 hours old, discard it and mix a fresh pint of redeveloper.

Each 100-foot roll of 16 mm film will require 2 quarts (2 litres) of redeveloper solution.

Water Rinses. The water rinses are included as processing steps to increase the life of the chemical solutions. The 10- to 15-second draining time mentioned below applies to the rinses as well as the solutions, to avoid undue dilution of the solutions following the rinses.

Processing Procedure

IMPORTANT: Drain the film 10 to 15 seconds after development and after each successive process step. This time is included in the process step time. The temperature recommended for all solutions is 20 C (68 F), but it can be changed as indicated in the section on processing temperatures.9

1. First Development. Develop the film for 8 minutes at 20 C (68 F). Be sure to agitate as recommended and to adjust the time if you are using a temperature other than 20 C (68 F). (*Note:* It is possible to process up to 100 feet of 35 mm film on a large spiral reel in a tank of suitable size. Develop for 6 minutes, using the agitation plan described in the section on motion picture processing. Agitate in the same way in other solutions, using the times given for small tank processing.)

The contrast of the final positive images *cannot* be changed appreciably by varying the developer temperature or the time of first development. Increasing the first development time produces an effect similar to overexposure—decreased densities and loss of highlight detail. Underdevelopment results in increased densities—dark highlights and other effects similar to those of underexposure.

When using spiral reels, take the usual precaution of tapping the small tank against the sink bottom to release air bells, or tapping the reel against the tank bottom if this is more convenient.

In processing 36-exposure rolls of 35 mm film, use a small tank that requires 240 to 300 ml (8 to 10 ounces) of solution and use fresh developer each time.

Drain the film for 10 to 15 seconds at the end of the development step. The drain time is included in the process step time.

2. Rinsing. Rinse the film 2 to 5 minutes in running water. Drain it for 10 to 15 seconds before placing it in the bleach solution, to prevent dilution of the bleach solution.

3. Bleaching. Bleach the film for 1 minute when using the 20 C (68 F) processing temperature. Agitate during bleaching. Drain.

WARNING: Because the bleach corrodes most metals, do not leave it in contact with metal equipment any longer than necessary. There is generally no noticeable effect on stainless steel reels, troughs, tanks, etc, if the bleach is in contact with them for only the processing time. Remove the bleach from metal tanks as soon after use as practical and store it in containers made of polyethylene, glazed earthenware or porcelain, glass, or baked enameled metal having surfaces that are free from cracks and chips.

4. Clearing. Immerse the film in the clearing bath for 2 minutes when using the 20 C (68 F) process. While the preceding steps are best accomplished in total darkness, this step and the following steps can be done under a Kodak safelight filter OA under the conditions described in the section on safelights.

Do not use white light at this stage or the transparencies may be fogged, causing too much density, which will be especially noticeable in the highlights. Exact timing of this step is important: too little time will result in inadequate clearing; too much time will dissolve the silver halide image, with a consequent loss of density in the final positive image. Two minutes (including a drain time of 10 to 15 seconds) is

correct for the 20 C (68 F) process, with agitation as described in the section on agitation.

5. Redevelopment. Redevelop for 8 minutes at 20 C (68 F) in a solution mixed from chemicals supplied in the outfit or from the formula for Kodak fogging developer FD-70a. Adjust the time for a different temperature process according to the instructions given earlier in this article on processing temperature.

CAUTION: The redeveloper solution must be prepared *immediately before use,* because it will keep for only 1 to 2 hours. For this reason, in order to process 8 rolls of 35 mm film in each Kodak direct positive film developing outfit, 2 rolls must be redeveloped in a pint of redeveloper simultaneously or in *rapid succession.*

Agitate and drain as discussed earlier.

6. Rinsing. Rinse the film for 1 minute in running water or Kodak stop bath SB-1 at 18 to 21 C (65 to 70 F), or ½ minute at 29 C (85 F). Agitate and drain.

7. Fixing. Fix for 5 minutes at 18 to 21 C (65 to 70 F) in Kodak fixer or Kodak fixing bath F-5 or F-6, or for 2 ½ minutes at 29 C (85 F). Agitate and drain.

For reel-and-trough processing, or where ventilation is poor, the use of the relatively odorless F-6 fixing bath is recommended to avoid the odor of sulfur dioxide which is given off by the other two fixers.

8. Washing. After fixing the film, wash it for 20 to 30 minutes with an adequate supply of running water (sufficient to replace the water in the tank once every 5 minutes). If the processing equipment will permit, wipe the surface of the film carefully under the water with a soft sponge or a Kodak photo chamois. After removing the film from the wash water, squeegee and dry it in a location that is as dust-free as possible. The tendency for water-spot formation will be minimized and uniform drainage of water from the film facilitated by immersing the film in Kodak Photo-Flo solution before drying.

To reduce washing time and conserve water, you can use Kodak hypo clearing agent. First, remove excess hypo by rinsing the film in water for 30 seconds. Then bathe the film in the clearing agent solution for 1 to 2 minutes, with moderate agitation, and wash it for 5 minutes, using a water flow sufficient to give at least one complete change of water in 5 minutes.

Mounting the Slides

After processing and drying, the film is ready for mounting as slides, or if a single-frame camera has been used, it can be left as a filmstrip. If used as slides, the individual frames must be cut from the roll and mounted for projection. Open-frame cardboard mounts—the Kodak Ready-Mount, for instance—will be satisfactory. It is preferable, however, to bind the transparencies made on black-and-white film in a glass mount if they are to be subjected to rough handling or if they are to be kept in automatic-changer magazines or trays.

Mounting Slides in Glass. Mounting slides in glass will keep transparencies flat and provide greater protection against dirt, scratches, and abrasion. However, it will not prolong the life of the transparencies, except by preventing physical damage. The necessary materials for mounting transparencies in glass are available from your local dealer in photographic supplies. It should be noted that mounting transparencies in glass may sometimes introduce new problems, such as the glass being too thick for some magazines or trays, moisture condensation occurring on the glass (especially in humid weather with high-intensity projectors), and Newton's rings. (*See also:* MOUNTING SLIDES AND TRANSPARENCIES.)

Motion Picture Processing

The following Kodak black-and-white 16 mm motion picture films may be reversal processed by the procedures described. The processing times are the same as for still films, except as noted here.

Kodak Film	First Development	Redevelopment
Plus-X reversal film 7276	6 min	8 min
Tri-X reversal film 7278	6 min	6 min
4-X reversal film 7277	6 min	8 min

Motion picture films may be processed either on large spiral reels in lengths up to 100 feet, or on rack-and-tank equipment. Different methods of agitation are required.

Agitation. *Large Spiral Reels:* Lower the reel into the solution, giving it a vigorous turning motion sufficient to cause the reel to rotate one-half to one revolution. Raise and lower the reel approximately ½ inch (keeping the reel in the solution) for the first 15 seconds, tapping it against the bottom of the tank to release air bubbles from the film.

Agitate once each minute by lifting the reel out of the solution, tilting it approximately 30 degrees to drain for 5 to 10 seconds, and immersing it again with a vigorous turning motion sufficient to cause the reel to rotate one-half to one revolution in the solution. Alternate the direction of rotation each minute. Just before the end of the development time, drain the reel for 15 seconds and proceed to the next step.

Rack and Tank: Agitate the film for 5 seconds under the solution when you first immerse it. At 1-minute intervals, lift the rack completely out of the solution, drain it for a few seconds, and reimmerse it. With this agitation, the developing time at 20 C (68 F) will be approximately 9 minutes. With the lower rate of agitation usually employed by commercial photofinishers, the developing time will be about 11 minutes.

Formulas for Reversal Processing Solutions

Kodak Developer D-67

Water, about 50 C (125 F)	500	ml
Kodak Elon developing agent	2.0	g
Sodium sulfite (anhydrous) .	90.0	g
Hydroquinone	8.0	g
Sodium carbonate (monohydrated)	52.5	g
Potassium bromide (anhydrous)	5.0	g
Sodium thiocyanate (liquid) (51% solution)	3	ml
Water to make	1.0	litre

This developer can also be made from a solution of Kodak developer D-19 (available in prepared form) as follows:

Kodak developer **D-19** solution . 1.0 litre
Sodium thiocyanate (liquid)
(51% solution) . . . . .3 ml

Kodak replenisher D-67R for use with Kodak developer D-67

Water (about 50 C)
(125 F) . . . . 750 ml
Kodak Elon developing
agent . . . . 2.0 g
Sodium sulfite (anhydrous) . 90.0 g
Hydroquinone . . . . 8.0 g
Sodium carbonate
(monohydrated) . . . . 52.5 g
Sodium thiocyanate (liquid)
(51% solution) . . . . 7.5 ml
Water to make . . . . 1.0 litre

Kodak fogging developer FD-70a

Part A
Eastman sodium dithionite
(90% minimum sodium
hydrosulfite)* (Cat. No. P533) . 6.0 g

Part B
Water . . . . 900 ml
Kodalk balanced alkali . . . . 15 g
Eastman 2–thiobarbituric acid
(Cat. No. 660)* . . . . 0.5 g
Water to make . . . . 1.0 litre

Dissolve 6 grams of Part A in 1 litre of Part B not more than two hours before use. Discard after one use. If using smaller quantities, proportion accordingly: 3 grams per half litre.

*Eastman organic chemicals can be obtained from many laboratory supply dealers.

CAUTION: Kodak fogging developer FD-70a contains compounds that are extremely active photographically. If the dry powder comes into contact with photographic materials, serious spotting may occur. Therefore, take care to prevent the powder suspended in the air from reaching photographic materials or areas where they are handled. Also, thoroughly wash your hands and the containers used for mixing and using this solution. Sodium dithionite is a flammable solid. Use caution.

Kodak bleach bath R-9

Water . . . . 1.0 litre
Potassium dichromate
(anhydrous) . . . . 9.5 g
Sulfuric acid*
(concentrated) . . . . . 12.0 ml

*CAUTION: Always add the sulfuric acid to the solution slowly, stirring constantly, and never the solution to the acid; otherwise, the solution may boil and spatter the acid on the hands or face, causing serious burns.

NOTE: Kodak Bleach for Kodak direct positive paper (supplied in packages to make 1 gallon) can be used instead of this formula.

Kodak clearing bath CB-1

Water . . . . 1.0 litre
Sodium sulfite (anhydrous) . 90.0 g

NOTE: Kodak clearing bath for Kodak direct positive paper (supplied in packages to make 1 gallon) can be used instead of this formula.

Kodak stop bath SB-1

Water . . . . 1.0 litre
28% Acetic acid* . 48.0 ml

*To make approximately 28% acetic acid from glacial acetic acid, dilute 3 parts of glacial acetic acid with 8 parts of water.

Kodak fixing bath F-5

Water (about 50 C) (125 F)	600	ml
Sodium thiosulfate (hypo), prismatic type (pentahydrated) ...	240.0	g
Sodium sulfite (anhydrous)	15.0	g
28% Acetic acid*	48.0	ml
Boric acid (crystals)† ..	7.5	g
Potassium alum, fine granular (dodecahydrated) ...	15.0	g
Water to make (cold) ..	1.0	litre

*To make approximately 28% acetic acid from glacial acetic acid, dilute 3 parts of glacial acetic acid with 8 parts of water.
†Crystalline boric acid should be used as specified. Powdered boric acid dissolves only with great difficulty, and its use should be avoided.

NOTE: Kodak fixer (available in prepared form) can be used instead of the above formula.

Kodak Fixing Bath F-6. In warm weather and in darkrooms where the ventilation is inadequate, the odor of sulfur dioxide given off by Kodak fixing bath F-5 may be objectionable. To eliminate this odor almost entirely, omit the boric acid and substitute twice its weight in Kodalk balanced alkali.

• *See also:* BLACK-AND-WHITE SLIDES AND TRANSPARENCIES; COLOR FILM PROCESSING; COLOR PRINTING FROM TRANSPARENCIES; DEVELOPERS AND DEVELOPING; DIRECT POSITIVE PAPER PHOTOGRAPHY, DUPLICATE SLIDES AND TRANSPARENCIES; DYE DESTRUCTION; COLOR PROCESS; FORMULAS FOR BLACK-AND-WHITE PROCESSING; MOUNTING SLIDES AND TRANSPARENCIES.

Dispersion

Dispersion is the separation of radiant energy rays into their constituent wavelengths. It results when energy, such as light, passes through a material which has a different refractive index for each of the various wavelengths in the energy. A similar effect results when energy is diffracted as it passes the edge of an obstruction. (*See:* DIFFRACTION.) If the energy being dispersed is white light, the dispersion creates a full visible spectrum from red through violet. In contrast, wavelength interference in phenomena such as thin-layer reflection produces only partial spectra. (*See:* DICHROIC FILTERS.)

Light which strikes glass at an angle perpendicular to its surface is not refracted and therefore not dispersed. But light which strikes the surface of glass at some other angles is both refracted and dispersed. The amount or degree of dispersion is related to the

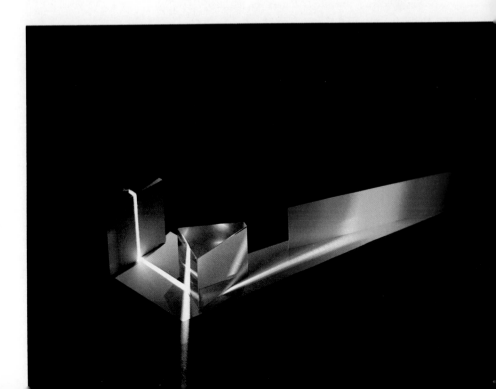

White light entering a prism is dispersed into a spectrum. Because a prism refracts blue light more than red, light bands of equal wavelength do not produce color bands of equal width in the resulting spectrum.

Dispersion

refractive index, which is different for various types of glass. Light which strikes the glass surface at angles less than the critical angle is totally reflected, so that none enters the glass to be refracted and dispersed.

Because of the front surface curvature, almost all light entering a lens strikes at an angle; thus, dispersion is unavoidable. If the lens is not corrected, dispersion produces chromatic aberration in the image formed by the lens. This is visible as rainbow fringing around the edges of objects in the image. Correction is achieved by using different types of glass for the various elements in a compound lens. In this way, the dispersion of one element is counteracted by the different refractive index and shape of another element. This is the case in all two-color (achromatic) and three-color (apochromatic) corrected lenses for photographic use.

A dispersion spectrum is created by means of a prism. A prism refracts blue light more than red, or short wavelengths more than long wavelengths. It does not have an even change in refraction with wavelength, so that equal wavelength bands do not produce color bands of equal width in the resulting spectrum. The spectrum produced by diffraction does produce bands of color proportionate to the change in wavelength because the narrow slit disperses all wavelengths equally by diffraction. This is useful in spectrography. A diffraction grating produces many separate spectra, which may not be visually complete because interference between overlapping spectra causes some wavelengths to be canceled.

• *See also:* ABERRATION; DICHROIC FILTERS; DIFFRACTION; PRISMS; REFRACTION; SPECTRUM; WEDGE SPECTROGRAM.

Disposal of Photographic Solutions

Photographic processing wastes and effluents can be considered generally safe and not destructive to the environment. Most processing effluents normally discharged are not of extreme concern because of any environmental regulations. A photographic processing effluent usually has little color or odor, its pH and temperature are almost always well within acceptable limits, and suspended solids are very low.

In addition, photoprocessing labs are generally regarded as being relatively small.

The items of concern are the oxygen demand and the concentration of certain metals, especially silver. Because it is economically advantageous to recover silver, much of it never reaches the sewer system or the environment.

Other toxic or potentially toxic substances that fall within the regulations such as cyanide and chromium are very low in concentration of the total effluent. On the other hand, oxygen demand is relatively high and is characteristic of both developer and fixer solutions. The actual oxygen demand concentration in the final effluent depends upon the other sources of water at the processing location. Fortunately, it is amenable to biological treatment and has no adverse effect on municipal treatment performance. Between the photography enthusiast who processes two or three rolls of transparencies a month in a one-pint tank and the commercial photofinisher who processes and prints hundreds of rolls of film a day, there are many users of photographic-processing solutions who, from time to time, must discard a quantity of these solutions. Printers, hospitals, law enforcement agencies, schools, portrait studios, serious amateurs, and many others fall into this category. How their solutions are disposed of is, to a large extent, determined by the size of the entire operation.

The casual user of a one-pint tank generally can pour the expended solutions down a household drain without ill effect. At the other end of the disposal spectrum, the large-scale processing laboratory frequently must provide some sort of pretreatment of its effluent before discharging it into municipal facilities or lakes, rivers, and streams. Between these extremes, consideration must be given by the user to the concentration of the chemical constituents and to the volumes of the solutions and wash waters generated in the processing operation before deciding how to dispose of them. The laboratory using a color process that has a ferricyanide bleach faces a different situation from the one who processes x-ray film that yields a large amount of silver compound as a by-product. The laboratory using trays or tube processors approaches the disposal problem differently from the laboratory using a 3½-gallon sink line. The concern for our environment within the photographic industry has led to the development of pretreatment techniques. These are techniques that the individual, laboratory or photo-processing plant can use before the processing effluent is discharged to a municipal treatment plant or waterway.

Replenishment

In sink lines and larger installations operated on a regular basis, adding new solutions to the partially used ones (replenishment) greatly reduces the amount of solution that must be disposed of. Only the small amounts of solutions that are carried by the film into the wash water enter the sewer. Replenishment must be done with care to prevent the processing solutions from becoming too concentrated or too dilute. Be sure to follow the replenishment instructions that accompany the chemicals. Even in replenished systems there are reasons for dumping solutions occasionally: excessive dirt or sediment, contamination, or a need to clean or repair the processing equipment.

Holding Tank

A simple way to reduce the concentration of chemicals in an effluent is to use a holding tank. This is particularly appropriate when your waste load is within the sewer code, but the concentration may be too high. The tank should be large enough to hold the total volume that might be expected to be dumped at one time. An even larger tank permits you to add wash waters and, consequently, begin the dilution right in the tank. The contents are then bled slowly into the waste line. The bleed rate should be low enough to allow plenty of dilution with other wastes from the building, but high enough to empty the tank before the next dump. Ideally, the tank should be drained while the other flow rates in the building's waste lines are close to, or higher than, normal.

Septic Tank

Septic-tank systems can maintain their efficiency in the treatment of sanitary wastes and a wide variety of photographic chemical solutions, provided that the ratio of sanitary waste to photographic waste (including wash water) is kept in the range of 10 or 15 to 1, for a manual processing method. As an example, the average daily volume of waste per person going to a home septic tank is approximately 50 gallons. A family of four would produce about 200 gallons of sanitary, kitchen, and washing effluent per day. Therefore, a correctly designed septic tank in this example could handle 13 to 20 gallons of photographic-processing waste and wash water per day (based upon 15-to-1 and 10-to-1 ratios, respectively). For automatic processing machines, the ratio of sanitary to photographic waste should be about 20 to 1.

Extreme caution should be taken not to introduce into a septic tank solutions that contain sodium or potassium dichromate, which are hazardous to the bacteria in the septic tank. In sufficient quantities, these chemicals may retard or stop the desired biochemical reactions. Dichromate in a solution can be reduced to a less troublesome form by first adding reducing agents such as sulfite or thiosulfate. Any alkaline material (including waste developer) can then be added to neutralize the acidity and precipitate the chromium. The solid chromium compound can be filtered out or allowed to settle before disposing of the solution. A second precaution is to avoid a sudden release of chemicals into the septic system, although pint-sized amounts are not likely to be harmful.

Silver Recovery

Recovering the silver from processing solutions is a good idea, not only because it removes silver from the effluent but because the recovered silver can be sold. Once again, for small processing operations, a holding tank is useful. If your operation is large, and you are using a continuous processing machine, a silver recovery unit can be connected directly to the overflow from the fixer or bleach-fix tank.

A convenient way of recovering silver from fixers and bleach-fixes in small-scale operations is to use metallic replacement. Metallic replacement occurs when a metal, such as iron, comes in contact with a solution containing dissolved ions of a less active metal, such as silver. The dissolved silver ions react with solid metal (iron). The more active metal (iron) goes into solution as an ion, and an ion of the less active metal becomes solid metal (silver). Because of its economy and convenience, steel wool is most often used for this purpose. Below a pH of 4, the steel wool dissolves rapidly, making it unavailable for silver replacement. If the solution is not sufficiently acidic, i.e., below a pH of 6.5, the replacement reaction may be too slow because a slight etching action by acid on the iron continually exposes a fresh surface to the solution. Most bleaches and bleach-fixes are within the pH range for good utilization of steel wool. One metallic replacement unit is the Kodak chemical recovery cartridge. It is described in Kodak publication No. J-9, *Silver Recovery with the KODAK Chemical Recovery Cartridge, Type P*. This cartridge usually can be justified if you are generating over 200 gallons of used fixer solution in six months.

After removal of the silver by metallic replacement, the spent solution must be discarded. This effluent has a high iron content that may exceed local sewer regulations. It may be advisable to return the effluent to a holding tank, where it can be discharged slowly into the sewer. Other silver recovery methods are discussed in Kodak Publication No. J-10, *Recovering Silver from Photographic Materials*.

Chlorination

The addition of household bleach (sodium hypochlorite) to waste effluents by the photographic processor should not be used as a treatment method except as a last resort in meeting chlorine-demand regulations. It is not recommended because it produces large amounts of ammonia when used with certain solutions. Unless the pH is controlled carefully, objectionable amounts of chlorine gas can be generated. Much of the chlorine demand in photo effluent is amenable to biological oxidation when the effluent gets to a municipal treatment plant.

Commercial Solution-Disposal Services

A chemical user can contract to have his wastes disposed of by having the wastes tanked and picked up by a company whose business it is to provide such a service. This enterprise has the knowledge and the equipment to meet local requirements for waste disposal and relieves the small user of this responsibility. Such an arrangement is especially useful when the photographic processor does not have the time, personnel, or equipment to treat wastes before discharging them into a sewer.

Small-Scale Activated Sludge Unit

If a processing operation is located where a municipal sewer system can be utilized, in-plant treatment of wastes may not be necessary to prevent stream pollution. Where no municipal system is available and wastes must be discharged into a body of water, an in-plant treatment system probably will be required by state or local law. For processing operations having waste volumes less than 100 gallons of processing solutions and wash water a day, a small-volume waste-treatment device can be built from inexpensive materials. The treated effluent from this type of device may be acceptable in a stream without further treatment, depending upon stream flow, type of photographic process, and other factors. It will lower the oxygen demand of the wastes, but it will have no appreciable effect upon nonbiodegradable chemicals.

The accompanying diagrams show a small activated-sludge treatment plant. The unit is made from a 55-gallon steel drum with the top removed. It will handle about 25 gallons of waste a day. Drums made of plastic or plastic-lined steel, which will not corrode, can also be used. Do not use galvanized or copper materials in the unit, because such materials may contaminate the system.

The baffle plate can be made from a 16-inch square steel plate or from a steel bucket cut in half vertically with the bottom removed. The plate is joined to the inside wall of the drum by welding, bolting, or cementing with epoxy cement. A polyethylene bucket cut in half vertically, with the bottom removed, can be used if it is attached to the drum with epoxy cement. The solution exit port is drilled through the wall of the drum, as a 1⅛-inch

Activated sludge unit; (1) air from compressor, (2) Hose, pipe, or metal tubing, (3) baffle plate (welded or cemented at sides), (4) exit port, (5) effluent (to next unit or to drain), (6) opening (7) plug in end (wooden dowel, pipe cap, etc.), (8) perforations, (9) 55-gallon steel drum, (10) waste in (flow rate—25 gal/day/drum), (11) entrance port.

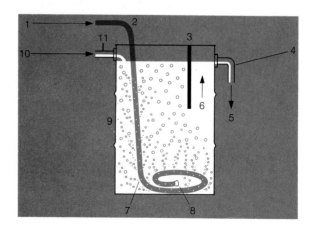

Disposal of Photographic Solutions

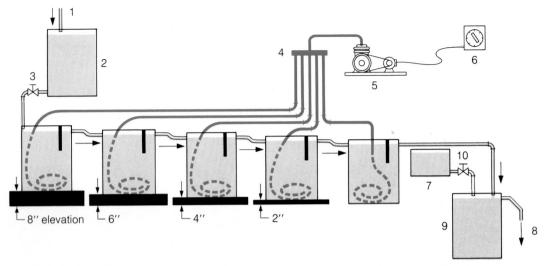

Waste-treatment system using five units in series: (1) waste in, (2) holding tank (to hold 16-hour supple), (3) pinch clamp or valve, (4) air lines, (5) air compressor, (6) timer switch, (7) 15 percent sodium hypochlorite solution (optional), (8) waste out (to each field, stream, etc.), (9) chlorine contact tank (optional), (10) pinch clamp or valve.

hole, behind the baffle plate, about 2 inches from the top of the drum.

The solution entrance port, also a 1⅛-inch hole, is drilled on the opposite side, slightly higher. A ¾-inch bulkhead fitting is fastened to each hole, and a reducer fitting or a short length of threaded pipe is screwed into the bulkhead fittings. Rubber or plastic hoses are then attached. Air is supplied to the drum through a length of pipe, tubing, or hose that is perforated with holes, plugged at one end, and coiled in the bottom of the tank. The unplugged end is attached to an air supply or compressor. One air compressor can be made to serve several units by the use of tees or Y-tubes.

A system capable of handling more than 25 gallons of waste a day can be constructed by joining several of the units in series. Once the system is in operation, the first tank should be fed uniformly at all times. Intermittent use can impair the functioning of the microorganisms that make this type of unit work. Details of operating the waste-treatment method described above are contained in Kodak publication No. J-43, *A Simple Waste-Treatment System for Small Volumes of Photographic Processing Wastes.*

Practices to be Avoided

Some practices should be avoided in handling photographic-processing wastes:

1. Wastes from photographic-processing solutions should not be disposed of in storm sewers, which are neither a method of disposal nor a means of treatment and merely carry surface water from rainstorms, etc, to the nearest stream or watercourse. Disposing of wastes in a storm sewer may create undesirable conditions in the receiving water.

2. Large scale or direct dumping of processing chemicals should be avoided. Holding tanks that bleed into the sewer line should be used whenever possible.

3. Do not attempt to dispose of spent solutions by pouring them back into the container they come from and letting your usual refuse collector pick up the filled containers. Most refuse trucks are compactors; plastic or glass bottles, when stoppered and full, or partly full, can burst under the great pressure exerted by the compactor mechanism. The result is that personnel standing behind or near the open part of the compactor could be sprayed with the solution in the bottle, which might be irritating to the skin and eyes, or even poisonous.

D-Log E Curve
D-Log H Curve

These terms are the names given to the graph depicting the response of a light-sensitive material, also known as the "characteristic curve" of response, in which density (D) is plotted against logarithm of exposure.

Originally, E was the symbol for photographic exposure, the product of light intensity and time: $E = I \times t$. Now, however, E is the internationally accepted symbol for illuminance, measured in lux (lumens per square meter). The international symbol for exposure in lux-seconds is H, the product of illuminance and time: $H = E \times t$.

Therefore, the preferred designation of the response graph is D-Log H Curve. Another name for this same curve is H&D curve, so called for Hurter and Driffield who originated the curve in their early studies of the sensitometry of films.

Most D-Log H curves are absolute in the sense that they show the results of one film, one developer at a particular dilution and temperature, with a particular degree of agitation, and for one length of time. A representative D-Log H curve is an averaged curve from several tests in which all the above factors remain constant, except that the films may have come from several manufacturing runs.

A family of characteristic curves shows what happens when only one variable is changed, such as the developing time.

• *See also:* CHARACTERISTIC CURVE.

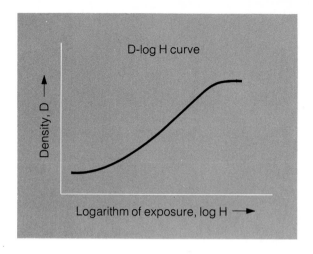

The graph depicts the response of a light-sensitive material, it is also known as the "characteristic curve" of response, in which density (D) is plotted against the logarithm of exposure.

Documentary Photography

To document something is to make a direct record of it. At a later time, the document can verify that the subject did in fact exist, or that the event did occur; the document may also preserve an explanation of why something was the way it was. Documents are not limited to dealing with the past; they may tell about how something is now, about what is currently going on. They are used to report, to verify, to convince, and sometimes to move to action.

Because photographs can record reality with great precision and apparent authenticity, they inevitably document the state of things at the time they were taken. They show how people dressed, what the city was like, the appearance of the landscape, the things people used, how they worked and played—every visible aspect of life and the world. Even photographs that do not deal with actuality, those that are made as artistic images, whether representational or abstract, document aspects of the esthetic taste and style of their period.

In this sense, every photograph becomes a document with the passage of time, for it records and verifies something about which we can no longer have direct knowledge or experience. But such a broad definition takes in all of photography, and the vast majority of pictures thus included are documents only by accident. For example, although the snapshots of 50 or 75 years ago are an increasingly valuable source of information for social historians, they were made for immediate purposes of personal interest and pleasure, not to become an archive for future generations. Similarly, the scenes of public life that accumulated in the files of a turn-of-the-century commercial studio are rich with information about things that have disappeared or been forgotten; but they were made to serve the purposes of clients at the time, not to become reference material.

Definition

Documentary photography consists of pictures taken for social purposes. Such documentary photographs are intended to record and report on how lives are lived and the conditions under which they are lived. When events are recorded, it is in terms of how they affect lives and living conditions. Although often considered to be limited to human beings, documentary photography may deal with the lives of animals, forests, rivers or any other aspect of the natural world. This has increasingly been the case in the past three decades as an understanding has grown of the complex interactions between the ecological balance in nature and the actions of man; life in both worlds is affected by every event.

Because their ultimate subject is always some aspect of life, the images of documentary photography include some of the most emotionally powerful pictures ever taken, for they usually deal with things of universal experience and concern.

Kinds of Documentary Photography

There are two kinds of social documentary photography: documentation for record, and documentary reportage. They are not completely separable, but can be distinguished in broad outline.

Social documentation for record. Photography for this purpose is usually undertaken to create a fund of material for later study and understanding. It results from a realization that a subject is changing or disappearing and that valuable information will be irretrievably lost unless it is documented now. Thus, the task is to collect and preserve as much data as possible. Documentation for record may also be required when the subject must be observed over a long period of time, or when a large number of individual observations must be made before information and understanding can be derived from the recorded material.

The work of Eugene Atget is an outstanding example of documenting a changing, disappearing subject. From about 1900 to 1927, Atget eked out a living in Paris photographing its streets, parks, monuments, and buildings. The old city he knew

Eugene Atget devoted almost thirty years to photographing his cherished Paris, which was rapidly disappearing as it grew and became modernized. This magnificent art nouveau facade, recorded in loving detail, is one of thousands taken during Atget's career. Photo courtesy International Museum of Photography at George Eastman House.

and cherished was rapidly changing under the impact of population growth and modernization. Digging from the surface to install the subway, the Métro, was destroying centuries-old streets and block after block of handsome buildings. The installation of electricity in homes and for street lighting, the broadening of streets to accommodate motor traffic, the spread of the powered streetcar, and many other developments were destroying or drastically altering things that reached back as far as the 15th century. Atget set out to record as much of the old Paris as possible before it was gone or no longer recognizable. He occasionally would sell some pictures to one or another bureau of the municipal government, or to an artist who might want reference images of details or various scenes. But for the most part, his record of Paris accumulated in his workroom and lodgings in the form of thousands of glass plate negatives and paper prints. Today, they comprise one of the most beautiful and moving records ever made of a time and a kind of place that have vanished.

The work of August Sander, a German portrait photographer, is a major example of a documentary record that had to be built up over a long period of time. In the course of operating a highly successful portrait studio in Cologne, Sander was struck by how often people of a certain visual aspect seemed to have similar roles in life. He began to take photographs to see whether certain kinds of people were the models or seemingly universal types for their roles. He was also interested in the degree to which people were identified and characterized by the public perception of their social roles, rather than their names or individual personalities.

About 1920, Sander began to actively seek out and photograph role types from every level of German society, looking for those aspects that were universal, those traits that seemed to repeat from generation to generation within a role. He called his project "People of the 20th Century"; it documented the kinds of people who became industrialists, artists, peasants, performers, laborers; the kinds of people who were failures and those who were successes. He believed that much more could be learned about human beings from visual records of them in their various roles than from verbal descriptions. Today his pictures provide an unequalled image of what Germans—and by implication, the structure of German society—was like in the first 40 years of this century.

Documentary recording of this sort is more than just making a photographic catalog of the subject. The pictures are taken and collected because there is much that their preservation and study can add to an understanding of life and social processes —how people live, and what they are like. The ultimate value of documentary records is how much can be learned, not just how much can be recorded.

Documentary reportage. By far the greatest amount of documentary photography is done for immediate purposes rather than to create a record for eventual study. Documentary reportage is concerned with bringing attention to its subject so that something can be done about it now, in time. Although not always intended to move people to action, the usual purpose of social reportage is to convince people that something ought to be done. Either a situation should be changed, or prevented from recurring, because it is damaging to life; or a situation should be supported and encouraged because it is beneficial.

Documentary reportage as distinguished from news reportage. Documentary photography is concerned with existing, continuing situations. News reportage deals with situations or events as if they were brief, isolated instances, and it concentrates on basic facts: what happened, to whom, when, and where. Documentary photography examines events and conditions in terms of the lives that are affected. It looks to the causes of an event, and the consequences for those involved or touched by it. Thus, the emphasis is not on what happened, but the results of what happened, or is happening. In contrast to the quick, overall view of a news report, the documentary report calls attention to the social aspects of a situation—how people and events interact—and tries to give an extended description.

Documentary reportage as distinguished from propaganda. Propaganda is often mistaken for, or masks itself as, documentary coverage. The aim of propaganda is to form people's attitudes and move them to action. It does not try to be objective, it tries to be convincing. To do that, it selects, arranges, and may even distort, the information it presents to insure that the subject is seen or interpreted in a particular way, so that a desired conclusion or line of

action seems inescapable. Documentary reportage attempts to be convincing by being truthful. Although it must make a selection (because to present everything would be total re-creation, which is an impossibility), it tries to select in balanced proportions so that the truth of the situation cannot be misinterpreted. Documentary photography arises from a feeling of identification, a sense of involvement and concern on the part of the photographer. He or she cares about what is being shown, and wants to bring others to understand and care as well, in the belief that if the human consequences are understood, an audience will be moved to appropriate humane action.

Subjects and Growth of Documentary Photography

Most often, documentary photography deals with human beings, but as noted before, it is not limited to humans. The subject may be a large social group, such as migrant workers, or the aged. Or it may concern itself with a small group—a family, or the personnel of a fire station, for example. It may even concentrate on one individual, but usually from the standpoint of how contact (or lack of contact) with outside factors is of importance. Whatever the size of the group, it is usually examined in terms of specific individuals and instances; the broad picture is created by presenting significant details.

As the use of photography for social purposes has grown, social documentation has come to use more and more pictures to explore a subject. Seldom do the pictures exist without accompanying words, but a single picture is not sufficient. The documentary approach creates an essay on its subject, and today often comprises an entire book.

In the beginning, single pictures were used to illustrate text material which provided the comprehensive description and explanation of the subject. Today, it is often the pictures which carry the major content, while the text provides additional comment or insight.

A major early example of the use of photography for social documentation is the work of John Thompson in *Street Life in London,* by Adolph Smith. This book, published in 1870–1871, consisted of essays and interviews with people who lived and worked on the streets. Thompson's pictures of chimney sweeps, flower sellers, tinkers, bill-posters, beggars, and a wide variety of others at the bottom end of the economic scale added great authenticity to Smith's text.

1880–1890. The pictures taken by two men who established the foundations of documentary photography, Jacob Riis and Lewis W. Hine, were also made to illustrate social-purpose writings. Today, their pictures stand on their own as impressive bodies of documentary work. Riis first used photography to accompany his newspaper articles about the crime-ridden slums of New York City in the 1880's and 1890's. The undeniable reality of the photographs added impact to piece after piece in his column, "How the Other Half Lives," and helped

convince people that slum problems were largely the result of conditions there, not the evil nature of the residents. The support his work gave to social movements in the city helped bring about the first public housing, social assistance, and governmental reform in decades.

1905–1915. From about 1905 to 1915, Lewis Hine's pictures of immigrants being processed through Ellis Island, and their subsequent lives in the tenements and sweatshops of New York, and the coal mining and industrial towns of Pennsylvania, helped focus attention on the origins and the desperate struggles of the laboring class. More importantly, his pictures of the exploitation of children in factories, and their neglect in poor sections, were used by various agencies to force passage of the first national child labor protection laws, and to improve public education and family assistance efforts throughout the major cities of the United States.

1920–1930. In the 1920's, Hine began a series, "Men at Work," which documented the individuality and dignity of those who worked in industrial

(Above) Lewis Hine's 1905 photo of an Italian family looking for lost baggage on Ellis Island is a well known example of his documentary work. (Right) Hine's photographs of the wretched working conditions endured by working-class children were instrumental in forcing passage of the first child labor protection laws. This photo of a young worker in a Tennessee knitting mill was taken in 1912. Photos courtesy International Museum of Photography at George Eastman House.

Documentary Photography

jobs. This series culminated in the early 1930's in a major project documenting the construction of the Empire State Building, from the first excavation to the placement of the topmost steel beam. It was Hine who first pointed out that the idea of completely factual, objective documentary photography was an impossibility. Although the photographer makes every effort to be as truthful as possible in the selection and presentation of a subject, the very fact that he or she is moved to deal with a particular situation or topic reveals involvement and concern on a subjective level. The potential mistakes such unconscious bias could lead to should prevent a photographer from claiming too much objectivity, he warned. So as not to mislead with his own work, Hine insisted on calling his pictures "photographic interpretations." Photographers have generally agreed that the documentary approach must involve commitment and concern. However, the fact that one cannot be completely neutral does not make it impossible to be truthful; rather, it is even more crucial to make every effort to be so, and to communicate that truthfulness in the pictures.

Europe and the United States experienced economic depression, agricultural disasters, and a great variety of other social problems in the 1920's and 1930's. The use of photography to record and report on these problems, and on the efforts to solve them, expanded enormously and included widespread use of motion pictures as well.

The largest coordinated project ever undertaken in social documentary photography was carried out by the Historical Unit of the Federal Farm Security Administration (FSA) during the Depression of the 1930's. Under the direction of Roy Stryker, a large number of photographers recorded the plight of the sharecropper, migrant worker, and small farmer through years of drought and economic collapse in

The Great Depression became the source of some of the greatest documentary photographs in existence. Arthur Rothstein, working under the auspices of the Farm Security Administration, produced this well-known document of a Cimarron County, Oklahoma, dust storm in 1936. Photo courtesy of the photographer.

Documentary Photography

Dorothea Lange's widely reproduced study of a destitute migrant mother in Nipoma, California, taken in 1936, illustrates with deep sensitivity the plight of the "Okies" in Depression-era America. Photo courtesy International Museum of Photography at George Eastman House.

the United States. Those who worked for the FSA at one time or another included Dorothea Lange, Walker Evans, Arthur Rothstein, Russell Lee, John Vachon, Marion Post Wolcott, Ben Shahn, and many others. Although their primary mission was to show how government programs were helping the agricultural poor, it is the pictures that recorded the struggles and human dignity of these people that are among the strongest photographs ever taken. In particular, Dorothea Lange's pictures of individual strength and character in the face of enormous hardship and suffering have achieved a seldom equalled

level of emotional, human communication around the world. And Walker Evans' studies of the unconscious evidences of inherited and invented style and taste in the environments and structures people created for themselves are recognized as masterpieces far more sublime and subtle than most photographs specifically created for artistic expression.

The documentary essay also flourished from the 1920's and after, because of the growth of the picture magazine. The leader among such publications was *Life* magazine, which published many of the finest essays ever taken. These essays include: "Life in a

Documentary Photography

Documentary Photography

Spanish Village," "Alabama Midwife," and "A Country Doctor," all by W. Eugene Smith; World War II coverage by Smith, Robert Capa, David Douglas Duncan, and others; and various essays by Henri Cartier-Bresson. Many of the stories undertaken as reportage or photojournalism were truly documentary because of the depth of human involvement and revelation they contained.

1950-present. In the 1950's and 1960's the picture magazines ceased publication one by one, but documentary photography continued to grow. It moved into television, the medium that had killed the magazines, and into books. Today, there are hundreds of hours of documentary programming on television each year. The documentary photographic book has largely followed from the work of a few young photographers who began observing the social landscape in the 1950's. Their pictures of the places people have built for their social activities—supermarkets, tract housing, drive-in movies, amusement parks, bars, resorts, and the like—began

with the publication of *The Americans* by Robert Frank.

The social evolution of the past 25 years—characterized in the United States by such events as the civil rights movement, school integration, and involvement in the Vietnam war—has been thoroughly documented by photography. Today, there is an enormous production of photographic books on social topics. The following list of some outstanding examples is by no means complete, but it gives some indication of the range of contemporary documentary photography.

> *The Destruction of Lower Manhattan,* by Danny Lyon; demolition of old neighborhoods for urban renewal, photographed in the direct tradition of Atget and Walker Evans.
> *Minimata,* by W. Eugene Smith and Aileen Smith; the suffering and struggle for justice of Japanese villagers poisoned by industrial pollution.

The social landscape of the 1950s and early 1960s—tract housing, suburbia, crabgrass, and station-wagons—provided a great wealth of material for the documentary photographers of that period. Bill Owens captured the feeling of the times in this photograph of a plump young family which he captions with the subject's self-description: "We're really happy. Our kids are healthy, we eat good food and we have a really nice home." Photo courtesy of photographer.

The youth rebellion of the late 1960s was characterized by anti-war protests, campus unrest, and a demand for total self-realization. This young woman was photographed at a peace rally in Washington, D.C. Somehow, she seems to represent many of the powerful and often confusing ideologies of the era. Photo by Michael Tzovaras for Editorial Photocolor Archives, Inc.

Gramp, by Mark and Dan Jury; coming to grips with old age and death within a compassionate, close-knit American family.

100th Street, by Bruce Davidson; life on a block in New York City's Spanish Harlem.

Circus Days, by Jill Freedman; the people and work of a small traveling circus.

A Kind of Life, Conversations in the Combat Zone, by Roswell Angier; strippers, dancers, bar girls and others who work in the Boston area zoned for "adult" entertainment.

Friday Night in the Coliseum, by Geoff Winningham; professional wrestling: the place, the fans, the performers.

Tulsa, by Larry Clark; hard-drug culture in a teenage group.

Pumping Iron, by Charles Gaines and George Butler; the art and sport of bodybuilding.

Documentary Photography

Suburbia, by Bill Owens; the people and their possessions in a middle class California community.

Commonplace, by David Plowden; small town buildings in the Plains States of America.

• See also: HISTORY OF PHOTOGRAPHY.

Further Reading: Abbott, Berenice. The World of Atget. New York, NY: Horizon, 1975; Akmakjian, Hiag E. The Years of Bitterness and Pride: FSA photographs 1935–1943. New York, NY: McGraw-Hill, 1975; Alland, Alexander, Sr., ed. Jacob A. Riis: Photographer and citizen. Millerton, NY: Aperture, 1974; Buckland, Gail. Reality Recorded: Early documentary photography. North Tomfret, Vermont: David and Charles, 1977; Capa, Cornell and Bhupendra, Karia, eds. Robert Capa. New York, NY: International Center of Photography, 1974; Doherty, R. J. Social Documentary Photography in the USA. Garden City, NY: Amphoto, 1976; Hurley, F. Jack. Portrait of a Decade: Roy Stryker and the development of documentary photography in the thirties. Baton Rouge, LA: Louisiana State University Press, 1972; Kirstein, Lincoln, afterword. W. Eugene Smith; His photographs and notes. Millerton, NY: Aperture, 1969; Sander, August. Men Without Masks. Greenwich, CT: New York Graphic Society, 1973; Shahn, Ben. The Photographic Eye of Ben Shahn. Cambridge, MA: Harvard University Press, 1975; Stott, William. Documentary Expression and Thirties America. New York, NY: Oxford University Press, 1976; Szarkowski, John. Walker Evans. New York, NY: Museum of Modern Art, 1971.

Document Examination by Photography

Documents may require detailed examination and investigation for a number of reasons. If they are to be used as legal evidence, their true nature and content must be known and verified. If they have potential artistic or historical value, they must be authenticated, and perhaps dated. If anything has been obliterated, either deliberately or by accidents of handling and storage, an attempt must be made to restore the concealed material. If the documents have been damaged or altered, the slightest remaining traces may lead to recovery of the changed or missing content. Photography can play a significant role in all these aspects of document examination; it is especially widely used for this purpose in criminal and legal investigations.

Documents under question can be divided into two general classes: (1) The erasure or alteration may be poorly executed and quite evident to the trained investigator but acceptable to the untrained eye, (2) the work of bleaching, erasing, and altering may have been done so cleverly that there is no visible evidence even to the trained eye of an experienced investigator.

Reproduction for Case Study

As soon as possible, photograph the document with either black-and-white or color film—the choice depending upon whether or not the original contained any color other than black. This photograph is not intended to show that a forgery has taken place. It is made with the intention that it will be a record of a document as it appeared to the eye at the time it was submitted for examination. The photograph can be used for the study of signatures and other comparisons, thus relieving the original document from repeated handling.

Court Exhibits

Document examiners rarely give the court an opinion concerning a handwriting or typewriting comparison or an alteration without supporting their statement with photographic exhibits. In no other type of expert examination is photography used so extensively in explaining points of evidence to jurors.

Preliminary Procedure

If the standard visual techniques fail to reveal evidence of an alteration, photograph the document using ultraviolet, ultraviolet fluorescence, infrared and infrared luminescence. Also photograph the document with Kodalith film (both with and without a Kodak Wratten filter No. 18A ultraviolet transmitting filter). Even if nothing shows up by any of these techniques, it is not safe to assume that the document has not been altered. Often, a new technique reveals that some material contains information which has gone undetected for years.

It is almost a necessity to make photographs by all of these techniques. Sometimes negatives made by ultraviolet, fluorescent, and infrared techniques will reveal entirely different evidence from the same document. If they are made at the exact same magnification, it is possible to superimpose two such negatives, print them together, and thus show information that is the result of both ultraviolet and infrared examination.

The fact that we are not able to predict in advance the use of any specific technique or formula is perhaps one of the factors which makes document examination so fascinating.

Photographic Equipment

Camera. Document copying requires a good copy camera and a high-quality, medium-speed, coated lens. An apochromat is essential for the most demanding work.

Lens Use and Care. In most cases, focus at $f/8$, stop down to $f/16$, recheck focus, and expose at $f/16$ if the lighting will permit it. In order to get the best performance out of your lens, keep the exposed glass lens surfaces surgically clean and use a deep lens shade to reduce flare.

Films and Developers. In the examination of questioned documents, one of the most important factors is the contrast control provided by the photographic process. High-contrast films, such as Kodalith, magnify small differences in subject contrast. Low-contrast films and developers work together to reduce contrast as in photographing the detail in a pen stroke. A particularly unique property of films is that prolonged exposure builds up density and reveals what the human eye cannot see.

Exposure, by itself, is a critical factor. Experience has shown that sometimes information in one part of a document is quite evident with underexposure and disappears completely with overexposure. At the same time, another area of the same document may show more information with a longer exposure than with a shorter exposure. The composite prints made from each of the two exposures may provide a great deal more information than would be obtained if an average exposure were given.

Lighting. Nearly anything that can be seen can be photographed. Therefore, examine the document in ordinary light, diffused lighting provided by a frosted bulb, specular light such as the beam from a microscope lamp, transmitted light from behind, and polarized light from a Kodak pola-light. Direct each light source across the document at a very low grazing angle. It sometimes helps to have all other lights in the room turned off. Examine the document through different Kodak Wratten filters with each lighting method. If some particular lighting and viewing angle will cause an erasure to become more visible, duplicate these conditions for the camera lens to see.

Erasures

Writings which have been erased by either mechanical or chemical means present the most diffi-

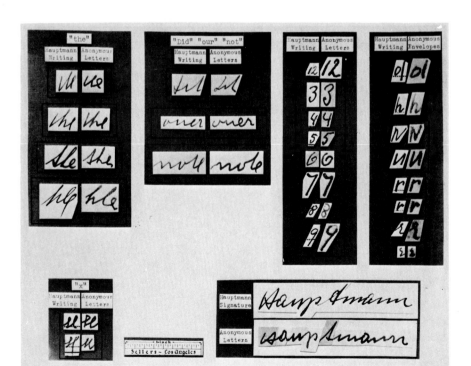

This display demonstrates similarities in handwriting from a famous kidnap-murder case of the 1930s. Documents attributed to the accused kidnapper were photographed and the similar parts of an anonymous letter were compared with these writings. Conviction was obtained largely on evidence such as this. Photography is used extensively in this type of court evidence; as a back-up to testimony concerning handwriting or typewriting, it is essential.

cult problem. There are chemical methods to restore the writing; but before these are attempted, every effort should be made to decipher the writing by visual means or the photographic methods given here. When chemical methods are used, photograph the document immediately because the results obtained chemically may not be permanent.

Use Kodalith film and the lighting which reveals the erasures the best. This is often a low, raking light across the surface of the material. Such illumination will throw the most minute surface variations into relief. Even in cases where no visible outline appears of any of the erased material, it is often possible with Kodalith film to magnify whatever small difference may be present and reveal the outline of the characters that have been erased. Kodalith pan film is often desirable because it can be used with a contrast filter to show differences between colors as well as recording the document with extremely high contrast.

Ultraviolet Radiation. This is particularly helpful with sized paper and chemical erasures. Many papers have a natural fluorescence which is easily disturbed by any attempt at erasing. The effect of ink eradicators is usually quite noticeable under ultraviolet light. Any effect seen by ultraviolet fluorescence can be photographed. There are two important precautions: The room must be dark; and an ultraviolet absorbing filter, such as a Kodak Wratten No. 2A filter, must be used over the camera lens. Without the 2A filter, the ultraviolet radiation reflected by the document may expose the film much more strongly than any weak fluorescence. Any film will record the fluorescence, but high-contrast film will help show small differences better.

Infrared Luminescence. Some materials used in the manufacture of inks and papers luminesce in the invisible infrared region of the spectrum when excited by blue-green light. This is the same kind of phenomenon as ultraviolet fluorescence except that it occurs with longer wavelengths. Infrared luminescence often has revealed considerable information from suspected documents that went undetected by all other techniques. However, experience so far indicates that only 10 to 15 percent of minerals and elements luminesce.

Photographic spotlights of 500–1000 watts are the most convenient light sources. It is necessary to eliminate infrared from the light, and a ¾-inch-thick plastic cell filled with a 10-percent copper-sulfate solution works well. If a lot of work is to be done a cold-light dichroic mirror (filter) that absorbs infrared radiation and transmits light can be purchased. A Kodak Wratten filter No. 87 is used over the camera lens with Kodak high speed infrared film, 35 mm, or a special infrared plate known as Kodak spectroscopic plate, type I-N. For luminescent photography, it is vital to eliminate all radiation except the blue-green light transmitted by the cell which is used to illuminate the suspect document. The room must be absolutely dark, and all stray light from the spotlight must be shielded. A tight-fitting, opaque tunnel is required between the lamp and the cell.

Trial exposures for infrared luminescence (emission) can be determined with an exposure meter, adjusted for an ASA speed of 80, by taking a reflection reading of the subject illuminated by the blue-green light. Multiply the exposure thus obtained by 20,000. Exposure may run between 8 and 15 minutes at $f/8$. In making tests, exposure should be increased or decreased until the luminescing area has a negative density of at least 0.9.

Focusing for Infrared. Infrared rays, because of their longer wavelength, do not focus in the same plane as visible rays. It is therefore necessary to make an increase in the lens-to-film distance to correct the focusing difference between infrared and visible rays. For best definition, infrared photographs should be exposed with the smallest lens opening that conditions permit. If large apertures must be used and the lens has no auxiliary infrared focusing mark, a focusing correction can be established by photographic focusing tests. A basis for trial is the extension of the lens by one-quarter of one percent of its focal length. A practical approach is to focus visually and then move the focus setting to a nearer distance by about the space between the infinity and 50-foot marks on the focusing scale.

Alterations and Differentiating Inks

Alterations can be so expertly done that they may be almost as difficult as erasures to prove. In some cases, the ultraviolet techniques described above prove useful. Photomicrography may reveal differences in the drying pattern of the two inks used. Infrared luminescence is also a valuable technique in detecting document alterations.

Obliterated Writing

Obliterations in a single document may be both intentional and unintentional. Usually the writing is covered or obscured by markings, overwriting, or haphazard scratching with ink, pencil, or crayon. In the case of checks, bank stamp imprints may obscure the signature and other important data. Photographic separation of color imprints by masking techniques is very useful.

Filters. If the upper markings and underwriting differ in color, use a filter of the same color as the top layer to photograph the bottom layer with panchromatic film. To select the correct filter, view the obliteration through filters of different colors.

Oblique Lighting. The difference in the reflecting characteristics of the upper and lower layers may permit the deciphering of the obscured writing. The pressure with which the lower layer was impressed is also important. If great pressure was used on thin paper, a legibly imbedded outline may be seen from the back. Oblique lighting should be used. Direct the light at varying angles and with varying intensities across the writing. If the writing can be read at a selected angle, photograph it with either Kodak Panatomic-X film, Kodak Plus-X pan professional film (Estar thick base), or Kodak contrast process panchromatic film.

Infrared and Ultraviolet. Both techniques may show up alterations, infrared especially, if the obliterating ink is transparent to infrared and the original ink is not. Ordinary tungsten lamps are used with the infrared film. A Kodak Wratten filter No. 87 must be used over the camera lens, and the camera must be focused for IR as described previously.

Masking Technique for Data Separation. Multiple bank stamp imprints often combine to create complete obliteration of any single bit of information. Masking is a photographic process which often permits separating the individual information wanted from such a maze.

If a photographic negative and a positive made from it are superimposed, all of the information will disappear. However, if the positive is made from a second negative which differs in some respect from the first, then some information can be made to disappear selectively while other information can be retained.

It is necessary to make two photographic negatives at the same magnification and that these negatives differ as much as possible in the ratio of image strength between the writing to be deciphered (wanted information) and that which is causing confusion. A film positive is made by contact from the negative containing the weaker image of the wanted information (or the stronger image of the unwanted values) and processed so that superimposition with the other negative will obliterate the unwanted information. A print made by exposing through the superimposed films will produce a greatly clarified picture of the information desired.

In order that the two negatives be obtained with maximum differences, the photographer should use ingenuity to exaggerate one image or the other. If two different-colored inks are involved, the use of selected filters will normally produce the desired result. The images may differ more in their reflected ultraviolet or infrared characteristics, or in fluorescence or luminescence, or in some other property, such as depth of indentation or ink penetration into the paper. In these latter instances, photographing the reverse side of the document often leads to a usable negative. It may even be possible to reproduce the overwriting (for instance, if a rubber stamp that had been used to make the overprint were still available). A photograph of a freshly stamped impression will lead to an excellent mask. Occasionally, documents will contain several different overprints, and techniques that work for one overprint are not good for another. A sandwich of a negative with more than one mask will often be beneficial.

The wide variety of situations which might be encountered precludes the formulation of a set of exact instructions. However, if the main principles are understood, then filters, choice of film, processing techniques, etc. will be found through a minimum of trial and error. The basic steps are:

1. Produce a negative with the strongest possible image of the wanted writing.
2. Produce one or more negatives which emphasize all of the overprinting and make a positive mask from each of these negatives.
3. Process the masks to a contrast so that registering each mask over the original negative will minimize the visual image of the overprint.
4. Make a print through the registered combination of films.

The usual photographic methods failed to reveal that this cleverly altered check had been raised from $10 to $17790. Macrophotography with 35 mm Kodacolor film showed that the letters J, H, and A had been written over the certification stamp.

Registration of the masks will be easier if they are slightly unsharp. This can be achieved by sandwiching a piece of Kodak diffusion sheeting (0.003 inch thick) between the film and the negative during exposure. The matte surface of the diffusion sheet should face the negative.

Wetting Method. Occasionally, the obliteration is made by pasting paper over the writing. To leave the paste-over intact, try wetting the reverse side of the original document with a volatile fluid, such as benzene. The writing will appear for a few seconds and again become invisible as the fluid evaporates. Be prepared to photograph it as soon as the image appears. Use Kodak Panatomic-X film with strong lighting. Wetting should not be attempted until all other techniques have been tried and have failed.

Indentations

The impressions left upon a pad of paper by writing on an upper sheet which has been removed will sometimes provide a legible copy of the message written on the missing page. By directing a beam of light from the side (almost parallel to the plane of the paper), the indentations can be brought into relief and the writing revealed. No special treatment of the paper is necessary. This should be done in a darkened room so that only the grazing light illuminates the paper.

Handle the pad very carefully before photography. Never put the suspect paper document between pages of a book or under any other pressure because any pressure will tend to smooth out the indentures and make it more difficult to photograph.

The photograph should be made at natural size (that is, 1:1) on Kodak commercial, Kodak contrast process panchromatic, or Kodalith film. If the outline is faint, use the film of greatest contrast. It is sometimes impossible to obtain a satisfactory image of all the writing in one photograph because different areas of the paper require different angles of illumination. In these instances, make one exposure with the lamp placed on one side, grazing across the paper; and then make a second negative at the same magnification with the lamp placed on the opposite side. When the two negatives are processed, they can be placed together in contact and if they are thrown slightly out of register, a relief effect occurs and the writing pops up so that it can be read without making a print.

Carbon Paper

A carbon paper discarded after the typing or writing of a document will sometimes reveal the original message. Try:

Oblique Lighting. With the carbon side of the paper facing the lens, direct a single lamp from the side until the light appears to be reflected from the writing. This method is especially useful if the carbon has been used only once or twice.

Carbon as a Negative. A much-used carbon that is thin and evenly perforated in spots may be used on the contact printer as a negative. The writing is then printed directly on photographic paper. This usually requires a long printing exposure.

Transmitted Light. By illuminating the carbon from the rear and using a red filter (Kodak Wratten No. 25), a satisfactory photograph of the writing or carbon paper can often be obtained with Kodak contrast process panchromatic film.

Blotting Paper

A blotter applied by the suspect to his ink writing sometimes picks up a legible copy of the text. Try a photograph with panchromatic film. If the blotter is colored, use a filter of the same color. If different inks have been blotted, the more sophisticated techniques, described previously, may separate the different writings.

The blotter writing is, of course, a mirror image of the original. Therefore, for court exhibit, make two prints: A straight print which will duplicate the appearance of the writing on the blotter and a reverse print of the negative so that the court or jurors can read the message.

• *See also:* ART, PHOTOGRAPHY OF; CLOSE-UP PHOTOGRAPHY; COPYING; CRIME PHOTOGRAPHY; EVIDENCE PHOTOGRAPHY; INFRARED PHOTOGRAPHY; PHOTOMACROGRAPHY; PHOTOMICROGRAPHY; POLARIZED-LIGHT PHOTOGRAPHY; ULTRAVIOLET AND FLUORESCENCE PHOTOGRAPHY.

Further Reading: Eastman Kodak Co. *Using Photography to Preserve Evidence,* pub. No. M-2. Rochester, NY: Eastman Kodak Co., 1976; Editors of Time-Life Books. *Documentary Photography.* New York, NY: Time-Life Books, 1972; Scott, Charles C. *Photographic Evidence,* 3 vols. 2nd ed. St. Paul, MN: West Publishers, 1969.

Dodging

Dodging is the procedure of shadowing a portion of an image to hold back light during part of the printing exposure. When the print is being made from a negative, the dodged area will be lighter than if it had received full exposure. If the print is being made on reversal material from a positive such as a slide, the dodged area will be darker than an equivalent undodged area. Dodging is also called holding back.

Like its opposite technique, burning in, dodging is used to adjust tonal relationships in a print. In negative-positive printing it is most often used to preserve visibility of details in areas that otherwise would print too dark.

Large areas are dodged during an enlarging exposure by inserting a piece of cardboard or the hands in the path of the projected light; the placement of the shadow can be seen in the image on the easel. Small areas are usually dodged by using a bit of cardboard, clay or putty, or red celluloid on the end of a wire. The closer such a tool is held to the surface of the printing paper, the smaller the size of the shadow it casts. The dodging device must be kept moving at all times so the edge of the dodged portion

Dodging, or holding back light, when printing from a negative, results in a print with the dodged area lighter than it would be if the area had received full exposure. As demonstrated by these before-and-after prints, dodging has eliminated some of the shadows to make the boy's face lighter.

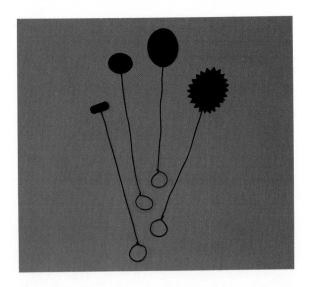

(Right) Small areas, such as the subject's face, are dodged with pieces of cut-out material on the end of a wire. The dodging device must be moved constantly to blend the edges of the dodged portion with the surrounding area.(Above) An assortment of dodging tools is useful for variously shaped and sized areas that may require dodging.

will blend with surrounding areas, and so that the shadow of the wire will not create a light line across the image.

Many contact printers have an internal glass shelf on which torn tissue shapes or other dodging material such as sawdust may be laid, or markings with a red material such as lipstick may be made, to hold back some light from selected areas of the negative being printed.

• *See also:* BLACK-AND-WHITE PRINTING; BURNING IN; COLOR PRINTING FROM NEGATIVES; COLOR PRINTING FROM TRANSPARENCIES; CONTACT PRINTING; ENLARGERS AND ENLARGING.

Dollond, John

(1706–1761)
English optician

Dollond was the first to show that Isaac Newton was in error concerning the relationship between the refractive index of glasses and their dispersive power.

Newton had abandoned the refracting telescope in favor of reflectors, believing that the chromatic aberration of lenses was quite incurable. Dollond, however, showed that combinations of crown glass, having a low refractive index and high dispersion, with flint glass, having a high refractive index and low dispersion, could produce an achromatic lens. This discovery (circa 1757) made practical large refracting telescopes and color-corrected camera lenses.

Draper, John William

(1811–1882)
American chemist and researcher, and associate of Samuel F. B. Morse

Draper made very early daguerreotype portraits and also did much research in the theory of the process; in this work, he discovered the law of photochemical absorption, now known as the Draper-Grotthus law. He produced the first daguerreotype of the moon and suggested the use of very small daguerreotypes, with subsequent enlargement of the image, both in 1840. He also observed the phenomenon of latent-image regression in the daguerreotype process—that is, as the time between exposure and development increases, the latent image progressively deteriorates to an undevelopable state.

Driffield, Vero Charles

(1848–1915)
English chemist

In association with Ferdinand Hurter, Driffield undertook to determine the relationship between the exposure and development of a silver emulsion and the resulting image densities. This was the beginning of what we call sensitometry today, but was then known as photographic photometry. In 1898 the two collaborators received the Progress Medal of the Royal Photographic Society for this work. The Royal Photographic Society issued a memorial volume of the collected papers of Hurter & Driffield in 1920 (published in facsimile by Morgan and Morgan in 1974).

• *See also:* DENSITOMETRY; HURTER, FERDINAND; SENSITOMETRY.

Drum and Tube Processing

Although color prints can be processed in a conventional tray setup, the procedure is often impractical for a number of reasons:

1. Some color processes have several solutions, requiring too many trays for the available space.
2. Trays require relatively large amounts of solution.
3. The large area of solution exposed to the air promotes oxidation, which quickly destroys the developer's effectiveness.
4. Exposed solutions rapidly change temperature, and temperature control devices for use with trays are not precise enough for consistent results.

These difficulties can be overcome by using either drum or tube processors in place of trays. These processors require a comparatively small amount of space, and use the minimum adequate amounts of solution. The solutions are used in containers that are closed or that have only a small open area, reducing oxidation and making temperature control easier and more precise. Because they provide constant agitation, processing time is reduced—a typical eight-minute process can be cut to five or six minutes.

There are two types of drum processors. In the first, the surface of the drum is textured, and the print is held emulsion-side against the surface of the drum as it rotates. The lower portion of the drum passes through processing solutions held in a tray below but close to the drum. The textured surface picks up solution and moves it rapidly across the surface of the print, providing continuous agitation.

In the second type of drum, the surface of the drum is smooth, and the print is held emulsion-side out against the surface of the drum. As the drum rotates, the print passes through the solution in the tray below the drum, providing agitation. The print goes in and out of the solution.

In both types of processors, the first steps must be carried out in total darkness, or in the light of a suitable safelight.

Tube processors are cylinders that receive the print and the processing solutions inside. The print is placed against the wall of the tube, emulsion facing inward. When loaded and capped, the tube is laid on its side and rolled or revolved so that the solution continually washes over the entire face of the print. Small tubes for prints up to 11″ × 14″ are commonly activated by hand; motor-driven processors are used for large prints of up to 30″ × 40″. Once capped, the tube can be used in full light. Some tubes have light-trapped filler caps that permit solutions to be poured without exposing the print.

Print and negative films can also be processed in drum or tube equipment, as can black-and-white prints. This approach is primarily useful for very large formats that cannot be accommodated in conventional tanks or trays. Since by far the largest use of such processors is for color work, the following sections describe their use for reversal and negative-positive color print processing.

Drum Processors

Two of the most widely used drum processors for prints up to 16″ × 20″ are the Kodak rapid color processors, model 11 and model 16-K; both are motor-driven. The model 11 will process 11″ × 14″, 8″ × 10″, or 8½″ × 11″ prints. The temperature of the processing solutions is maintained manually, unless auxiliary equipment is used.

The model 16-K will process one 16″ × 20″, one 14″ × 17″, two 8½″ × 11″, or two 8″ × 10″ prints at one time. A coated net blanket holds the print on the revolving textured-metal drum surface. A hinged tray receives the three processing solutions. The revolving drum constantly picks up and transfers fresh solution to the emulsion of the print with vigorous agitation. Processing solutions are changed by tilting the tray, rinsing the print and tray, and refilling the tray with the next solution. A processing temperature of 37.8 C (100 F) is thermostatically controlled by the recirculating water system.

The epoxy-coated net blanket for the model 16-K processor may have to be trimmed in size. The full-size blanket, overlapping the print being processed, may cause additional tension and may result in nonuniformity of development at the ends of the print. If this happens, or if streaking occurs, trim the blanket to the same width as (or slightly smaller than) the paper to be processed.

The rough coating on one side of the net blanket grips the smooth base side of the paper and prevents the paper from slipping off the drum. Be sure that the blanket is installed on the bar assembly so that the rough side will face the drum during operation, with the green end in the bar (one bar width) and the white end trailing.

IMPORTANT: After each process, rinse blanket, drum, and tray with running water to remove all traces of processing chemicals. Wipe excess water from drum and tray before starting next process.

The power cords on all three Kodak rapid color processors are fitted with three-prong plugs; if you

(Left) In tube processors, such as this Unidrum 11, the print is curled with the emulsion facing in; as the tube revolves, processing solutions wash over the print. (Right) Once the tube is loaded, it is capped, often with a light-trapped filler cap which permits addition of the solution in full light. The tube is then agitated either by hand or, as shown here, with a motor-driven device (this base is a Uniroller). Photos by Bob Nadler.

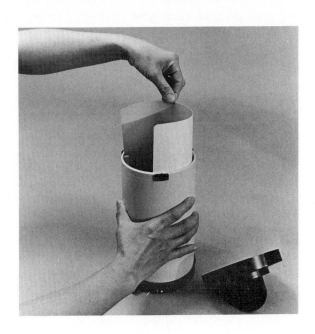

Two Kodak drum processors: the model 11 (left) and the model 16-K (right). The model 11 will process prints up to 11" × 14"; the 16-K processes larger prints, or two prints at a time up to 8½" × 11". A net blanket holds the print, emulsion side down, on the textured drum surface. The drum revolves through the tray below, which is filled with the processing solutions.

do not have a grounded three-wire outlet in your darkroom or processing area, you should have one installed by an electrician. *Do not use a two-wire outlet and an adapter plug.*

The elevated temperatures required for color print processing are maintained by placing water of the correct temperature inside the drum just before processing is started.

Drum Processing: Negative-Positive Prints

Kodak Ektacolor 37 and 74 RC papers are used for prints from color negatives. The chemicals recommended for drum processing are:

> Kodak Ektaprint 300 developer
> Kodak Ektaprint 3 bleach-fix and replenisher
> Kodak Ektaprint 3 stabilizer and replenisher or their equivalent

For best results, do not use solutions that have been stored for longer than the following times:

Note that a special developer—Ektaprint 300—is recommended for processing in Kodak rapid color processors. The other chemicals are the same as those used for tank and tray processing. Mixing instructions are included with the chemicals. Use 120 ml (4 ounces) of each solution in the Model 11 processor; use 240 ml (8 ounces) in the Model 16-K processor.

Processing Steps. The processing of Kodak Ektacolor 37 RC paper on the model 11 or 16-K processor requires a minimum time of 5 minutes. The processing steps are charted below. *Always con-*

Solution	Partially Filled, Stoppered Glass Bottles	Full, Stoppered Glass Bottles
Developer	3 weeks	6 weeks
Bleach-fix	6 weeks	8 weeks
Stabilizer	8 weeks	Indefinite

Processing Step	Drum Temperature		Time in
	C	F	Minutes*
Steps 1–4, total darkness.			
1. Prewet	21–39	70–102	½
2. Developer	37.8 ± 0.3	100 ± ½	2
3. Wash†	37.8 ± 1	100 ± 2	½
4. Bleach-fix	37.8 ± 1	100 ± 2	1
Remaining steps can be done in normal room light.			
5. Wash†	37.8 ± 1	100 ± 2	½
6. Stabilizer	37.8 ± 1	100 ± 2	½
7. Dry (forced air)	Not over 107	Not over 225	——

*Include drain time of 10 seconds for prewet step; 5 seconds for all other steps.
†Water flow of 7.5–9.5 liters (2–2½ gals) per minute.

sult the instruction sheet packaged with the Kodak Ektaprint 300 developer for the latest information.

Drum Processing: Reversal Prints

Kodak Ektachrome RC paper, type 1993, used for prints from slides or transparencies, can be drum-processed using Kodak Ektaprint R-500 chemicals. A set of chemicals consists of:

Kodak Ektaprint R-500 first developer
Kodak Ektaprint R-500 stop bath
Kodak Ektaprint R-500 color developer
Kodak Ektaprint R-500 bleach-fix
Kodak Ektaprint R-500 stabilizer.

Mixing directions are included with each package and must be followed carefully.

Store solutions at a room temperature of 24 to 29.5 C (75 to 85 F). For best results, do not use solutions stored longer than the following times:

Solution	Partially Filled, Stoppered Glass Bottles	Full, Stoppered Glass Bottles
First developer	2 weeks	4 weeks
Stop bath	8 weeks	8 weeks
Color developer	2 weeks	4 weeks
Bleach-fix	8 weeks	8 weeks
Stabilizer	8 weeks	8 weeks

Use 200 ml (7 ounces) of each solution in the model 11 processor; use 325 ml (11 ounces) in the Model 16-K processor.

Processing Steps. Processing with either model processor requires a minimum time of 12 ¾ minutes. The processing steps are charted below. *Always*

Processing Step	Drum Temperature C	F	Time in Min*
Steps 1–3, total darkness.			
1. Prewet	21–39	70–102	1
2. First developer	38 ± 0.3	100 ± ½	1½
3. Stop bath	38 ± 0.6	100 ± 1	½
For steps 4 & 5, use safelight No. 10 or OA.			
4. First wash†	38 ± 1.1	100 ± 2	2
5. Color developer	38 ± 0.6	100 ± 1	3
Remaining steps can be done in normal room light.			
6. Second wash†	38 ± 1.1	100 ± 2	½
7. Bleach-fix	38 ± 0.6	100 ± 1	1½
8. Final wash†	38 ± 1.1	100 ± 2	1½
9. Stabilizer	38 ± 0.6	100 ± 1	1
10. Rinse	38 ± 1.1	100 ± 2	¼
11. Dry	49–66	120–150	——

*The time for each step, except the prewet, includes a 5-second drain time. The drain time after the prewet should be 10 seconds. In each case, start draining in time to end the processing step and start the next one on schedule.
†Water flow of 7.5—9.5 litres (2—2½ gals) per minute.

Some small tube-type processors have leak-proof end caps for use in a temperature control bath. This is the Colourtronic Turbo-Drive Processor, Model TD 800. Photo by Bob Nadler.

consult the instruction sheet packaged with the Kodak Ektaprint R-500 developer for the latest detailed information.

Small Tube Processors

Small plastic tube-type processors have become very popular for use in darkrooms where only a few color prints are made at a time. They are inexpensive and very easy to use, but are generally limited to a maximum print size of 11" × 14". Two distinctive types of small tube-type processors are available:

Type A. These tubes are designed to be used without a constant-temperature water bath. Their solution inlets and outlets are open and would allow water to enter if they were used in a water bath.

Type B. These tubes are designed for processing in a constant-temperature water bath. Their solution inlets and outlets are either closed or positioned in such a way that the tempering water is prevented from entering the tube.

It is essential that none of the tempering water enter the tube during the processing procedure.

Owing to the variety of tube-type processors available, several portions of the processing cycle have to be calculated or determined by the user for the particular processor. Select the processing procedure that is appropriate for the type of tube you are using.

Motor-driven processors for large-format prints are discussed in a later section.

Basic Procedures for Small-Tube Processing.

Depending on the size and type of small tube processor used, the volume of solution, number of washes, temperature of control bath, and other factors will vary.

Determining processing solution and wash water volumes. The volume of chemical solution and wash water necessary to process a sheet of color print material properly in a tube-type processor depends upon the size of the tube. The size of the tube is defined by the largest single sheet that can be processed in it. For example, a tube that can process nothing larger than an 8" × 10" sheet is an 80-square-inch tube.

The processing solution volume is calculated by multiplying the tube size by 0.8 ml and rounding off to the nearest 10 ml. For example, 80 in.² × 0.8 = 64 ml rounded off to 70 ml of processing solution for an 8" × 10" sheet of paper.

The wash water volume is twice the processing solution volume rounded up to the nearest 50 ml. Thus wash water volume for an 8" × 10" sheet of paper is 150 ml.

The accompanying chart outlines the liquid volumes for popular sheet-sizes of paper.

Paper Size	Tube Size (square inches)	Liquid Volumes in ml	
		Processing Solution	Wash Water
8" × 10"	80	70	150
11" × 14"	154	130	300
16" × 20"	320	260	550

Conserving Chemicals: With some processing tubes it *may* be possible to use less than the suggested volumes of each chemical solution. The suggested volumes contain sufficient safety factors to accommodate the wide variety of tube-type processors available. They also are sufficiently large to minimize agitation effects. A user may, for a particular processor, reduce the volumes of solutions used per run in an attempt to maximize solution usage. If you do this, be aware that as the solution volumes are reduced, agitation becomes more and more critical and repeatability becomes harder to maintain. *Do not reduce the wash volumes, and do not reduce the chemical solution volumes below 0.6 ml per square inch of paper.* In order of increasing sensitivity to volume reduction, the chemical solutions are: stabilizer, stop bath, bleach-fix, color developer, and first developer.

Determining the necessary number of washes after the bleach-fix. In reversal-print processing it is important that the bleach-fix solution be washed away after it has removed all traces of residual silver from the emulsion. Use the following procedure to determine how many times the wash step after the bleach-fix must be repeated to provide the proper removal of chemicals:

Load the tube with a sheet of scrap photographic paper. Wet the paper and the interior of the tube with water. Drain the tube for 10 seconds and then add a solution volume of bleach-fix. Agitate the tube according to the manufacturer's instructions for 90 seconds. Drain for 10 seconds and add a wash volume of water. Agitate for a 30-second wash that includes a 10-second drain. Drain into a clear glass or bottle. Repeat the washing step a second and a third time and drain each wash into a separate clear glass or bottle. Look at the three containers against a white background. If the second container is as clear as the third, only two washes are required after the bleach-fix. If not, repeat the washing step and drain into another clear glass or bottle. Compare the fourth wash with the third. If they are equally clear, the processor requires three washes after the bleach-fix.

Determining the proper water bath temperature. The recommended processing temperature for processing a number of Kodak color print materials is 38 C (100 F). The type of processing tube that you are using will determine which of the following tempering procedures you will use:

Procedure A (for processing tubes designed to be used without a tempering bath): The processing steps, including agitation recommendations, should be done on a level surface (not in the constant temperature bath). The tube *must* be level (flat) to allow an even distribution of each solution.

Since this procedure is run outside the constant temperature bath, heat can be transferred between the processor and the surroundings. To obtain an average temperature of 38 C (100 F), conduct the following test:

1. Place a previously processed sheet of print paper in the tube (this can be a scrap print).
2. Follow the prewet and first developer portions of the processing cycle (Steps 1 and 2), using the correct volumes and times. The prewet and first developer solutions (water can be substituted in the test) should be at the temperature of the constant temperature bath before the process is run.
3. At the end of the first developer step, collect the solution discarded from the tube and measure the temperature. For a 24 C (75 F) room temperature, the constant temperature bath is typically about 43.3 C (110 F) and the temperature of the first developer after the processing step would be about 32.2 C (90 F). The average of 43.3 and 32.2 is 37.8; the average of 110 and 90 is 100.

4. Repeat this test procedure, raising or lowering the temperature of the constant temperature bath until the average of the first developer bath temperature, before and after the cycle is 37.8 C (100 F).

This test procedure need only be done once for a given processor, provided the room temperature remains fairly constant. Use the bath temperature established by this test for all future processes. If the temperature of the room varies more than about 5 F for any reason (or season), repeat this test as experience dictates.

Procedure B (for processing tubes that are designed for use in a tempering bath): The processing steps, including agitation recommendations, should be done with the tube placed in the constant temperature bath. For complete, even processing of the paper, the tube *must* remain level (flat) while in the constant temperature bath to allow an even distribution of each solution.

With an average room temperature of 24 C (75 F), the constant temperature bath should be 38 ± 0.3 C (100 ± ½ F).

Agitation. Agitation is very important. Be sure to follow the procedure recommended by the manufacturer of the processing tube that you are using.

Miscellaneous recommendations:

1. Do not reuse chemicals.
2. Always mix full volumes of solutions as received from the manufacturer. Do not attempt to mix fractional volumes. The ingredients may not be evenly distributed in the containers.
3. Thoroughly wash and dry the processor and containers after each process.
4. Make sure that the tube is drained after each step. In some cup-type tubes it may be necessary to (a) drain the tube, (b) tilt the tube 180 degrees, and then (c) tilt the tube back to the draining position.
5. Become totally familiar with the processing tube you are using. It may help you to run through a processing cycle using water only (no paper in the tube).

IMPORTANT: Always clean and dry the processing tube thoroughly after each process to help prevent contamination.

Small-Tube Processing: Reversal Prints. For prints from slides or transparencies, Kodak Ektaprint R-500 chemicals are recommended for processing Kodak Ektachrome RC paper, type 1993, in small tube-type processors. The addition of approximately 0.2 gram per litre of potassium iodide to the wash water preceding the bleach-fix is recommended to prevent excessive stain. Since the amount of potassium iodide required in the wash is not critical, it is convenient to add the potassium iodide to the water in the form of a stock solution, just prior to processing.

To prepare a stock solution, completely dissolve 8 grams (approx. ¼ ounce or 1 teaspoonful) of potassium iodide crystals in 946 ml (32 ounces) of water. Add 30 ml (1 ounce) of this stock solution to each 946 ml of wash water preceding the bleach-fix.

Small-Tube Processing: Negative - Positive Prints. The general method of tube handling with the two types of tubes is the same for negative-positive print processing as for the reversal process just described. A set of chemicals consists of:

Kodak Ektaprint 2 developer (1 gallon)
Kodak Ektaprint 2 bleach-fix
    and replenisher (1 gallon)
Kodak stop bath SB-1 mixed from
    Kodak 28% acetic acid.

The developer and bleach-fix are mixed according to the directions on the package. The stop bath is mixed as follows:

Kodak stop bath SB-1

1. Start with 1 litre (33.8 fluid ounces) of water.
2. While stirring add 48 millilitres (1.63 fluid ounces) of Kodak 28% acetic acid.
To make 28% acetic acid from glacial acetic acid, add 3 parts of glacial acetic acid to 8 parts of water, while stirring.

CAUTION: Add the acid to the water, never water to acid.

GENERAL PROCESSING SPECIFICATIONS (*KODAK EKTAPRINT* R-500 CHEMICALS)

Nominal Solution Temperature of 38 C (100 F)

Processing Step	Time in Minutes*	Accumulated Time in Minutes
1. Prewet (water)	½	½
2. First developer	1½	2
3. Stop bath	½	2½
4. Wash	½	3
5. Wash	½	3½
6. Color developer	2	5½
7. Potassium iodide wash	½	6
8. Bleach-fix	1½	7½
9. Wash	½	8
10. Wash†	½	8½
11. Stabilizer	½	9
12. Rinse (water)	¼	9¼

*All times include a 10-second drain (to avoid excess solution carryover). Some processing tubes may require a slightly longer drain time. Be sure to allow enough time to make certain that the tube is drained and to add the next solution on time for the next step. The next step begins when the solution contacts the paper.

†An additional step (new Step 11) may be required, depending on the processing tube you are using.

GENERAL PROCESSING SPECIFICATIONS (*KODAK EKTAPRINT* 2 CHEMICALS)

Solution Temperature of 33.0 + 0.3C (91 ± ½ F)

Processing Step	Time In Minutes	Accumulated Time in Minutes
1. Prewet	½	½
2. Developer	3½	4
3. Stop bath	½	4½
4. Wash	½	5
5. Bleach-fix	1	6
Remove print from tube and wash in tray.		
6. Wash	½	6½
7. Wash	½	7
8. Wash	½	7½
9. Wash	½	8

Dry at room temperature, on racks. For faster drying, use forced warm air, not exceeding 93 C (200 F), as from a hand-held hair dryer. *Never ferrotype prints on water-resistant papers.*

NOTE: All of the processing times include a 10-second drain to avoid excess solution carry-over. Some tubes may require a slightly longer drain time. Allow enough time to be sure the tube is drained and the next processing step starts in time.

Store the solutions at room temperature of 24 to 29.5 C (75 to 85 F). For best results, do not use solutions stored longer than the following times:

	Partially Filled, Stoppered Glass Bottles	Full, Stoppered Glass Bottles
Developer	3 weeks	6 weeks
Bleach-fix	6 weeks	8 weeks

Large Tube-Type Processors

One of the most versatile tube-type processors for large format color prints is the Kodak rapid color processor, model 30A. When used with a 3040A processing tube, it will process a 30″ × 40″ print. A print that ranges in size from 16″ × 20″ to 20″ × 24″ can be processed if a 2024A processing tube and adapter are used.

The same color print processing chemicals are recommended for use with drum processors. The model 30A processor is used in normal room light. The loading of exposed paper into the processing tube is done in a darkroom under the recommended safelight. The processing tube has two lighttight traps, one at each end, through which water and processing solutions are introduced into the tube and drained from it. After the exposed paper has been placed in the tube and the cover is in place, the tube can be carried into normal room light and placed in the movable processor cage. With the tube in the vertical position, solutions or washes are poured into the lighttight cover and are held in the cup beneath the cover. At the same time, used solutions or washes will drain from the bottom of the tube into a sump.

When the cage and tube are pivoted to the horizontal position, the solution in the cup flows into the tube and is distributed evenly over the paper emulsion as the tube automatically rotates within the cage. One litre (one quart) of each solution is required for each 30″ × 40″ print. Solutions and wash water are held in individual containers in a tempering unit at a thermostatically controlled processing temperature of 37.8 C (100 F). No solution exhaustion problems are encountered, since each solution is used once, drained, and discarded. Smaller-size prints (16″ × 20″ to 20″ × 24″) can be processed using 383 millilitres (13 fluidounces) of each processing solution in the 2024A processing tube and adapter.

General Procedures. The model 30A processor uses timing disks that provide an audible signal at the end of each processing step. There are separate disks for Kodak reversal print paper and negative-positive print paper, and for use with either 60-Hertz or 50-Hertz current. Be sure that the proper disk for the process to be carried out is in the timer.

Loading the processing tube. The manual for the processor explains in detail how to load the tube. The processing tube must be loaded in complete darkness. Once the processing tube cover is in place, the tube can be exposed to room light without danger of fogging the paper. Handle the tube carefully to avoid disturbing the position of the paper.

Place the loaded processing tube vertically in the cage of the processor. Check the temperature of the tempering unit water bath and the temperature of the contents of the containers. The "prewash" legend should be visible in the window of the timer.

Fill the solution containers with water or processing solutions in the proper numbered sequence, as outlined in the specific procedures below.

Processing. Start by pouring the water of container No. 1 into the processing tube cover. Avoid splashing by holding the container inside the rim of the cover. (The solution will stay inside the cup of the processing tube cover until the tube is pivoted to the horizontal position.) Gently pivot the tube to the horizontal position and immediately press the process start button. The processing tube will start revolving and the process will be under way. When the timer buzzer sounds, immediately return the tube to the vertical position and add the solution in container No. 2 to the tube. Repeat this sequence for the remaining steps.

Tube Cleaning. After each process, rinse the processing tube and cover with warm water, not above 43.5 C (110 F). Before loading the tube for the next process, be sure that the inside of the tube is dry. Wet surfaces can prevent correct positioning of the paper.

Temperature. The temperature for Kodak reversal and negative-positive print processing is nominally 37.8 C (100 F). Although the specific temperature of the first developer is 43 ± 0.3 C

(110 ± ½ F), it will gradually drift down to a nominal 37.8 C (100 F) when processing ambient at 24 C (75 F) conditions. The water in the tempering unit must be adjusted, depending upon the ambient air temperature. The user will not normally adjust this temperature, since it is done automatically by the thermostat and temperature controls of the Kodak rapid color processor, model 30A. The thermostat is factory-adjusted to control the water in the tempering unit when the room temperature is 24 ± 4.2 C (75 ± 7 F). Any ambient conditions beyond this range will require adjustment of the thermostat adjusting screw. Carefully follow the procedures outlined in the processor manual for this adjustment.

Large-Tube Processing: Reversal Prints. To process Kodak Ektachrome RC paper, type 1993, in the Model 30A processor, the spiral design processing tube (2024A or 3040A) is recommended to produce satisfactory results. Load the tube in total darkness.

The color developer contains a chemical fogging agent that eliminates the need for a separate white light reexposure step. Never remove the processor tube cover until after the final rinse, otherwise there may be chemical streaks on the final print.

Kodak Ektachrome RC paper requires large volumes of wash water. A sufficient supply of water should be available to refill the containers.

Use a squeegee or sponge to remove moisture gently from both sides of the processed print. This provides faster drying and eliminates drying marks.

The processing of more than one sheet of Kodak Ektachrome RC paper at a time in the model 30A or model 30 is not recommended.

Filling the Containers. Use Ektaprint R-500 chemicals mixed according to the directions on the packages. The stainless-steel containers of the processor are numbered and should be used for the processing solutions and water washes corresponding to the step number. To avoid contamination, do not interchange containers or container positions in the tempering bath.

Fill the containers (No. 1, 7, 8, 9, and 10) to the appropriate level (see summary of steps) with warm water and place each container in the proper compartment of the tempering unit. With the 2024A processing tube, one full container of water is needed for the third wash (container No. 9). To this wash, add 30 ml (1 fluidounce) of potassium iodide stock

solution (8 grams potassium iodide crystals dissolved in 946 ml water). Container No. 10 can be used for the fourth wash; immediately after use it should be refilled with warm water for the fifth wash.

Fill the remaining containers to the appropriate level with chemical solutions as follows:

Container	Solution
2	First developer
3	Stop bath
4	Color developer
5	Bleach-fix
6	Stabilizer

Extreme care should be taken to avoid contamination of one solution by another. Wash the containers immediately after each step, and use the same container for the same solution each time.

With the 3040A processing tube, use container Nos. 7 and 8 for the first wash, and refill the same containers for the second, fourth, and fifth wash steps. Containers 9 and 10 are needed for the third wash and require the addition of 30 ml (1 fluidounce) of potassium iodide stock solution to each container.

Because of the large volumes of wash water required, it may be difficult to get all the water into the cup of the processing tube cover within 10 seconds. If water is slow in draining from the top section of the cover, gently strike the side of the processing tube near the cover. This will displace the air pocket formed and allow the wash water to drain more rapidly.

Large-Tube Processing: Negative-Positive Prints. The following chemicals are required to process Kodak Ektacolor 37 RC paper in the Model 30A processor:

Kodak Ektaprint 300 developer
Kodak Ektaprint 3 bleach-fix and replenisher
Kodak Ektaprint 3 stabilizer and replenisher.

PROCESSING STEPS WITH *KODAK EKTAPRINT* R-500 CHEMICALS

Processing Temperatures: (75 F ambient room temperature)	First Developer Solution	**43.5 ± 0.3 C (110 ± ½ F)**
	Other Solutions	**43.5 ± 0.6 C (110 ± 1 F)**
	Washes	**37.8 to 46 C (100 to 115 F)**

Processing Step	2024A Processing Tube Solution Volume		3040A Processing Tube Solution Volume		Time (min)*	Total Min at End of Step
	ml	fl oz	ml	fl oz		
1. Water prewet	385	13	945	32	½	½
2. First developer	385	13	945	32	1½	2
3. Stop bath	385	13	945	32	½	2½
4. First wash	945	32	1890	64	½	3
5. Second wash	945	32	1890	64	½	3½
6. Color developer	385	13	945	32	2	5½
7. Third wash†	945	32	1890	64	½	6
8. Bleach-fix	385	13	945	32	1½	7½
9. Fourth wash	945	32	1890	64	½	8
10. Fifth wash	945	32	1890	64	½	8½
11. Stabilizer	385	13	945	32	½	9
12. Rinse	385	13	945	32	¼	9¼
13. Dry—see instructions—49 to 66 C (120 to 150 F).						

*All times include a 10-second drain time.
†Add 1 fluidounce (30 ml) of potassium iodide stock solution to each 32 fluidounces (946 ml) of wash water.

Note that the stabilizer is also used as a stop bath solution in Step 3 of the process. Mix all solutions according to package instructions.

Fill containers 1, 4, 6, and 7 with warm water to the appropriate level. Fill container number 2 with Ektaprint 300 developer, containers 3 and 8 with stabilizer, and container 5 with bleach-fix solution. Use one litre (one quart) for each 30″ x 40″ print. For 16″ x 20″ to 20″ x 24″ prints (in the 2024A processing tube) use 383 ml (16 ounces) of solution in each container.

Be sure the proper timing disk is in the timer and that the "prewash" legend is visible.

• *See also:* COLOR PRINTING FROM NEGATIVES; COLOR PRINTING FROM TRANSPARENCIES; DARK-ROOM, PROFESSIONAL; LARGE COLOR PRINTS AND TRANSPARENCIES.

Further Reading: Carroll, John S. *Amphoto Color Film and Processing Data Book.* rev. ed. Garden City, NY: Amphoto, 1975; Nadler, Bob. *Color Printing Manual.* Garden City, NY: Amphoto, 1978. Eastman Kodak Co. *Processing Sheets of* KODAK EK-TACOLOR *37 RC Paper,* pub. No. E-79. Rochester, NY: Eastman Kodak Co., 1976; Vickers, John. *Making and Printing Colour Negatives.* New York, NY: International Publications Service, 1973.

PROCESSING STEPS FOR NEGATIVE-POSITIVE PRINT PROCESSING

Processing Step	Container Number	Temperature Remarks	Time in Minutes*
1. Prewash	1	The temperature	½
2. Developer	2	of this process is	2½
3. Stop†	3	nominally 37.8 C	½
4. Wash	4	(100 F).	½
5. Bleach-fix	5		½
6. Wash	6		½
7. Wash	7		½
8. Stabilizer†	8		½
9. Dry (forced air)	——	Not over 107 C (225 F).	——

*Include a 10-second drain time in each processing step.
†Use *Ektaprint* 3 stabilizer for this step.

Drum and Tube Processing

Drying Films and Prints

When films and prints have been thoroughly washed to remove chemicals absorbed by the emulsion and base materials, they must be dried before they may be used and stored away without fear of damage or deterioration.

During drying, the wet material gives up water to the surrounding air or absorbent medium (such as blotters) until it reaches a state of equilibrium in which it contains the same relative amount of moisture as the surroundings. There are two major concerns in achieving effective drying of photographic materials: (1) removing surface water without injuring the image, and (2) removing the absorbed water. The first must be done with extreme care because the soft, swollen gelatin of a wet emulsion is easily damaged, and because wet base material can be easily wrinkled or crimped to a degree that cannot be corrected. The second step must be carried out in a place and manner that prevent dust or dirt from coming in contact with the emulsion while it is soft, and that permit drying to progress at an even rate throughout the material. Uneven drying may cause physical distortion of the size or shape of the image, and uneven density in areas that should be uniform.

Protecting Emulsions

Films and prints that have been processed in conventional solutions at normal temperatures (18–24 C, or about 65–75 F), can be handled without damage throughout all stages of washing and drying if ordinary care is exercised. This assumes that a standard acid hardening fixer is used.

However, an emulsion that has been processed at high temperatures, as in rapid processing or under tropical conditions, may be very soft. A separate hardening prebath or a post-fixing bath may be required to protect the emulsion during washing and drying. Suitable formulas and procedures are given in relevant articles (*See:* FORMULAS FOR BLACK-AND-WHITE PROCESSING). Some chemical solutions may also cause problems. For example, certain print toners leave an emulsion soft enough to be easily damaged during drying. Protection can be obtained by using either of the following hardeners.

Post-toning hardener

Kodak liquid hardener . . . .   1 part
Water . . . .   13 parts

Kodak hardener F-5a

Water, about 50 C (125 F)	600	ml
Sodium sulfite (anhydrous)	75	g
28% Acetic acid	235	ml
Boric acid, crystals	37.5	g
Potassium alum, fine granular (dodecahydrated)	75	g
Cold water to make	1	litre

After toning, rinse the prints thoroughly in water. Then immerse them in either hardening solution for three minutes at 20 C (68 F). After hardening, wash the prints thoroughly before drying.

Removing Surface Water

Prints and films, even when well drained after washing, retain surface drops of water that must be removed for even, spot-free drying to take place. This may be accomplished in one of three ways:

1. Using a wetting agent to promote drainage and evaporation—suitable for films; not generally used for prints.
2. Using a sponge, chamois, or squeegee to absorb or wipe away the water—suitable for both films and prints.
3. Using blotters to absorb the moisture—suitable for prints, but not for films.

Wetting Agent. An aerosol wetting agent reduces the surface tension of water so that it flows freely off smooth surfaces such as film emulsion and base materials. It also speeds up evaporation of the remaining moisture. A very dilute solution of wetting agent is used as a final bath, after complete washing. Only a small amount of wetting agent is required; for example, Kodak Photo-Flo 200 solution is intended to be diluted 1:200 with water for use. With some water supplies, even further dilution may be necessary.

It is important not to create bubbles or foam on the surface of the dilute solution when it is mixed or used; they may cling to the film when it is withdrawn and cause drying marks. If bubbles do appear because of too vigorous stirring when the solution is mixed, or because of agitation when the film is in the solution, add enough water to bring the solution to a level that overflows the container. The bubbles will float off, or may be wiped off the surface of the liquid with the side of a finger.

Films may be immersed in the dilute solution while still in their processing holders. They should remain in the solution without agitation for 30 seconds before they are drained, removed from their holders, and hung to dry. *Do not wipe the surfaces of films treated in a wetting agent solution:* wiping counteracts the effect of the wetting agent and can cause drying streaks.

Wiping Films. Films may be wiped with a soft viscose sponge or chamois of fine quality specially prepared for darkroom use; household materials are too harsh and may be impregnated with chemicals that will affect the image. The sponge or chamois should be thoroughly wet to soften it completely, then squeezed to eliminate as much excess moisture as possible. As the illustrations show, it may be folded so that no raw edges are drawn over the emulsion. A soft-blade squeegee can be used on large-format films and is preferred for use on prints, but it is not practical for lengths of roll or 35 mm film.

Films should be handled one at a time, as shown in the following:

1. Remove from wash water and drain.
2. Remove from processing holder and hang in a clip that grips firmly with a pin or teeth that puncture the base or grip through a sprocket hole.
3. Hold the film steady by the lower end and wipe down from the top. Wipe slowly and steadily, with as much of the chamois or sponge in contact with the film surface as possible; this permits absorption of the maximum amount of water in a single pass. It should not be

necessary to wipe over the surface a second time. It is especially important not to wipe the emulsion side more than once in order to avoid damage.

4. Wipe only one side of the film at a time; after wiping one side squeeze the absorbed moisture out of the sponge or chamois before wiping the other. Do not try to fold the absorbent material around the film in order to wipe both sides at once. The use of sponge-tongs or other devices designed for this purpose should be done with great care. It is easy to squeeze the film unevenly or too tightly and cause damage to the emulsion.
5. To use a squeegee blade, hold the bottom of the film and wipe down each surface just once with a slow, steady motion. Wipe the blade free of water between sides.
6. Move the wiped film to the drying location before proceeding to the next film that is still in the wash water. Do not hang or wipe wet films next to those that have already been wiped; there is too much danger of spattering drops onto moisture-free surfaces.

A drop of water may collect at the lower corner of a film after it has been hung to dry for a few minutes. Do not try to wipe it away; instead, touch the corner from below with a sponge or chamois to absorb the water without contacting either film surface. If the drop is not removed, that corner will remain soft and moist long after the rest of the film has dried.

Wiping Prints. Although prints may also be wiped over with a sponge or chamois, it is far more effective to use a rubber-bladed squeegee. There must be a flat, smooth surface to support the print during wiping. A sheet of thick glass or plastic is suitable, or an old ferrotype sheet. The smooth bottom of a photographic tray is also suitable, but only if it is absolutely free of chemical contamination. A tray reserved only for washing is preferred; one that is used for fixer solution should never be used for this purpose.

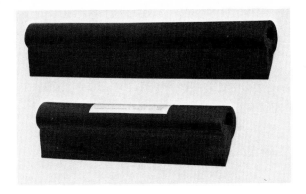

Rubber squeegees made especially for photographic use, such as these Kindermann products, are highly effective for wiping surface water from prints and large-format films. The blade of the squeegee should be wiped free of water between each pass. Photo courtesy Ehrenreich Photo-Optical Industries, Inc.

Stand the wiping board at an angle so that it is firmly supported in a location where water running down it can easily be collected or drained away. Handle prints one at a time in the following steps:

1. Rinse the board with clean water to remove any chemicals or dirt.
2. Remove a print from the washer—or from the stabilizer in the case of color prints—drain it thoroughly, and place it emulsion-side-down on the board.
3. Hold the top edge or corners of the print firmly with one hand to prevent sliding, and wipe down across the back of the print with the squeegee blade. Make more than one pass if necessary to remove all surface water. Use firm, steady pressure so as not to wrinkle the wet print or press a crease into it.
4. Peel the print from the wiping board; use the squeegee to wipe all moisture from the surface of the board before replacing the print with the emulsion facing outward.
5. Wipe the water off the blade, then squeegee the drops off the face of the print. Again, hold it at the top edge to prevent slipping or wrinkling. Do not wipe the emulsion more than is necessary; the wet emulsion is delicate.
6. Remove the print and place it in the drying location; then rinse off the board with clean water and repeat the above steps for the next print.

Blotting prints. Only paper prints may safely be blotted to remove surface water without damage; film emulsions are too delicate. After draining, place a print between two blotters and use hand pressure to make sure they contact every portion of both sides of the print. After about thirty seconds, remove the print and place it in the drying location. Blotters can be used for only two or three prints before becoming too saturated with water to be effective. It is important to use only photographic quality white blotters; ordinary blotters are commonly bleached with chemicals that can adversely affect photographic images. Preliminary "wet blotting" of this sort is a good way to use blotters that have become too warped and wavy to be suitable for final drying, so long as they are kept clean and chemically uncontaminated. Do not use newsprint, paper towels or tissues, or similar materials; they are chemically impure for this use.

Removing Absorbed Water

Gelatin emulsion may absorb as much as 20 grams of water per square foot during processing; conventional paper base material may absorb a great deal more. Drying removes this moisture by evaporation, displacement, absorption, or by a combination of these effects. Prints and films are considered to be dry when their moisture content has been reduced to about 15 percent; a lower content makes the gelatin emulsion brittle.

Moisture will evaporate readily into drier air. Evaporation is improved by a flow of air so that the material being dried is not surrounded by a stagnant layer of high humidity after the first evaporation has occurred. Moderately heated air, or heat applied to a print also encourages evaporation.

Extra-rapid drying can be achieved (at a cost) by treating materials to replace absorbed water with a faster-evaporating solution such as dilute alcohol, or by using a compound such as potassium carbonate to chemically absorb the water.

Drying is also accomplished by using absorbent materials such as blotters in contact with both sides of a print. Once saturated, the blotters must be changed or drying will drop to the very slow rate at which the blotters can evaporate the moisture they contain. Air flow and heat also increase the efficiency of such direct-absorption drying.

Drying Films

High volume, automatic processing machines variously use hot air jets, microwaves, infrared radiation, and other methods to dry films. The best method for small scale use is air evaporation.

Do not dry films in their processing holders. The channels, grooves, and other parts of the holders may retain drops of water that can run over the drying emulsion, causing streaks, or that may keep the edges of the film soft and damp long after the image area has dried. Drying lengths of film in spiral holders encourages curling.

After surface water is removed, hang films in a dry, dust-free location, using a puncture-type clip or hook at the top. Hang sheet films by one corner; use a weighted clip at the bottom end of long strips of film so that they cannot curl up on themselves. Wet film surfaces must not touch one another at any time during drying; at the least, permanent marks will result, and it may be impossible to separate the films without damaging the emulsion.

The drying area should be closed off to prevent air currents from carrying dust onto the wet films. A drying cabinet, an enclosure improvised out of plastic sheeting, or a room that will not be used are all suitable. Wipe the area with a damp (not wet) sponge or cloth to remove dust before use.

Air flowing into the drying area should be filtered to remove dust; a glass-fiber filter of the type used in small air conditioning units can be placed across the air inlet. The best flow is produced by air entering at the bottom of the enclosed area and exhausting near the top. If a fan is used it should not be directed onto the films; there is too much danger of driving dust or dirt into the emulsions, or causing films to swing and touch one another. An inlet fan should be positioned so that it blows air through the

protective filter into the drying area. A better arrangement is to use a fan at the outlet to pull moist air away. This also creates pressure to prevent dust from drifting in at the exhaust opening. The drying enclosure is easier to keep dust-free if the outlets are in the sides near the top, rather than the top being open.

Heating the air used for drying will cause an upward flow by convection. Screw-in electric resistance coils or even 100-watt light bulbs can be mounted in standard sockets at the bottom of a cabinet to heat the air as it enters. If the enclosure is made of plastic sheeting or other flexible material, it must be secured so it cannot possibly touch the heat source.

Avoid excessive heat; a temperature of about 38 C (100 F) is suitable. Higher temperatures may cause the surface of the gelatin to dry before lower layers, or may soften the gelatin; in either case the emulsion is likely to be damaged in normal handling after-

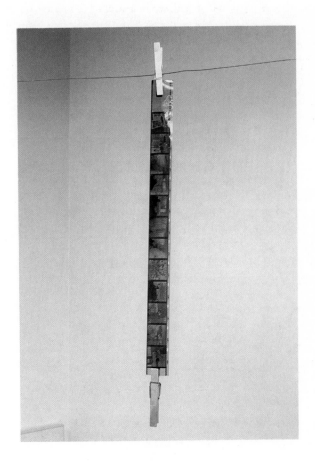

After surface water is removed, film should be hung to dry in a dust-free location. While special clips are manufactured for photographic use, many photographers use ordinary wooden clothespins. Film strips should be weighted at the bottom to prevent curling.

ward · Films will dry in 15–60 minutes, depending on emulsion thickness and the relative humidity of the drying air.

A small handblower hair dryer can be used as the source of both heat and air for a small film drying cabinet. One that has several heat levels is convenient to control the air temperature.

Rapid Drying. Although the following methods can be used for prints, they are primarily intended for drying films quickly. Samples should be tested before trying the alcohol method with water-resistant print materials. Rapid drying of one or two prints at a time with heated air can be accomplished by using a household handblower hair dryer. Set it for minimum heat and low blower speed, and move it continuously so that all portions of the print surface are equally covered by the stream of warm air. This is a convenient expedient for use with color test prints which must be first dry before they can be evaluated.

Alcohol Displacement. Alcohol will partly absorb and partly replace water in a film, reducing the drying time to 3–4 minutes. Use the solution:

Ethyl or isopropyl
   alcohol* . . . . . . 400 ml
Water . . . . 100 ml

* *Do not* use methyl alcohol; it attacks film base.

Treat films that are thoroughly wet; if some portions of the emulsion have dried significantly, marks may result. Drain the film and wipe the water off both surfaces. Soak it 1–2 minutes in the alcohol solution at about 20 C (68 F). Drain it with one corner or edge still in the solution to help the alcohol flow off. Hang to dry without wiping at a temperature no higher than 27 C (80.6 F). Soaking a film in undiluted alcohol and drying it with air that is too hot may cause the gelatin to become opalescent. If this occurs it can usually be corrected by soaking the film in water and drying slowly. The alcohol solution may be used several times, but must eventually be discarded because it is progressively diluted by the water removed from each film.

NOTE: Because some films may be affected by this treatment, it is wise to test a scrap negative before alcohol-drying valuable work.

Chemical Absorption. A saturated solution of potassium carbonate will rapidly dehydrate a gelatin emulsion. This method of drying is only temporary; it provides a negative that may be used immediately, but which must be thoroughly washed at the first opportunity to remove all traces of the carbonate if the image is to be preserved.

Potassium carbonate . . 500 g
Water . . . . 500 ml

Add the carbonate in small quantities, stirring continuously to be certain that it is entirely dissolved.

Remove a film from the wash water, drain it, and soak it in the carbonate solution for 1–2 minutes at about 20 C(68 F). Remove and drain the negative; wipe all surface water away with a sponge or chamois, and complete drying with a soft cloth or wad of cotton. The emulsion will be hard and shiny; the negative may be used at once for printing.

When rewashing to remove the carbonate, use just enough water to cover the negative and pour it off after about one minute. Repeat four or five times before washing in the normal way. This procedure avoids reticulation of the gelatin which might result from too rapid a change in the carbonate concentration in the emulsion.

This drying solution may be used repeatedly, and may be restored by dissolving more carbonate in it when required.

Drying Prints

Prints on all kinds of materials may be dried in the air. Conventional paper prints are also easily dried between blotters or in equipment which places them in contact with a heated surface, but such dryers pose special problems for water-resistant papers. However, because these paper bases absorb little or no water, they dry much more quickly than conventional papers and so there is often less need for direct-heat drying.

Air Drying. Prints can be hung by their corners to dry, but that takes unnecessary space and encourages curling of the free corners. The best method is to lay squeegeed prints face down on an open frame covered with cheesecloth, muslin or plastic screening. The plastic material is easier to keep clean and dust-free, and it does not generate lint. A large number of prints can be dried on frames arranged in a stack. They must have spacer pieces or be placed on separated guides in a rack or cabinet to allow suffi-

Prints may be dried on stacked, plastic-screen frames in a drying cabinet. Heated air blown across the frames will increase drying speed.

cient air flow between them. A fan blowing heated air across the frames will speed drying. Temperatures up to 88 C (190.4 F) may be used; the air flow must not be so strong that it moves the dry prints.

There are small, self-contained dryers especially intended for use with water-resistant papers which use radiant heat. The print is placed on a screen or rack a few inches below an electrical resistance element or infrared heat source. Some models incorporate a low speed fan to create air flow; others use a continuously moving belt to carry the print past the heating element.

The use of a household hair dryer was discussed in the section on rapid drying.

Blotter Drying. Use only clean white blotters that are chemically pure. Those used for the final stages of drying must be completely free of warps and wrinkles so as not to distort the print. As blotters do become warped, they may be used for the earlier, wetter stages of drying. Do not place water-resistant papers between blotters or with the emulsion in contact with a blotter; the soft, wet emulsion will adhere.

Remove all surface water from prints and pile them up with interleaving blotters for two or three minutes. Then transfer them to clean, dry blotters, with at least two blotters between prints so that moisture absorbed from one print is not directly transferred to the next. After about 10 minutes these blotters will be saturated. Transfer the prints to clean, flat blotters, again with at least two sheets between prints. Pieces of corrugated board inserted in the stack every five or six prints promote air flow. A fan blowing heated air onto the stack will speed drying. After about an hour, check the middle of the stack; if the blotters seem excessively damp, transfer the prints to dry blotters once again.

Blotter rolls provide good air circulation because of the length of corrugated material that rolls up with them, especially when heated air is blown through. Blotters in spiral-bound books do not receive adequate air circulation. It is better to remove the blotters and use them individually.

Some warping may be removed by dampening blotters thoroughly and pressing them with a handheld iron or in a dry mounting press at a moderate temperature.

Direct-Heat Drying. Most print dryers consist of a rotating metal drum or a flat box with two large metal sides; they are electrically heated from within. A canvas belt or apron holds prints in contact with the heated surface while allowing moisture to evaporate. Conventional paper prints may be dried face up or face down. Face-down drying, in contact with a very smooth surface, such as a chromium plated metal sheet, will produce a glazed finish on glossy surface papers (*See:* FERROTYPING). Face-up drying produces a smooth but unglazed finish on glossy papers and is also suitable for matte, lustre and other paper surfaces.

Prints on water-resistant papers must be dried face up, otherwise moisture in the emulsion cannot evaporate through the base. To prevent the base from sticking to the drum, a double-belt dryer must be used. A special liner must also be attached to prevent the emulsion from sticking to the canvas belt. The liner is used in such a way that the emulsion side of the print faces away from the drum surface. Belt tension must be adjusted so that the

(Left) The small, low-priced Durst FRC 200 print dryer, designed for 8" × 10" water-resistant papers, dries by means of filtered, electronically heated forced air. Prints are loaded on two plastic-coated (non-sticking) grids and inserted into the front of the unit; single-print drying time is from 3½ to 4½ minutes. (Right) The Durst RC 3400 print dryer will dry prints up to 12.8" by any length; it can dry up to eighty-six 8" × 10" prints per hour. The print is fed into the front of the machine where squeegees automatically remove excess water; it is then moved through the dryer by a transport mechanism and deposited in a tray at the back of the machine. It is designed to prevent any contact with the emulsion of water-resistant papers. Photos courtesy Ehrenreich Photo-Optical Industries, Inc.

texture of the liner is not embossed into the emulsion coating.

Maximum operating temperature with direct-heat dryers should be about 88 C (190 F).

Drying Problems

Surface Deposits. Scum may result from un-clean wash water or from an excess of wetting agent in the final rinse. White powdery deposits are usually caused by the presence of lime or other alkaline salts in the water. Rewashing will frequently remove them, if they are not imbedded in the gelatin. A final rinse in a one-percent solution of acetic acid will usually prevent their occurrence.

To mix an approximate one-percent solution, combine:

Acetic acid
Glacial (99%) . . . . 5 ml
　　or (28%) . . . . 18 ml
Water . . . . 500 ml

Uneven Density. Water drops may leave spots of different density because the gelatin remained swollen long after the surrounding emulsion had dried. This occurs whether a water drop is on the emulsion or the base side of a film. Larger areas of density variation may result from an uneven flow of heated air, which causes some parts of the emulsion to dry faster than others. Thorough rewetting of the emulsion and careful, even drying may eliminate the problem, but this method is usually successful only when a hardener has not been used in the fixer or some other bath.

Curling. Gelatin emulsion gives up moisture at a different rate than base materials. While drying, the side that loses moisture more rapidly contracts faster and causes the print or film to curl in that direction. In the case of films most of the curl usually disappears when drying is complete. Many films have an anti-curl layer of gelatin coated on the base side. This layer counteracts curl because it dries and contracts at essentially the same rate as the opposite side of the film.

Print materials do not have an anti-curl layer on the back so that prints have a tendency to retain drying curl. This can be minimized by drying prints under weight or pressure, or by weighting them down for a few hours after drying. Single-weight papers present greater curling problems than double-weight papers because the thinner base presents less resistance to the contraction of the emulsion.

Drying Films and Prints

Conventional paper prints may have a great tendency to curl immediately after being removed from a heated dryer because the gelatin will have contracted significantly faster than the base. Usually the curl will disappear if the prints are placed face down on a flat surface until the emulsion has a chance to absorb enough atmospheric moisture to equal the base moisture content. If the curl in a conventional paper base print remains after the print is cool, it can sometimes be removed by gently pulling the back of the print down over a smooth edge such as the side of a tabletop or counter. This is preferable to placing a ruler across the back of a face-down print and pulling the print up and outward, because it avoids the possibility of scraping the emulsion.

To correct persistent overall curl, slightly dampen the entire back of a paper print and press it between protective papers with a heated hand iron or in a dry mount press. The back of the print should face the heat source.

Prints made on water-resistant papers tend not to curl as much as conventional base prints because the paper base does not tend to absorb water during processing.

Negatives and prints may change their degree of flatness during storage and use as the moisture content of the emulsion varies according to the humidity of the surrounding air. The anti-curl layer on films will effectively counteract this problem. A flattening solution for prints prevents curling by filling the emulsion and base with a constant-moisture material (usually glycerine) that is unaffected by humidity changes. Such solutions leave an emulsion relatively soft and therefore more susceptible to damage. They may also promote chemical reactions with atmospheric pollutants that can affect image quality. Although very effective for many kinds of work, a flattening solution should not be used with prints that are to be stored for long periods, nor with materials that have been processed to meet archival standards.

Distortion. Almost all major changes in the shape and size of images result from too much heat during drying. In the case of films, by the time the temperature is high enough to distort the base, the emulsion is likely to have been damaged.

Rapid, uneven heating is the cause of most print distortions. If the center of a print dries faster than the edges—often the result of a hot spot in the dryer surace—it will contract at a greater rate, causing the edges to wave or flute. If the edges dry more rapidly, their contraction will cause the expanded center to bulge and ripple. Similar bulging results when moisture is trapped under water-resistant prints that have been placed face down on a heated surface. The remedy is to use a lower temperature and to make certain that the dryer is heated evenly over its entire surface.

• *See also:* Developers and Developing; Ferrotyping; Formulas for Black-and-White Processing; High-Temperature Processing; Toning; Washing.

Further Reading: Hattersley, Ralph. *Beginner's Guide to Darkroom Techniques.* Garden City, NY: Doubleday & Co., 1976; Jacobsen, C. I. and L. A. Mannheim. *Developing: The Technique of the Negative.* Garden City, NY: Amphoto, 1972; Langford, Michael J. *Basic Photography; A primer for professionals.* 3rd ed. Garden City, NY: Amphoto, 1973; Pittaro, Ernest M., ed. *Photo Lab Index.* Dobbs Ferry, NY: Morgan & Morgan, 1974; Sussman, Aaron. *The Amateur Photographer's Handbook.* Cornwall, NY: T. Y. Crowell Co., 1958.

Two film drying tunnels from Kindermann are designed for 35 mm roll films. (Left) The Porta-dri 20 has a capacity of forty 20-exposure rolls or fifteen 36-exposure rolls. (Right) The Porta-dri 40 will hold forty-two 36-exposure rolls.

Ducos du Hauron, Louis

(1837–1920)
French scientist and pioneer in the science of color photography

In his book, *Les Couleurs en Photographie,* published in 1869, he outlined the basis of almost every possible system of color photography, even though many of them could not at that time be experimentally demonstrated for lack of the proper sensitized materials. He did, however, demonstrate some additive color photographs, and with his brother Alcide, published a pamphlet *Photographie des Couleurs* in 1878, describing the methods by which these pictures were produced. In 1891, he proposed the anaglyph system of three-dimensional photography, and in 1900, he received the Progress Medal of the Royal Photographic Society. When panchromatic emulsions became available, he was successful in making separation negatives in sequence and reasonably successful color prints from these by a pigment process similar to the carbro process.

Dufaycolor

Dufaycolor is one of the most technically sophisticated methods of creating additive color photographic images, using an integral mosaic of regularly spaced color elements. The first version of a Dufay system film, Dioptichrome, was developed about 1910. It produced color still transparencies. A variety of improved versions were introduced in suceeding years under a number of names; they culminated in Dufaycolor film for both motion and still pictures, in 1934. At first this was only a reversal process, but a method of negative-positive printing was subsequently developed.

Additive color motion picture systems have not been successful on the level of theatrical film production because they produce far less brilliant projected images than subtractive color systems, and because the degree of enlargement of the projected image makes the pattern of the integral line screen or mosaic objectionably apparent. However, Dufaycolor films produced a relatively high quality image

A Dufaycolor photograph, produced by recording the subject on black-and-white film through red, blue, and green filters. Photo courtesy of Dr. Walter Clark.

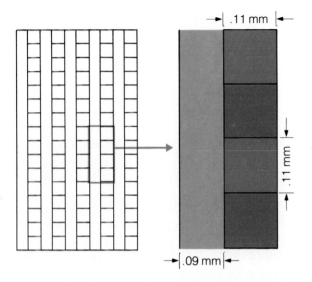

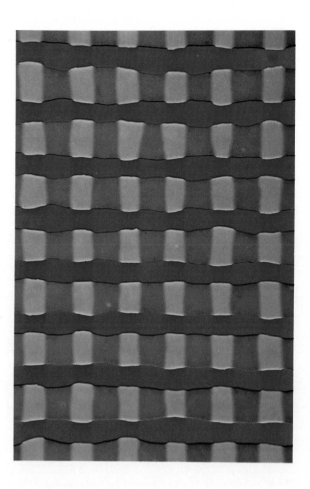

Mosaic in dufaycolor films consists of dye lines laid down in a right-angle pattern to create rectangles with a maximum dimension of 0.002 inch. Each mosaic element group contains three primary color rectangles, as shown in detail. The regular pattern and tiny size of the color elements insures that very small details of image-forming light passing through the mosaic to the black-and-white emulsion behind would be analyzed in terms of their red, green, and blue content. After reversal processing or printing onto positive film, light from the positive silver image passing through the mosaic projects an additive full-color image on the screen.

for amateur use and remained available in some versions until the late 1940's.

Additive color photography depends on recording a subject on black-and-white film with separate exposures through red, green, and blue filters. In an integral additive system, the filter elements are built into the film structure so that a single exposure produces the three individual color records in small spatial increments. As explained in separate articles, *line screen* and *lenticular* systems cover the entire image area with parallel lines of red, green, and blue filter elements. *Mosaic* systems use intermingled spots or dots of the three filter colors. A random mosaic, such as used in the Lumière Autochrome systems, is one in which the dots are laid down with little or no control over their shape and size, or over

the distribution of the colors. A regular mosaic is one created by methods which control dot formation and placement so that every area of the film is covered with an equal number of dots of each color, evenly distributed. The Dufay method used a combined screen mosaic composed of lines and rectangular dots, at a frequency of 500 per linear inch or, in some films, up to 750 per inch. The methods by which transparencies and negative-positive printing were accomplished are explained further in the various articles in the following list of cross references.

• *See also:* ADDITIVE COLOR SYNTHESIS; COLOR THEORY; DIFFUSION TRANSFER PROCESS; LENTICULAR SYSTEMS; LUMIERE COLOR PROCESSES; MOSAIC SYSTEMS.

Duplicate Black-and-White Negatives

In photographic work, it is often convenient and even necessary to use a duplicate negative instead of the original. A duplicate negative can be made in any desired size. Its contrast or density can be adjusted to suit the printing system or the paper in use. Another reason for duplicating is that sometimes negatives suffer abrasion during a long run of contact prints; a duplicate negative is the answer to this problem. Also, you can retain the original negative and send duplicates elsewhere for printing.

Direct Duplicate Negatives

The simplest way to make a duplicate negative is to use Kodak professional direct duplicating film (Estar thick base) SO-015, in sheets. The film may be exposed to the original negative by contact printing, or with a camera or an enlarger. (Various setups and techniques are explained in the article DUPLICATE SLIDES AND TRANSPARENCIES.)

This film has been designed to make duplicate negatives without the necessity of a reversal process. Instead, the normal develop-stop-fix procedure used for regular black-and-white negatives is employed for either tray or tank processing. It has an orthochromatic (red blind), medium-contrast emulsion. It may be handled under a light red (No. 1A) safelight filter in a suitable lamp with a 15-watt bulb. The safelight must be kept at least 1.2 metres (4 feet) from the film.

A similar film available in 35 mm long rolls and 36-exposure magazines is Kodak rapid processing copy film SO-185.

Exposure The exposure time for Kodak professional direct duplicating film should be determined by making a series of test exposures for the actual conditions under which the film is to be used. The amount of exposure controls the duplicate negative density (increased exposure reduces density, decreased exposure increases density), while development controls contrast.

Example of exposure for trial: Using a tungsten light source producing 3 footcandles at the exposure plane, expose for 40 seconds. Exposed film should be kept cool and dry. Process the film as soon as possible after exposure.

Processing.

1. Develop Kodak professional direct duplicating film at 21 C (70 F). Large tank (agitation at 1-minute intervals): Kodak developer DK-50 (full strength) —7 minutes.

    Tray (continuous agitation): Kodak Dektol developer (1:1)—2 minutes.

    Development times may have to be adjusted to obtain desired contrast.
2. Rinse at 18.5 to 24 C (65–75 F) with agitation. Stop bath—30 seconds.
3. Fix at 18.5 to 24 C (65–75 F) with frequent agitation (continuous for first 15 seconds). Standard fixer—5 to 10 minutes; rapid fixer—2 to 4 minutes.
4. Wash for 20 to 30 minutes in running water at 18.5 to 24 C (65–75 F). To minimize drying marks, treat in solution of wetting agent after washing. To save time and conserve water, use a washing aid such as Kodak hypo clearing agent.
5. Dry in a dust-free place.

Duplicate Negatives from Prints

When a duplicate is needed only occasionally, a simple way to proceed is to make a copy negative of a print made from the original negative you wish to duplicate. If you adopt this method, make a fairly dark print with considerably lower-than-normal contrast. A print of this quality retains most of the detail in the negative. Then, by increasing the contrast of the copy negative, you can obtain a very satisfactory result. A print made especially for copying should, of course, be printed on a glossy, smooth-surface paper. For further information, see the article COPYING.

Duplicate Negatives from Intermediate Positives

Since the density scale of a print is necessarily short, a duplicate negative of better quality can be made from an intermediate film positive, which has a much longer density scale.

To make an intermediate positive and then a duplicate negative from it, follow this procedure:

1. Make sure that the original negative is free from dust or fine lint. The latter is often invisible in room light, but it can be removed with a camel's-hair brush or with Kodak dust and static eliminating equipment.

2. Use a diffused-light enlarger to make an enlarged positive on Kodak commercial film. Other kinds of film can be used, but commercial film is relatively slow and can be handled in a red safelight. An 8 × 10-inch positive is suggested because this size is easy to spot or retouch. The positive should have higher density than one made simply for viewing. This is to make sure that all essential highlight detail is recorded on the straight-line part of the characteristic curve of the film emulsion for good tonal reproduction.

3. From the positive, make the duplicate negative on Kodak commercial film—or on Kodak Ektapan film (Estar thick base)—if you intend to make a big enlargement. The negative can be enlarged or reduced by projection, or it can be made by contact in a printing frame.

   As an alternative, you can set the positive up, illuminate it from the back, and then photograph the illuminated positive with a copy camera or a view camera. It is important to keep the surface of the positive in darkness during exposure; otherwise, reflection of light may spoil the negative.

Black-and-White Negatives from Color Transparencies

Excellent black-and-white reproductions can be made from color transparencies or color slides. The

transparency should be of good quality, although a dark, underexposed transparency often yields a good negative. On the other hand, a thin, overexposed transparency gives a reproduction lacking in highlight detail. The main problem in this work is the inherently high contrast given by a color transparency reproduced in black-and-white. However, contrast in the negative can be controlled by using a moderately low-contrast film and a suitable devel-

This black-and-white print was made from a color transparency. The black-and-white negative was made on Kodak Super-XX pan film (Estar Thick Base). Ideally, the original transparency should be of high quality, although some underexposed color transparencies may be converted to good black-and-white negatives.

oper and developing time. To make the negative, follow this procedure:

1. Make sure that the transparency is clean and free from dust.
2. If the transparency is original—that is, if it was exposed in a camera and processed by a reversal process—place it in the enlarger carrier, emulsion side towards the light. Otherwise, the reproduction will be laterally reversed.
3. Use Kodak Super-XX pan film (Estar thick base) to make the negative. At a $4 \times$ magnification, a transparency of average density needs an exposure of about 1 second at $f/16$ on an ordinary condenser enlarger with a photo enlarger lamp No. 212.
4. Develop the film in a tray for about 3½ minutes in Kodak HC-110 developer, dilution D. Contrast can be controlled by varying the time of development.

Color transparencies that are high in contrast or slightly unsharp yield a better quality black-and-white negative if masks are used. Generally, two masks are needed—a highlight mask and a principal, or contrast-reducing, mask. The highlight mask prevents the specular highlights from being gray in the print. The principal mask reduces contrast and so improves both shadow and highlight detail. This mask is purposely made unsharp to help register it accurately with the original.

Use Kodalith pan film 2568 (Estar base) and Kodak developer D-11 for the highlight mask. For the principal mask, use Kodak pan masking film (Estar thick base) and Kodak HC-110 developer, dilution F. Instructions for making the masks are given in the instruction sheets that accompany the films, and in the article MASKING.

Black-and-White Negatives from Color Negatives

You can, of course, make black-and-white prints from color negatives with Kodak Panalure paper, but when many prints are needed from a color negative it is easier to make them from a duplicate black-and-white negative.

To make a black-and-white negative from a color negative, follow this procedure:

1. Make a black-and-white film positive from the color negative. Since color negatives generally yield low contrast on black-and-white materials, use a film of moderately high contrast and develop it for the maximum time. Kodak Ektapan film, developed in Kodak developer HC-110 Dilution B for 4 minutes, is satisfactory in most cases. However, if you need greater contrast, use Kodak separation negative film, Type 2, and develop it for 4 minutes in Kodak developer D-11. These developing times are for tray development at 20 C (68 F). To make spotting and retouching easier, make enlarged positives from small negatives. The positive should have good contrast, but it should be somewhat darker than one intended simply for viewing.
2. Make the black-and-white negative from the positive either by contact or projection, according to the size you need. Kodak commercial film—tray-developed in Kodak HC-110 developer, dilution B, at 20 C (68 F) for 2¼ minutes—generally yields a good negative, but you can vary this developing time to get the contrast you require.

• *See also:* COPYING; DUPLICATE SLIDES AND TRANSPARENCIES; INTERNEGATIVE; MASKING.

Duplicate Color Negatives

Duplicate color negatives may be needed for a number of reasons. A photographer may have to release his or her original negative, but may wish to retain one for the files. Sometimes duplicate negatives have to be maintained at different locations. Having a number of identical negatives can be useful if a large quantity of color prints has to be made.

The following method can be used to produce duplicate color negatives. The original negative is used to make an enlarged print on a color paper, such as one of the Kodak Ektacolor papers. An N-surface paper is recommended for several reasons. As in many copying processes, the contrast tends to increase at each step. N-surface paper has a shorter density range than F-surface paper, and so helps control contrast. When F-surface paper is held flat by a sheet of glass in the copyboard, Newton rings can form. This does not happen with the N-surface paper. The N-surface paper is easier to spot or retouch, in case that is necessary.

In enlarging this intermediate print, it is wise to hold back shadow areas and to burn in highlight areas to maintain exceptionally good highlight and shadow detail. Not only does this help control contrast, it also improves tone separation in the highlight and shadow tonal areas. A good intermediate print looks a little flat and only the specular highlights are white. Diffuse highlights should be printed a light gray. There should be some black in the shadow areas, but the shadows should appear full of detail.

When the intermediate print is finished (including spotting, if necessary), it is copied on a color internegative film, such as Kodak Ektacolor internegative film. This film is available in the common sheet sizes, as well as in long rolls. It is balanced for tungsten light (3200 K), so it should be copied with light of this type, or the light should be balanced with filters as indicated in the following table.

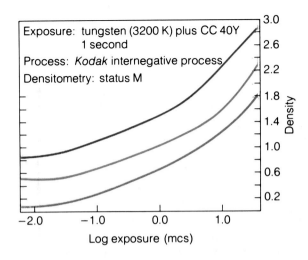

Characteristic curves of Kodak Ektacolor internegative film.

BALANCING LIGHT FOR COLOR INTERNEGATIVE FILM

Illumination	Color Temperature	Filter
Tungsten	3200 K	None
Photolamp	3400 K	81A
Pulsed-xenon Electronic flash Carbon arc	5500 K	85B

The contrast can be controlled, within limits, by varying the exposure. Increasing the exposure raises the contrast; decreasing the exposure lowers the contrast. As can be seen in the accompanying illustration of the characteristic curves, the film has two contrast slopes. Areas receiving lower exposures are reproduced with lower contrast. Those exposed on the upper part of the curve are recorded with an increased contrast. The ideal exposure places the highlights and lightest tones on the upper part of the curve. This compensates for the compression of highlight tones that always occurs when these tones are printed on the toe of the paper curve.

Kodak Ektacolor internegative film is processed in C-22 chemicals, but with a special developer made up from Kodak internegative starting solution and Kodak internegative replenisher.

• *See also:* INTERNEGATIVES.

Duplicate Slides and Transparencies

It is easy to make as many prints as may be required, whenever required, from a negative, but slides and transparencies are one-of-a-kind images. To obtain additional copies, it is necessary either to make several exposures of the original subject, or to make duplicates from an existing image. When the subject is no longer available, making a duplicate is the only possible way. Even if the subject could be rephotographed, the duplicating process offers the opportunity to improve the picture; that is, to produce a larger or smaller transparency, to crop the image for changed composition, to increase or decrease the density, or to use filtration to change color rendition.

Duplicates can serve a number of valuable functions. They make it easy to share slides with family and friends. They enable a photographer to make up two or more sample collections of his work for showing to more than one prospective client at a time. They may be used for inspection, projection, and reproduction purposes, keeping the originals protected from handling and repeated projection or viewing, which promotes fading of color images. Many photographic agencies and stock libraries use duplicates—and many photographers will submit only duplicates—for this reason.

Duplicates make it possible to issue multiple sets or collections of work, as for classroom use throughout a school system. And they make it possible to have identical reference collections in a number of locations—at several branches of a library, for example. In addition, enlarged duplicates may provide a more impressive presentation of work in a sample book or portfolio. Small-format images duplicated as 4″ × 5″ or 8″ × 10″ transparencies can easily be included in a portfolio of prints, avoiding the problems presented by a sheet or separate tray of slides.

Most commercial color processing laboratories offer duplicating services. However, there is much to be gained in the way of economy, control, and special results by making duplicate slides and transparencies yourself. It can be done with ordinary photographic equipment and perhaps a few accessories. The techniques are simple; they may also be used to make duplicate color or black-and-white negatives.

Basic Methods

Duplicates are produced either by:

1. Copying the positive image on a reversal or direct positive film, or by
2. Making an intermediate negative (internegative) and printing from that onto film.

Since a key problem in duplicating is a potential increase in contrast at each copying step, the first method is preferred because it consists of only one step. The second method is a better choice when a large number of duplicates must be made of a single image. The internegative protects the original from excessive handling and, especially, from repeated printing exposures which will accelerate the tendency to fade. It also provides greater opportunity for control and correction in making enlarged duplicates from small originals.

Whichever method is used, the best results will be obtained by using low-contrast films which are especially designed for the production of duplicates and internegatives. However, it is also possible to use conventional camera films to achieve good results. This article discusses duplicating methods using reversal films. For information about the internegative method, see the articles INTERNEGATIVE and TRANSPARENCIES FROM NEGATIVES.

Equipment

Cameras. A camera that provides through-the-lens viewing and focusing eliminates parallax problems. View cameras for large-format photography have this kind of viewing, and most can be equipped with adapter backs for roll and 35 mm films. Single-lens reflex cameras for smaller formats are widely used for duplicating because of their convenience and versatility.

Cameras with other viewing systems are more difficult to use. It may be possible to improvise by opening the camera back, opening the shutter for a time exposure, and placing a piece of ground glass, frosted acetate, or tracing paper across the film gate. But this allows you to make only one framing and focusing set-up, at the beginning of a roll of film. If a different set-up is required for later pictures, you must first remove the film in a darkroom, or rewind it and later advance it to a point beyond the previously exposed portion. The impracticality of this procedure (except for a very small number of duplicates) is obvious.

A few small-format cameras may accept an accessory "rack-over" back. This device is a light-tight sliding track that is used on a copy stand. In one position, a ground-glass viewer is positioned over the lens that will take the picture. After framing and focusing, the viewer is moved to one side, which slides the camera body into position over the lens. When the exposure has been made, the ground glass is racked over into viewing position again.

Lenses. Virtually all good quality photographic lenses will produce good duplicates. At the close focusing distances used for same-size (1:1) and enlarged images, better results may be obtained by reversing a camera lens so that its rear element faces the image being copied. Many manufacturers offer adapters for this purpose. If a great deal of duplicating is to be done, a macro lens is a worthwhile investment. Such a lens is especially designed to produce flat-field images at extremely close focusing distances.

In any case, it must be possible to extend the lens to greater than normal distances from the film plane; this requires built-in macro-focusing capability in the lens barrel, extra bellows extension, or extension tubes or rings. Although supplementary lenses may be used in front of a normal lens to achieve a close-focusing capability, they generally will not produce as good results as a macro lens or a standard lens. For further information, see the articles CLOSE-UP PHOTOGRAPHY and PHOTO-MACROGRAPHY.

Accessories. If the camera does not have built-in extra bellows extension, an accessory bellows will provide the greatest flexibility in focusing at various close distances. Fixed-length extension tubes and rings are limited to only one or a few distances, according to their individual and combined lengths.

A number of slide copying attachments are available for 35 mm and roll film cameras. They range from a slide holder with a light-diffusing back which mounts on a standard lens, to adjustable tubes or bellows with a built-in macro lens. The slide holder may permit the transparency to be shifted left, right, up or down to adjust framing, and may allow for the insertion of filters for color compensation or light balancing. If you will be duplicating just one size of slide onto just one size of film, such an accessory makes the job quick and easy.

A copy stand or tripod, coupled with a light box or other illuminator provides a great deal of flexibility. Some ways of achieving such a set-up are explained in the section on techniques in this article. Commercial units of this sort provide sophisticated control in duplicating. They generally consist of an illuminator with adjustable electronic flash light output, provision for corrective filtration, and built-in metering calibrated for various image magnifications. A widely used unit of this type is the Bowens Illumitran. It simplifies the production of large numbers of duplicates from a variety of originals.

Light Sources. Tungsten or electronic flash illumination may be used with equal success so long as it is matched to the color balance of the film emulsion being used. Electronic flash eliminates the need for heat protection for the original being duplicated, but requires filtration if used with other than daylight-type color films. Enlarging bulbs and tungsten-halogen lamps are good continuous light sources, as are photolamps and photoflood bulbs. Fluorescent light and cold light enlarger tubes should not be used with color films because of their discontinuous spectral output. Few set-ups make it practical to use actual daylight.

When light is placed behind a slide or transparency so it may be rephotographed, the illumination

Slide copying adapters, such as these two by Nikon, are designed to attach to a bellows unit. Duplication of same-size or enlarged 35 mm or smaller slides and negatives, as well as film-strips, 8 mm, super-8, and 16 mm movie films, is possible with these adapters. The deluxe model at left permits cropping by shifting slide holder up to 6 mm vertically and 9 mm horizontally. Photo courtesy Ehrenreich Photo-Optical Industries, Inc.

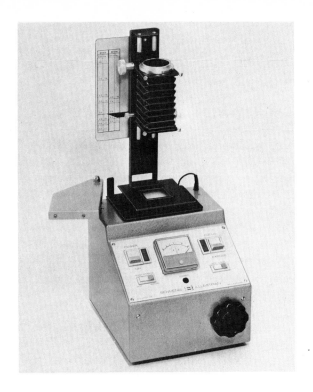

low the instructions included in the Kodak direct positive film processing outfit.

You can also copy black-and-white slides by using a color reversal film. However, duplicates may have a bluish cast if color balance during exposure and processing procedures are not under precise control.

Color Duplicates. For best results, and to make large numbers of duplicates, use Kodak Ektachrome duplicating films, which are available in 35 mm and 46 mm widths and standard sheet sizes. These films are discussed in detail in a later section. Conventional color reversal films may also be used; they are convenient when duplicates are made only occasionally, or on a small scale.

Although the accompanying table lists filtration for various light sources, it is best to use illumination that matches a film's color balance. Other filtration often will be required to compensate for characteristics of the image being duplicated, and it is desirable to keep total filtration to a minimum for the greatest accuracy and the shortest exposures.

Techniques

There are a number of methods of duplicating a positive image from a film. They include:

1. Contact printing.
2. Photographing the image projected on a screen—either a normal front-projection screen, or a rear-projection screen.
3. Photographing a transilluminated image.
4. Projecting the image directly onto the duplicating emulsion, as in enlarging.

These approaches are all discussed individually here. However, there are two factors common to them all, getting the correct exposure and the need for cleanliness.

Exposure Tests. No matter which method of slide duplicating you choose, you will need to make some exposure tests. Use a slide of average contrast

---

must be thoroughly diffused. This can be accomplished by reflecting the light off a white surface, or by shining it through a white diffuser behind the slide. A ground-glass diffuser does not spread the light evenly or sufficiently. Kodak opal flashed glass is a good material to use; a sheet of white plastic about ⅛″ thick may also be suitable with electronic flash, but is likely to be damaged by continuous light sources at close distances. Transillumination with a diffuser reduces the light intensity less than does reflecting it off a white surface. That may be a significant factor in choosing one method over the other when compensation for extra lens extension and for filtration is taken into account.

Films

Black-and-White Slides. To make black-and-white duplicates from either color or black-and-white transparencies, use Kodak direct positive panchromatic film, or Panatomic-X film. Both films are available in 35 mm size, and Panatomic-X film is also available in 120-size rolls. Rate these films at an exposure index of 80 for use with either tungsten or electronic flash illumination; no filtration is required. Reversal-process exposed films as described in the article DIRECT POSITIVE PROCESSING, or fol-

and brightness for your tests. The discussion of each duplicating method tells how to determine the *basic* exposure. However, in *every* instance you should bracket exposures at least 1 stop on either side of the basic exposure.

Depending on the duplicating set-up, you can take incident-light meter readings of the exposing or projecting light, reflected-light readings from an 18% gray card placed at the image position in the light, or reflected-light readings of the image itself. If it is difficult to get sufficient meter response from a gray card reading, use a white card instead, or read from a matte white screen. Reset the meter to an exposure index one-fifth of normal (for example, EI 20 instead of EI 100) when using the white card method.

When you see the processed slides, choose the best exposure and use this as the basic exposure for future duplicates. If you duplicate other slides that are lighter than average, use a 1 stop smaller lens opening than your test indicated. Use 1 stop more exposure for duplicating slides that are darker than average. (See later section "Evaluating Results.") You may wish always to bracket exposures of each slide, even after you have completed exposure

tests for your setup. That insures getting a duplicate with an exposure that is exactly right every time in spite of variations from original to original. It does take more film, of course. You will have to decide whether that is more important than the time and effort of reshooting if you are not satisfied with a single-exposure attempt.

NOTE: For bracketing, you may find that a + ½ and − ½ stop exposure will be adequate and will give a more exact exposure than you will get by using full-stop increments.

Preflashing. Pre-exposure of a film—preflashing—is a way to control (by lowering) contrast in a duplicate. It is especially useful when making duplicates on normal camera films, because the duplicate will have more contrast than the original. Sometimes the added contrast is acceptable. But if you duplicate a contrasty original, the added contrast will likely be excessive. In this case, you can preflash the film to reduce the contrast of the duplicate. In preflashing, the film is given a uniform exposure before the copy exposure is made. The preflashing exposure lowers the maximum density and the contrast of the shadows.

KODAK COLOR FILMS FOR DUPLICATING SLIDES AND TRANSPARENCIES

Film	Light Source—Film Speed—Filter		
	3200 K	3400 K	Electronic Flash (5600 K) or Daylight
Ektachrome duplicating films	See section: *Kodak Ektachrome* duplicating films		
Kodachrome 40 film 5070 (type A)	ASA 32 82A	ASA 40 None	ASA 25 85
Ektachrome 50 (tungsten)	ASA 50 None (at ½ sec.)	ASA 40 81A (at ½ sec.)	ASA 40 85B (at 1/60 sec.)
Ektachrome 160 (tungsten)	ASA 160 None	ASA 125 81A	ASA 100 85B
Ektachrome 64 (daylight) *Kodachrome* 64 (daylight)	ASA 16 80A	ASA 20 80B	ASA 64 None
Ektachrome 200 (daylight)	ASA 50 80A	ASA 64 80B	ASA 200 None
Kodachrome 25 (daylight)	ASA 6 80A	ASA 8 80B	ASA 25 None

The most convenient method of preflashing is to expose the film to the same light source used for copying the slide, but without the slide in place. This exposure should be approximately $\frac{1}{100}$ of the exposure for duplicating the slide. You can easily accomplish this by placing a 2.0 neutral density filter over the camera lens and making an exposure with the same lens opening and shutter speed that you'll use for making the dupe.

When you use neutral density filters, be sure not to confuse their density values. For example, a 2.0 neutral density filter reduces the light 100 times, while a .20 neutral density filter reduces the light by only 1½ times.

As with any unfamiliar procedure, make a series of test exposures to determine the best exposure for preflashing film.

A Clean Original. To help obtain a spotless duplicate slide, keep the original as clean and dust-free as possible. Never touch a transparency with your fingers; handle mounted transparencies by their mounts, unmounted transparencies by the edges. Remove dust or lint particles from slides with a clean, dry, camel's-hair brush. You can also use pressurized air, an anti-static brush, or other methods used in the darkroom to clean a negative for printing. To remove light fingerprints or oily smudges, apply Kodak film cleaner sparingly with a plush pad or a wad of cotton.

Contact Printing. Same-size duplicates of large-format transparencies can be produced by contact printing; trying to align and manipulate short lengths of small-format films is extremely difficult.

There are certain drawbacks to contact printing without special equipment. Unless a vacuum frame is used, the two sides of the pressure glass as well as the four film surfaces must be scrupulously clean. When the duplicate is being made on a panchromatic or color film, all operations must be carried out in total darkness. It is not as easy to add corrective filtration over the light source as over a camera lens, and larger filters are required. When placed emulsion-to-emulsion with the original for maximum sharpness, the duplicating film produces an image that is reversed left for right. It must be viewed or projected from the opposite side as the original. If the films are placed base-to-emulsion to

avoid lateral reversal, image definition may be reduced to a degree that is objectionable, especially if the duplicate is to be projected.

In spite of these problems, it is possible to achieve excellent results if care is taken in contact printing. Be sure that only direct light from the exposing source reaches the films. If an enlarger is used, it is easy to filter the exposing light to adjust color balance, using the same methods as you would for color printing. But use only the center of the projected circle of light to avoid any variation at the edges of the field; mask off the unused area to eliminate flare. An easy way to do this is to insert an empty negative carrier and adjust the enlarger until the projected rectangle of light just covers the films. Place a piece of black paper beneath the duplicating film so that light will not be reflected back into it from the easel or from the back of the printing frame or film holder. The transparency being copied goes on top of the film being exposed. Other factors in controlling stray light from an enlarger are discussed in the section on the "Direct Projection" method of duplicating.

To determine exposure, take a reflected-light reading from an 18% gray card at the film position, or take an incident-light reading with the meter cell pointed toward the exposing light. Do this before placing the films in position.

Front-Screen Projection. If possible, project the slide to be copied on a matte white screen. Hard composition board such as Masonite painted with several coats of flat, white paint makes a good screen. A pad of several large sheets of artists' watercolor paper also makes a good projection surface. Avoid beaded-surface screens, smooth finish poster board, and the like; they will cause glare and hot spot problems.

Arrange the projector and the camera so that the camera is as close as possible to the axis of the projection beam. This will help avoid distortion in the duplicate. If the focal lengths of the camera lens and the projector lens are approximately equal, you can set up the tripod-mounted camera to straddle the projector. For example, a 3″ projector lens and an 85 mm camera lens work fine in this manner. If the camera has a shorter focal-length lens, set it up in front of the projector, just under the projector beam. After you project the slide on the screen, you can move the camera back and forth to crop the

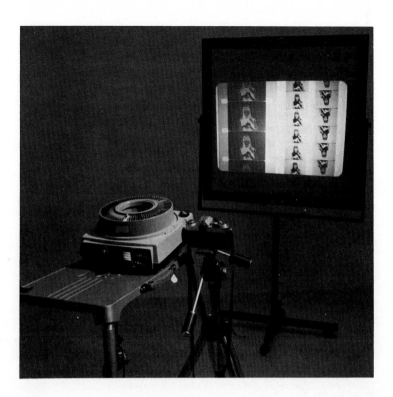

Position the camera on the same axis and as close to the projector lens as possible to photograph a front-projected image. If the tripod cannot be arranged to straddle directly the projector, the camera may be placed next to the projector, as illustrated here.

picture any way you like. You can also crop the picture by using a longer focal-length lens on the camera.

Work in a darkened room. Determine the basic exposure by taking a reflected-light reading from the projected image. Take an overall reading—hold the meter so that it doesn't shadow the screen or read the dark border around the image. You can also base exposure on a reflected-light reading of an 18% gray card held at the screen without a slide in the projector. Or, you can read from the white screen surface; in that case you must divide the exposure index of the film by five or use some other method to compute an exposure one-fifth of normal.

Make a record of the test exposures and the projector-to-screen distance. For the exposure test to be useful, the projection distance must be the same each time you make a copy. The brightness of the image will change if the projection distance is changed, or if a zoom projection lens setting is changed. The smaller the projected image, the brighter it will be. Choose a convenient setup for testing and use exactly the same arrangement whenever you make duplicates.

Rear-Screen Projection. This method of duplicating slides uses a translucent rather than an opaque screen. Place the projector behind the screen and photograph the projected image from the front. The slide must be reversed in the projector so that it will be properly oriented on the screen.

An excellent material to use as a rear-projection screen is a blackish translucent material called Lenscreen which at this writing is available from Polacoat, Inc., and Edmund Scientific Co. Also, a 20″ × 20″ Kodak day-view screen (No. 762355) works well. You can send a price request and an order to Eastman Kodak Company, Parts Services, 800 Lee Road, Rochester, New York 14650. These rear-projection-screen materials are rigid and can easily be held in place with blocks of wood.

Another material that can be used for a rear-projection screen is matte acetate tacked or stapled to a wooden frame. Matte acetate is colorless, has a fine grain, transmits light well, and is less expensive than the special materials listed above. It is usually available through art-supply shops. The only disadvantage in using matte acetate is that the projected image appears brighter at the center, causing a "hot

spot" in the center of the duplicate. To compensate for this effect, place a dodger a few inches in front of the lens in the center of the projection beam. A half-dollar or similar-sized opaque object glued to a piece of glass makes a good dodger. Adjust the dodger-to-lens distance until the projected image no longer appears brighter at the center.

To check for even illumination, take reflected-light readings from the camera side of the screen. Hold the meter cell very close to the screen and compare the center reading with those taken at the outer edges of the image; there should be no more than a ⅓-stop difference.

You can also use commercially available tabletop rear-projection screens for copying slides. Most of these units include a mirror to orient the image, so it is not necessary to reverse the slide in the projector.

Determine the basic exposure by taking an overall meter reading from the projected image. Alter the camera-to-screen distance to crop the picture. Always keep the projector-to-screen distance constant so that exposure tests will be useful at later times. Work in a darkened room to eliminate reflec-

tions on the surface of the screen and to avoid washing out detail in the projected image.

Transillumination. In this method of duplicating, light is shone through the slide, from behind, so you can copy the slide directly, not the projected image. Slide-copying accessories which attach directly to the camera lens mount, or to extension tubes or bellows, use transillumination. If you are putting together your own setup, the camera should be equipped with a close-up lens, extension tubes, or bellows focusing so that you can locate the camera close enough to the slide to make a same-size (1:1) copy. If you wish to copy only a portion of the original, it must be possible to focus even closer. However, that usually gives the best results only when the original is a medium- or large-format transparency. There can be a significant loss of quality in copying only part of a 35 mm slide unless the original slide is very sharp.

When using extension tubes or bellows, you must allow for the change in effective aperture. If you are making a same-size copy, either open the lens 2 stops more or increase the exposure time by a factor of 4. If you use close-up lenses, no exposure compensation is necessary. When you work at these short subject distances, use a lens opening of $f/8$ or smaller. For more information about close focusing and exposure compensation, see the article CLOSE-UP PHOTOGRAPHY.

The light source for making duplicates by transillumination can be a photoflood lamp, electronic flash, or a light box.

Using a Photolamp. Set the camera on a copying stand or on a tripod with an adjustable pan head so that the camera can be aimed straight down. For convenience, place the light near the floor; a reflector photolamp in a clamp-on socket is a flexible arrangement. Place a piece of diffusing glass, such as Kodak flashed opal glass, several feet above the light. One simple arrangement is to turn a stool upside down and place two pieces of wood across the leg brace to support the diffusing glass. Another easy setup is to place two chairs back-to-back about a foot apart, and use the chair backs to support the glass.

Next, cut an opening, slightly larger than the picture area of the slide, in a piece of cardboard. Lay the cardboard on the diffusing glass and position your slide over the opening. Work in a darkened room to avoid reflections on the surface of the slide.

If you place the light less than about 2 feet from the diffusing glass, position a heat-absorbing glass several inches below the diffusing glass. The heat-absorbing glass, usually available from plate-glass shops, will protect the diffusing glass and the slide from the heat of the lamp. Heat-absorbing glass may introduce a slight shift in color balance, which you can correct with filters.

Be sure the color temperature of the lamp matches the color balance of the film you are using. Most tungsten color films are balanced for 3200 K illumination; however, Kodachrome 40 film 5070 (type A) requires a 3400 K light source.

You can determine the basic exposure with an incident- or reflected-light meter. With a reflected-light meter, place the cell directly against the illuminated slide. The exposure indicated by the meter should be quite accurate if the meter cell is no larger than the slide area. If you use an incident-light meter, hold it so that the cell is in the position that the slide will occupy, but without the slide in place. Face the meter cell toward the light source.

Using Electronic Flash. The setup with electronic flash is basically the same as with a photolamp. Place the flash unit behind the slide, pointed directly at the slide, and arrange a piece of diffusing glass between the flash and the slide. You will need a cord long enough to connect the flash unit and camera. Since electronic flash closely approximates daylight, use daylight-type color film and work in subdued room light.

It is not possible to give specific camera settings for good exposure because of the variety of flash units in use today. Make a test carefully with your equipment—about five or six trial exposures. Use a shutter speed of 1/60 sec. and aperture settings of f/4 to f/16. With compact flash units, place the flash 18″ to 24″ from the slide—for larger units, 36″ to 48″.

Record the aperture setting used for each frame number. Measure and note the exact distance from the flash to the slide being copied. Remember, exposure will change as the distance is altered.

If your tests are all overexposed (too light), move the flash farther away or use another thickness of diffusing glass and repeat the tests. Do the opposite if they are all underexposed.

Using a Light Box. If you plan to duplicate quite a few slides at different times, you may want to build a special light box. Such a box offers the convenience of a standard copying setup. When you

Commercial tabletop rear-projection screens include a mirror to orient the image. Reversal of the slide in the projector is not necessary when using such a device.

Duplicate Slides and Transparencies

want to duplicate some slides, just plug in the box and set up the camera.

Construct the box as shown in the accompanying illustration. While the dimensions are not critical, the box should measure about 10″ square. Make the box from wood. The opening in the top should be large enough to illuminate the slides you plan to copy. If you expect to copy slides of different sizes, make the opening large enough to accommodate the largest slide. Then cover the opening with glass so you can lay smaller slides on the glass. Use a black opaque mask around the slide on the illuminator to keep stray light from reaching the camera lens.

If one side of the box is a hinged door, it will be much easier to replace the lamps when necessary. Paint the inside of the box with a matte white paint. Install a lamp socket in the center of the bottom of the box. Use either a photoflood lamp or a photo enlarger lamp, No. 211 or 212. These lamps have a color temperature of approximately 3200 K, which is suitable for most Tungsten and color duplicating films. Make provisions for including a heat-absorbing glass and a diffusing glass between the lamp and the slide. To allow air circulation, there must be some space between the sheets of glass and the sides of the box. You can best achieve this by using sheets of glass about ¾″ smaller than the inside dimensions of the box. Nail small blocks of wood to the nonmovable sides of the box to support the glass.

Drill an air-intake hole above the diffusing glass, and another opening for an exhaust hose near the bottom of the box at the opposite corner. Make a light baffle for the air intake out of a small box open on two adjoining sides. One open side will fit against the light box, and the other open side will face the base of the box. Attach a small exhaust fan, or even a tank-type vacuum cleaner, to the exhaust opening with a flexible hose. The flexible hose will help prevent vibrations from being transmitted to the light box.

Install a household dimmer switch in the wiring of the box so that you can reduce the brightness and heat while you position the slide and adjust the cam-

A light box of this sort can also use a small electronic flash unit as an exposing light source. In that case, an incandescent lamp should be included to provide illumination for focusing and framing.

era. *Be sure to switch to full brightness to take the pictures.*

Determine the basic exposure as described in the section "Using a Photolamp." Work in a darkened room to avoid reflections on the slide.

If you plan to duplicate many slides of equal size at one session, position the first slide and the camera, and mark the *exact* position of the slide with tape. This will make positioning successive slides easier, faster, and more precise. It will also allow you to accurately position several slides for making multiple exposures—a technique you can use to make titles or montages.

Direct Projection. Enlarged or same-size duplicates can be obtained by placing the original in an enlarger and projecting the image onto duplicating film in a film holder at the easel position. To obtain a 1:1 image, it must be possible to extend the enlarger lens twice its own focal length from the slide or transparency that is being copied. The duplicating film must then be that same distance below the lens. If you cannot lower the enlarger head close enough to the baseboard, raise the film holder on a box or a thick book to bring it within focusing range.

Tape wooden or cardboard guides in position to give you a means of registering film holder locations accurately. Use a separate holder loaded with a sheet of white paper for focusing. In order to get a right-reading duplicate image, insert the original with the emulsion facing away from, not toward the lens.

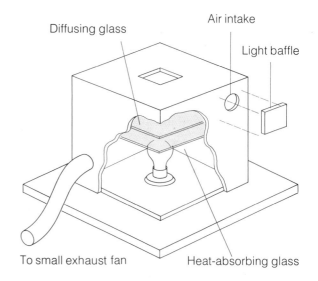

Diffusing glass Air intake Light baffle

To small exhaust fan Heat-absorbing glass

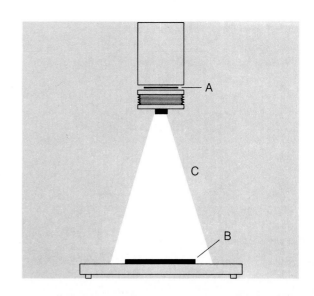

Direct projection duplicating: (A) Original in enlarger, base side toward lens; (B) Holder loaded with duplicating film; (C) Opaque cone (black paper) to eliminate stray light. Note that cone does not have to reach completely to lens or to narrow down to diameter of lens barrel. This greatly simplifies putting cone in position in total darkness after the slide has been removed from the film holder, just before exposure.

After focusing, close the lens to a medium aperture —at least two stops smaller than the maximum—to make exposure tests.

Determine exposure in one of three ways:

1. Read the projected image on the white paper with a reflected-light meter;
2. Remove the slide from enlargers, read the reflected light intensity from the white focusing paper and compute an exposure one-fifth of that indicated;
3. Make an incident light reading from the film holder position with no slide in the enlarger.

For a test series, change the lens *f*-stop setting; do not change the enlarger timer setting because it is hard to repeat various settings accurately at a later time.

You can work under normal room light for all the setup operations, and under subdued illumination or any safelight for focusing. But you must be in total darkness when you remove the dark slide from the film holder and make the exposure. All enlargers emit some stray light around the edges of the negative stage and at lamphouse ventilation ports. This is insignificant during normal printing, but it may have a fogging effect on films. Although you can place something over the enlarger head just before the exposure to block the light, this may not be practical during an exposure of several seconds because of heat buildup. An opaque cone between the lens and the film holder, as shown in the accompanying illustration, is an easy way to shield the film from unwanted light.

If the enlarger has built-in filtration, or accepts color-printing filters in the light head, it is easy to add corrective filtration as required. It is also possible to use color compensating filters below the lens, but they may affect image quality and they make it more difficult to put the stray light shield in place.

Evaluating Results

Examine each duplicate slide by projecting it in a darkened room. Larger transparencies should be viewed on a standard illuminator (5000 K, as recommended in ANSI Standard PH2.31–1969). Such an illuminator provides the correct light intensity and the spectral distribution characteristics necessary for the critical analysis of color transparencies.

Density. It is usual to make three trial exposures (normal; one stop more; one stop less). When evaluated, it is likely that one of the three exposures will be close to correct, producing the proper density level. If all three exposures produced densities that are too great (dark), give *more* exposure by changing the aperture (not the time) in making a new exposure series. It is important to keep the exposure time relatively constant in order to maintain a consistent filter pack. If the exposure series produced transparencies that are too low in density (light), make a new test-exposure series with less intensity (smaller apertures).

Color Balance. If the color balance of the duplicate is not what you want, you can correct it by using filters when you reshoot the original. Color compensating (CC) filters can be used over the camera or enlarger lens, or between the original and the light source. Do not use more than three filters over a lens, as image sharpness may be impaired. You can use any number of filters between the original and the light source, so long as they are protected from the effects of heat. In fact, you can use less expensive color printing (CP) filters between the original and the light source because in that position they do not affect the sharpness of the duplicate.

CC and CP filters are available in densities from .025 to .50. Various densities may be combined to achieve a desired result; for example, .20 + .10 = .30. If you made the duplicate without any filtration, you need only add filters to make a correction when you reshoot. Generally, densities of .10 or .20 will be sufficient. However, if you did use filters originally, it may be necessary to add or subtract various densities and colors from the filter pack to achieve the desired correction.

Adjusting Color Balance. First, determine the color or colors that are present in excess. This can be done by viewing the test transparencies through various CP or CC filters. The Kodak color print viewing filter kit is convenient for this purpose. When making judgments, look at the middletones instead of the shadows or the highlights. The required filter-pack adjustment involves removing a filter of the color that is present in excess in the transparency or adding a filter of a color complementary to the excess color. The amount of change is approximately the amount of the viewing filter that is required to make the middletones of the test transparency appear balanced.

For example, if a transparency is too red and requires a 20 cyan viewing filter to make it appear balanced, 20 red filtration should be removed from the original filter pack or 20 cyan filtration should be added to the pack. Whenever there is a choice, remove filters rather than adding them. The accompanying table may be useful in determining filter adjustment.

As a general rule, keep the number of filters in the filter pack to a minimum. Where CP filters are being used between the light source and the transparency, this is not critical. Some users find the use of just C, M, and Y filters convenient, because they do not have to stock red, green, or blue color printing filters. In using the CC filters in the image forming beam, the use of more than three filters may lead to loss of definition in the duplicate, and to lowered contrast due to flare.

When some filters of all three colors (C, M, Y) are in the pack, the pack in effect contains some *neutral density,* which can be removed without changing the basic correction of the pack. For instance, if the pack contains 40C + 40M + 20Y, the amount of the lowest value filter can be removed from all three colors, leaving only two colors in the pack.

$$
\begin{array}{ll}
\text{Filter pack} & 40C + 40M + 20Y \\
\text{Subtract} & \underline{-20C - 20M - 20Y} \\
\text{Reduced} & \underline{20C + 20M} \quad 0Y \\
\text{Filter Pack} & \qquad 20B
\end{array}
\left.\begin{array}{l} \\ \\ \\ \end{array}\right\} \begin{array}{l}\text{(remove} \\ \text{neutral} \\ \text{density)}\end{array}
$$

As can be seen in the filter adjustments table, C + M is equivalent to B, so that the 20C + 20M can be replaced by a 20B filter to obtain the minimum number of filters.

Filter Effect on Exposure

Filters have an effect on exposure, of course. To find the exposure change from one filter pack (old pack) multiply the filter factors for the new pack by each other, and divide this number (the pack factor) by the number found by multiplying together the filter factors for the filters in the old pack. Then

FILTER ADJUSTMENTS

If overall color balance is:	View through these filters:	Remove these filters from pack:	OR	Add these filters to pack:
Yellow	Magenta + Cyan	Yellow		Magenta + Cyan
Magenta	Yellow + Cyan	Magenta		Yellow + Cyan
Cyan	Yellow + Magenta	Cyan		Yellow + Magenta
Blue	Yellow	Magenta + Cyan		Yellow
Green	Magenta	Yellow + Cyan		Magenta
Red	Cyan	Yellow + Magenta		Cyan

Duplicate Slides and Transparencies

FACTORS FOR *KODAK* CC AND CP FILTERS

Filter	Factor	Filter	Factor
05Y	1.1	05R	1.2
10Y	1.1	10R	1.3
20Y	1.1	20R	1.5
30Y	1.1	30R	1.7
40Y	1.1	40R	1.9
50Y	1.1	50R	2.2
05M	1.2	05G	1.1
10M	1.3	10G	1.2
20M	1.5	20G	1.3
30M	1.7	30G	1.4
40M	1.9	40G	1.5
50M	2.1	50G	1.7
05C	1.1	05B	1.1
10C	1.2	10B	1.3
20C	1.3	20B	1.6
30C	1.4	30B	2.0
40C	1.5	40B	2.4
50C	1.6	50B	2.9

multiply the original exposure time by this result. The filter factor for each filter can be found in the above table.

Example:

Old pack	10Y + 5Y + 5M
New pack	20Y + 5Y + 20M
Exposure time	10 seconds

New pack factors $\dfrac{1.1 \times 1.1 \times 1.5}{1.1 \times 1.1 \times 1.2} = \dfrac{1.8}{1.45} = 1.25$
Old pack factors

1.25×10 seconds $= 12.5$ seconds (new exposure time)

Kodak Ektachrome Duplicating Films

There are two Kodak color reversal films especially designed to make high-quality duplicate slides and transparencies. Kodak Ektachrome slide duplicating film is available in long rolls of 35 mm and 46 mm width, and in 135—36 magazines. Kodak Ektachrome duplicating film is available in standard sheet sizes from 4″ × 5″ to 16″ × 20″. Both films are intended for processing in Process E-6 chemicals; they may be processed along with conventional camera films without any adjustments in time or procedures.

Kodak Ektachrome duplicating films may be exposed in a camera, or printed by contact or projection. Generally, camera exposure is most suitable for the 35 mm size, and contact or projection printing for larger sizes. Depending on the film size and the duplicating setup, copies may be made same-size, larger, or smaller. Because of their special contrast characteristics, no masking or other means of contrast control is normally required in exposing and processing. If somewhat lower contrast is acceptable in the duplicate, they also can be used to copy color prints or other colored reflection copy.

The duplicates are suitable for projection, for display on illuminators, or for use as originals for graphic reproduction. They can be separated by conventional film methods or by color scanner for use in catalogs, magazines, and other publications. The thickness of the duplicating film base in sheet sizes is the same as that of camera sheet films, so that both original and duplicate transparencies can be joined by cutting and butting operations. Retouching is possible with Kodak E-6 transparency retouching dyes.

Light source and exposing equipment. The Ektachrome duplicating films are intended primarily for exposure with tungsten illumination such as that supplied by photo enlarger lamps No. 212 or 302, or with tungsten-halogen lamps. Electronic flash or pulsed-xenon light sources can also be used, but fluorescent light sources are not recommended. Appropriate light-balancing filters are usually required with sources other than tungsten.

An enlarger is a convenient light source for making exposures by either contact or projection. The exposing equipment should have a heat-absorbing glass and an ultraviolet absorbing filter such as the Kodak Wratten filter No. 2B or a CP2B color printing filter. A constant-voltage power source minimizes short-term changes in light intensity and color balance.

As a starting point for color correction with a pulsed-xenon light, add CC25M and CC85Y filters to those recommended for tungsten light exposure. See the supplementary data sheet packaged with each emulsion for suggested color correction filters for tungsten illumination.

Exposing sheet film. Mask any unwanted portions of the original transparency with black paper. The intensity of the light should be controllable to allow an exposure time of approximately 5 seconds. Exposure is usually then controlled by the lens diaphragm; neutral density filters can be used if the illumination level is too high. Changes in voltage *must not be used* because the color balance of the exposing light changes with changing voltage. As a guide in determining the correct exposure conditions, make the initial exposure as follows:

Illumination at the Exposure Plane. ½ footcandle, without color correction filters in the light beam. Use a light integrator to measure pulsed-xenon illumination.

CC Filter Pack. Starting point recommendations are given in the data sheet packaged with each emulsion (for pulsed xenon, add CC25M and CC85Y to the filter pack recommendations given in the data sheet).

Trial Exposure Time. 10 seconds at three intensity levels: normal, 1 stop above normal, and 1 stop below normal. Normal is at the aperture that produces ½ footcandle illumination on the exposing plane.

While 10 seconds is recommended as a convenient exposure time for many situations, shorter times can also be used satisfactorily without getting uncontrollable color shifts. Avoid exposure times which are much shorter than 5 seconds or longer than 20 seconds.

Slide Duplicating with 35 mm Camera

A 35 mm single lens reflex camera having a through-the-lens metering system and equipped with a slide duplicating attachment is a convenient unit for making small numbers of duplicate slides. As a starting point, use a tungsten exposure index of 8 (with meters calibrated in ASA Speeds) and the following filters:

Original on this *Kodak* film	Use these *Kodak* color compensating filters, or equivalent
Kodachrome (process K-12)	CC10M
Ektachrome (process E-4)	CC20R
Ektachrome (process E-6)	CC10R + CC10M

Place the filters between the transparency and the 3200 K tungsten light source. Make sure that the filter pack is in place when metering or making exposures. Make a filter ring-around and an exposure series to determine the correct color balance and exposure for each new film emulsion used.

Exposing 35 mm and 46 mm Film. Make a series of exposure tests to determine the proper exposure level. For a tungsten light source, the exposure time should be about 1 second. For electronic flash, the exposure time will be about 1/1000 sec. Start with the suggestions given and vary the intensity of the light at the film plane until the slide density is correct. The reciprocity effect with this slide duplicating film is minimal. Adjustment in light intensity may be necessary to maintain correct slide den-

SLIDE DUPLICATING WITH ELECTRONIC FLASH PRINTERS*

When you duplicate from originals on these *Kodak* Films†	Use a filter pack containing these *Kodak* filters, or equivalent	And this exposure
Kodachrome (Process K-12) *Kodachrome* (Process K-14) Intermixed *Ektachrome* (Process E-4) *Ektachrome* (Process E-6)	Infrared cutoff, No. 304 + *Wratten*, No. 2B + Color compensating, CC115Y + Color compensting, CC50R	f/5.6 High beam
Ektachrome (Process E-4)	*Wratten*, No. 2B + Color compensating, CC120Y + Color compensating, CC10C	f/8
Kodachrome (Process K-12) *Kodachrome* (Process K-14) *Ektachrome* (Process E-6)	*Wratten*, No. 2B + Color compensating, CC110Y	High beam

*Such as Bowens Illumitran.
†Each listing includes all original camera films intended for the processing method noted in parentheses.

Duplicate Slides and Transparencies

sity if extremely short or long exposure times are used.

Starting filter pack. Ektachrome slide duplicating film has significant sensitivity to both ultraviolet and infrared radiation. An ultraviolet absorber, such as the Kodak Wratten filter No. 2B, is needed in the basic filter pack. The dye systems of Kodachrome and Ektachrome films (both older films and recently improved products) display differing degrees of infrared absorption. This can lead to a difference in the color quality of duplicates made from a mixture of original transparencies. A Kodak infrared cutoff filter No. 304 is recommended to compensate for this variability of infrared absorption.

This filter is a multilayer dichroic interference filter on glass. For effective results with an interference filter, position it *with care* in the light beam. Place the filter close to the light source, perpendicular to a specular, collimated part of the beam. Tipping the filter or allowing the light to pass through the filter at an angle changes the spectral transmittance characteristics of the filter. The Kodak infrared cutoff filter No. 304, is available in 70 mm (2¾″) filter size to fit several slide duplicating units.

Copying with Sheet Film

When used for copying color prints or other colored reflection copy such as paintings or drawings, Kodak Ektachrome duplicating film yields transparencies of somewhat lower contrast than duplicate transparencies. A standard copy setup can be used for copying on this film, with great care being taken to assure even illumination on the copyboard.

When incandescent illumination is used (3000 to 3200 K), start with the filter pack recommended on the instruction sheet packaged with the film, and make changes based on results. Use only CC filters (gelatin) and *not* CP filters (acetate), because the filters are used in the image forming beam. When using pulsed-xenon for illumination, start with an 85B filter only, and then make changes based on results. See the section given earlier in this article on color balance adjustments.

Processing. Process Kodak Ektachrome duplicating films in Process E-6 chemicals. Process the duplicating film separately or along with camera films; no adjustment in the process is necessary. Use the standard first developer time for all films.

Follow the process control methods recommended for Process E-6. Eastman Kodak Company supplies process control strips for Process E-6. Complete information is included in Kodak publication No. Z-119, *Using Process E-6.*

• *See also:* CLOSE-UP PHOTOGRAPHY; COLOR PRINTING FROM NEGATIVES; COLOR PRINTING FROM TRANSPARENCIES; CONTACT PRINTING; COPYING; DIRECT POSITIVE PROCESSING; DUPLICATE BLACK-AND-WHITE NEGATIVES; DUPLICATE COLOR NEGATIVES; INTERNEGATIVE; PHOTOMACROGRAPHY; TRANSPARENCIES FROM NEGATIVES.

Further Reading: Eastman Kodak Co. *Kodak Ektachrome Duplicating Film (Fact Sheet),* pub. no. P3-643. Rochester, NY: Eastman Kodak Co., 1974; ———.*Kodak Ektachrome Slide Duplicating Film 5071,* pub. no. E-39. Rochester, NY: Eastman Kodak Co., 1976; ———.*Kodak Ektachrome Duplicating Film 6121,* pub. no. E-38. Rochester, NY: Eastman Kodak Co., 1976; ———.*Storage and Care of Kodak Color Films,* pub. no. E-30. Rochester, NY: Eastman Kodak Co., 1976; ———.*The Third and Fourth Here's How,* pub. no. AE-104. Rochester, NY: Eastman Kodak Co., 1975; Spencer, D.A., L.A. Mannheim, and Viscount Hanworth. *Color Photography in Practice.* Garden City, NY: Amphoto, 1976.

Dye Destruction Color Process

In conventional color photographic print materials, the subtractive dyes that compose the final image are formed during processing in proportion to the silver image developed in each of three emulsion layers. It is also possible to create a color image in the opposite manner, by destroying rather than forming dyes. In material for this procedure, there is a maximum amount of dye in each emulsion layer before exposure. During processing the unwanted dye proportions are removed by chemical destruction, or bleaching.

Materials designed for dye destruction or dye-bleach processing use azo dyes which appear brighter and purer than other color photographic dyes because they are closer to the ideal spectrophotometric standards for cyan, magenta, and yellow. Azo dyes also have superior resistance to fading under usual viewing and display light conditions. However, because of the presence of the dyes, greater exposure is required to enable the printing light to penetrate to all emulsion layers sufficiently. Exposure speed is too slow for practical camera use.

Dye destruction emulsions can be coated on an opaque white base to produce a print for reflected-light viewing, or on a translucent or transparent base for viewing or projection by transmitted light. Materials may be made for direct positive (positive-to-positive) or for negative-positive printing; however, only direct positive materials (Cibachrome) are currently manufactured.

Principles

Like other color print materials, the emulsion is composed of three silver halide layers of selective color sensitivity: blue, green, and red, from top to base. A complementary color dye is also present in each layer: yellow:blue, magenta:green, cyan:red. As a result, under white light, unprocessed material appears black because all colors of white light are ab-

(Top) White printing light is colored as it passes through a slide or transparency. Halide in each emulsion layer of print material can be exposed by only one primary color of light. Dyes are complementaries of layer color sensitivities. (Center) Exposed halides are developed to a negative silver image. Then, dyes accompanying them can be bleached. (Below) The silver image is bleached and dissolved along with the unexposed halides. Remaining dyes correspond to a positive image of the subject. They subtract colors from white light so that those reaching the viewer's eye are the same as the original.

Direct Positive Printing

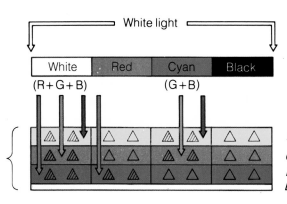

△ Unexposed halide
▨ Exposed halide
▲ Developed silver

Dye Destruction Color Process

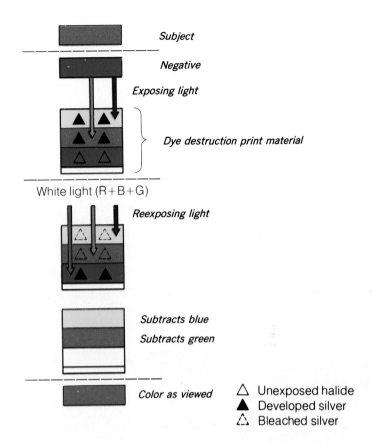

(Above) A red subject is recorded as cyan in a color negative. Thus, exposing light is green and blue and affects only halides in layers with those sensitivities. The silver image must be reversal-processed before dyes are removed. The first step is the development of the exposed halides to form a negative image. (Center) The negative silver is bleached. Reexposure to white light then exposes halides in the red-sensitive layer. Development produces a silver image and makes the dye in that layer bleachable. (Below) The dye is bleached. Then, the silver image is bleached and removed along with previously bleached compounds. The remaining dyes produce a red image by subtractive action on the white light. Other subject colors would be similarly reproduced by varying the proportions of dyes left in the emulsion at the end of processing.

sorbed by the dyes. The top layer dye gives the black a slight yellowish cast. Each dye is normally stable, but can be made bleachable by the process of silver halide development. After a silver image is developed, the accompanying dye is bleached; then all silver compounds are removed. The dyes which remain are in the proper proportions to form the desired positive color image.

Direct Positive Printing

The accompanying diagrams illustrate the following steps in positive-to-positive printing with a dye destruction material.

1. Exposure affects silver halides to form a latent negative image in each emulsion layer that corresponds to the primary color (blue, green, red) composition of each area of the slide or transparency being printed.

2. Development produces a negative silver image and makes the accompanying dyes bleachable in proportion to the amount of silver developed.

3. A bleach makes the dyes corresponding to the negative image colorless. Depending on the bleach composition, it may also bleach (rehalogenize) the silver image to a soluble state, or that action may be performed by the next solution.

4. A fixer dissolves all the unexposed halides and the silver bleached in the preceding step. Or, if the negative silver image was not bleached along with the dye, a combined bleach-fix solution is used in this step to dissolve and remove it along with the unexposed halides.

5. Washing removes all chemicals and processing byproducts from the emulsion. The remaining dyes correspond to the positive aspect of the original. They act subtractively on white viewing light to create a full-color image.

Negative-Positive Printing Principles

Although materials are not available, negative-positive printing by the dye destruction process would proceed as follows:

1. A red subject area appears cyan (green plus blue) in the color negative. Exposure through the negative affects the blue- and green-sensitive layers of the dye destruction print material. The negative silver image is developed there.

2. The negative silver image is bleached without affecting the dyes, and the material is reexposed to white light. This exposure affects only the red-sensitive emulsion layer.

3. The exposed halide in the red-sensitive layer is developed, producing a positive silver image and making the accompanying cyan dye bleachable.

4. The cyan dye and the positive silver image are bleached to a colorless state.

5. The emulsion is fixed to remove all silver compounds. Only yellow and magenta dyes remain; they subtract blue and green from white viewing light, producing a red positive image.

• *See also:* COLOR PRINTING FROM NEGATIVES; COLOR PRINTING FROM TRANSPARENCIES; COLOR THEORY; DEVELOPMENT; DIRECT POSITIVE PROCESSING; FORMULAS FOR BLACK-AND-WHITE PROCESSING; TONING.

Dye Toning

Dye toning is a method of changing the black silver image to one of a wide variety of colors by attaching a dye to the silver image or by substituting a dye image for the silver image. It differs from tinting in that the white paper base is not colored; for example, dye toning would produce a blue image on white paper, and tinting would produce a black image on a blue paper base. Dye toning is not much used any more; it was very popular for coloring the image on lantern slides and motion-picture films, but has been largely superseded by color film processes, even where a single colored image is desired.

• *See also:* FORMULAS FOR BLACK-AND-WHITE PROCESSING; TONING.

Dye Transfer Process

The Kodak dye transfer process is a method of producing color prints of the highest quality. It can result in either reflection images on paper or transparent ones on film base, in almost any size and quantity.

The starting point of this process can be a positive color transparency, a color negative or internegative, or black-and-white separation negatives made directly in the camera. The versatility to translate color information from various types of originals into a uniform finished product is one of the attractions of the dye transfer process. The accompanying diagram illustrates the various methods by which a subject may be reproduced.

Although more direct methods of making color prints are available, the dye transfer process continues to have important advantages in many professional applications. Since it has the capability of

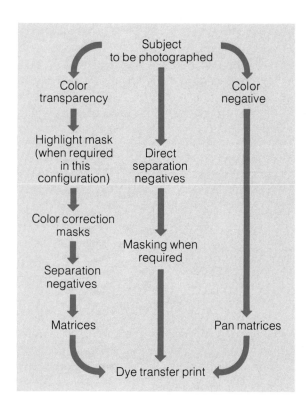

Dye transfer matrices are aligned in a register punch. The cyan matrix remains in place as a guide when the magenta and yellow matrices are punched.

color balance and contrast control in every step of the process, dye transfer offers unique possibilities for unexcelled photographic quality.

If the starting point is a positive color transparency, color-separation negatives are made on a suitable panchromatic sheet film by exposures from the transparency through red, green, and blue filters. Masking may also be used for improved reproduction. Then, three matrices on Kodak matrix film 4150 (Estar thick base) are made from the separation negatives by white-light exposures. Direct color-separation negatives can be made successively in a camera if the subject is a still life.

An original color negative or a color internegative is, in effect, a set of color-separation negatives in the form of dye images on one sheet of film. Three matrices, therefore, can be exposed directly from the negative through tricolor filters onto Kodak pan matrix film 4149 (Estar thick base).

Regardless of the starting point, the actual matrix processing and printing procedures are substantially the same. After exposure through the base side, the matrix films are developed in a tanning developer, fixed, washed in hot water to remove the gelatin in the unexposed areas, and dried. The images that remain are gelatin reliefs, in which the thickness varies with the degree of exposure. The matrices—which are, in effect, red-, green-, and blue-record separation positives—are soaked in solutions of cyan, magenta, and yellow dye, respectively. Each matrix takes up dye in proportion to the thickness of the gelatin. When the three dye images are transferred in register to a sheet of Kodak dye transfer paper, a color print is produced. Alternatively, the dye images can be transferred to Kodak dye transfer film 4151 (Estar thick base) to make "day-night" prints, suitable for viewing either by reflected light or by a combination of transmitted and reflected light.

Making Matrices using Pan Matrix Film

Kodak pan matrix film 4149 (Estar thick base) can be used to make dye transfer prints from color negatives and internegatives. This film must be handled and processed *in total darkness.* It is punched during manufacture to fit the register pins on a Kodak vacuum register board and the Kodak transfer register board.

Matrices are exposed with the emulsion side of a color negative or the base side of a color internegative facing the base side of the pan matrix film. The matrix images then appear in their correct left-to-right positions when seen through the base of the matrix film, and the dye images are correctly oriented on a paper print.

The matrices of a set include one made through each of the following filters: Kodak Wratten filters No. 29 (red), No. 99 (green), and No. 98 (blue). A Wratten filter No. 47B (blue) can be substituted for the Wratten filter No. 98, if the exposure time proves to be too long.

An enlarger is normally used as the light source for either enlarging or contact printing. In either case, the enlarger head should be equipped with baffles to prevent any stray light from reaching the matrix film. After each matrix is exposed, it should be identified to prevent mistakes from occurring in the later operations.

Pan Matrices by Enlargement. Check the enlarger head and its support thoroughly for rigidity. Any movement of the enlarger head during or between exposures will cause misregister. Avoid jarring the enlarger head while changing the filters.

An opaque mask must be used around the negative to prevent white light from getting past the desired image area of the negative and thus affecting the matrices.

A practical method for composing the picture on a Kodak vacuum register board is to place a sheet of paper on the board (Kodak dye transfer paper or other kind) that is larger than the widest vacuum channel. Locate the paper in such a way that one end extends under the raised clamps and over the register pins. When the clamps are lowered, the pins will perforate the paper. Draw a line lightly with pencil along the location of each of the vacuum channels; then compose the picture within the proper channel. The paper can be kept and reused by replacing it over the pins.

Keep the picture margin ½ inch or more away from the register pins; otherwise, difficulty may arise during transfer of the dye images. On the other three sides, provide for a narrow, unexposed border to facilitate handling the matrices without damage.

When the register board has been positioned properly for the negative to be printed, clamp or tape it securely to the enlarger baseboard to prevent any movement between exposures.

Pan Matrices by Contact. If matrices are to be made by contact printing, attach a strip of film containing register perforations to the negative so that it can be positioned identically with three sheets of Kodak pan matrix film. The strip of film can be obtained from a discarded matrix; if a Kodak register punch is available, it can be used to punch a discarded sheet of some other type of film. In either case, the perforated strip of film should be wide enough to bring the edge of the negative at least ½ inch away from the pins on the register board.

Having attached the strip of film to the negative, fasten an opaque mask on the base side of the negative to prevent the edges of the matrix film from being exposed. If the register punch is used to perforate the register strip, it is convenient to mask the image area first, and then to punch both the register strip and the opaque mask simultaneously.

A Kodak register printing frame can be used to expose matrices by contact. A Kodak register board or a vacuum register board can also be used in conjunction with a clean cover glass to maintain contact between the color negative and the matrix film. However, the vacuum channels are of no use in this operation. Use an enlarger as the light source, and if a register board is used to hold the negative and matrix film, place it on the easel. With the red separation filter over the enlarger lens, place a sheet of pan matrix film, emulsion down, over the register pins. Place the color negative on top, over the pins, emulsion down. (If the negative is an Ektacolor internegative, made by contact from an original transparency, place it, emulsion up, over the pins.) Lay a clean sheet of plate glass over the negative to hold it in contact with the matrix film, and make the exposure. Repeat the same procedure with the green and blue separation filters.

Determining Exposures for Pan Matrix Film. A correctly exposed matrix will show, after processing, a just-perceptible density in the diffuse white highlights of the subject. The exposure necessary to produce this density is found by making a trial exposure through the red separation filter, as will be described here.

The red-filter exposure, found by trial, determines the overall density of the final print. The color balance of the print depends upon the relative exposure received by the other two matrices. A balanced set of matrices shows equal densities in those areas that correspond to the neutral areas (white, gray, and black) in the subject originally photographed.

The blue-black pigment cannot be removed from the image on the pan matrix film. It is helpful in making exposure evaluations visually.

Gray Scale. A Kodak neutral test card, or a Kodak gray scale, or the gray scale found in the KODAK Color DATAGUIDE will be helpful in printing if it is included in the original scene when the color negatives are exposed. If it is inconvenient to include such a test image in each negative, a separate negative can be made. In either case, the test image will serve as a reference area only for other negatives made under the same exposure and processing conditions. At least one test exposure should be made for each group of negatives exposed under similar lighting conditions, and at least one test image should be developed in each processing batch.

Proper use of the neutral test card or gray scale provides reliable matrix-exposure information. If a test image is not available, select an area of the negative that probably represents a neutral object.

Master Negative. For the first negative to be printed, select one exposed to a typical subject containing a Kodak neutral test card or a Kodak gray scale. This negative is termed the "master negative." Before other negatives are printed, it is necessary to establish, as described in the next section, a printing relationship between the master negative and the emulsion number of the pan matrix film in use. The printing times for other negatives can then be calculated from density readings made with a photometer, a densitometer, or a Kodak video color negative analyzer, Model 2.

Test Procedure for New Emulsions. The following procedure must be carried out once for each new emulsion number of Kodak pan matrix film used:

1. *Make a mask.* Using interleaving paper from the pan matrix film box, make a mask that adequately covers the projected negative image on the vacuum register board. For large prints, two or more sheets of interleaving paper can be taped together. Mark the area of a diffuse highlight and the area of the gray card on the mask. Cut out these areas from the mask and reposition the mask on the easel. Tape one edge of the mask to the easel so that it can be folded back.

2. *Tape the diffuse highlight area.* With the mask folded back, position a piece of tape on the vacuum register board alongside the projected diffuse highlight area so that the tape can be used as a guide to positioning a matrix test strip. If the diffuse highlight and gray-card areas are in widely separated portions of the projected image, place another piece of tape alongside the gray-card area.

3. *Make the red-filter exposure.* Clip one end of the matrix test strip so that the first-exposure area can be later identified, and place the clipped end under the mask in the area of the diffuse white

highlight. The base side of the film should face the lens. If the gray-card area is close to the highlight area, position the film so that both areas will be exposed. If the gray-card area is not close to the diffuse-highlight area, cover the gray-card opening in the mask by taping a small piece of black paper over it. With the red filter over the lens, the trial exposure might be 15 seconds at $f/8$ for a $2\times$ enlargement. If the gray-card area was not exposed, move the test strip so that the image of the gray card will fall adjacent to the already exposed highlight image. Remove the black paper covering the gray-card area and place it over the highlight aperture, if this area is likely to cause an exposure on the test strip. Make another 15-second exposure.

4. *Make the green-filter exposure.* With the test strip in a lighttight drawer, replace the red filter with the green filter. Now, position the test strip under the gray-card mask aperture so that the green exposure will fall adjacent to the red exposure on the strip. Make a 25-second exposure. Repeat, using the blue filter, and give a 45-second exposure.

5. *Process the test strip.* It should show four exposed areas, readily identifiable by their positions in relation to the clipped end. If the green- or blue-filter areas are lighter or darker than the red-filter area, the time of exposure for these two must be lengthened or shortened until all three areas have the same density. Then the overall exposure level should be determined as follows: With your fingernail, scratch the diffuse-highlight area; place the test strip on the bottom of a white tray; the unscratched area should be noticeably darker than the scratched area.

On-Easel Exposure Determination with a Photometer. Once matrix exposure times from the master negative have been established by the test procedure just described, times for exposing other negatives on pan matrix film of the same emulsion number can be determined with an easel photometer having suitable response to red, green, and blue light.

1. With the master negative in the enlarger, the magnification and lens at the same settings as for the test strip, and the photometer probe on either a gray-card or a flesh-tone area, adjust the photometer potentiometers so that the exposure times determined for the red, green, and blue filters are indicated on the meter time scale.
2. Place the new negative in the enlarger and set the lens and magnification at the same settings used for the master negative. Place the photometer probe on either a flesh-tone or a gray-card area, whichever was used with the master negative. With the red-reading filter in place, adjust the lens opening so that the meter scale reads the same exposure time as for the master negative; then read the new green and blue exposure times directly.

Off-Easel Exposure Determination with an Electronic Densitometer. An electronic densitometer can be used as follows to determine matrix exposure times for subsequent color negatives once the times have been established for the master negative, and as long as the same emulsion number of pan matrix film is used:

1. Read and record the red, green, and blue densities of a flesh-tone or gray-card area in the master negative.
2. Read and record either the flesh-tone or gray-card densities of the new negative.

When a flesh tone is used instead of a gray card, both of the preceding exposure-determination procedures tend to reproduce all flesh tones alike, regardless of individual variations in skin color or in the character of the lighting falling on the original scene. Similarly, all images of a gray card tend to be printed alike, regardless of the position of the card relative to the main light.

Making Matrices using Matrix Film

Matrix exposures are made *through the base* of the Kodak matrix film 4150 (Estar thick base), with the color-separation negatives placed so that each matrix image will appear in its correct left-to-right position when seen through the base of the film. The dye images will then be oriented correctly when they are transferred to paper or film. After each matrix is exposed, it should be identified to prevent mistakes in the later operations.

Matrices by Enlargement. To prevent misregister or color wedging, and to provide the maximum useful picture area in the finished prints, place each color-separation negative *in the same position* in the enlarger negative holder. The simplest procedure is to tape an oversized sheet of thin white paper on the enlarger easel. Trace a few key lines and points of the projected image of one of the negatives on the paper. The next negative can then be positioned by moving it in the negative carrier until the image falls approximately on the marks; *do not move the easel.*

Mask the film so that there will be an unexposed border about 3/8 inch wide to facilitate handling the matrices without damage to the relief images. Use a clean piece of plate glass to hold the film flat during the exposure.

The necessity for using a sheet of glass can be avoided by exposing the film on a Kodak vacuum register board. However, the Kodak matrix film cannot be punched and placed over the register pins unless the enlarger head has a provision for pin or edge register of the separation negatives. In this case, punch the unexposed sheets of matrix film, one at a time, and expose them in register.

To expose unpunched film on a register board, place a sheet of white paper, the same size as the matrix film, in position over the vacuum channels, with one edge butted against the register pins. Mark the position of an adjacent edge with a piece of masking tape. After composing the picture on the white paper, position the films in the same way for exposure, using a black mask to keep the borders clear.

Place the separation negatives in the enlarger, emulsion side toward the light source. The enlarged images will then be in their correct left-to-right positions as seen on the enlarger easel. Since the matrices are exposed through the base of the matrix film, the matrix-dye images will also be correctly oriented when they are transferred in final printing operation.

Matrices by Contact. For contact printing, an enlarger or a modified safelight lamp can be used as the light source. An enlarger is more convenient, because it allows easy exposure control. Whatever the light source, the matrix film should be masked to provide an unexposed border or "safe edge" about ⅜ inch wide.

For matrices by contact, orient the separation negative so that the matrix film will be exposed through the back. Maximum sharpness in the matrices is obtained by using a small light source at considerable distance from the printing frame. A Kodak register printing frame can be used if the separation negatives have been exposed on the same pin system.

Effect of Exposure on Print Quality. When a correctly exposed and processed matrix is dyed, and the dye image is transferred to paper, any diffuse white highlight area shows a just-perceptible transfer of color. The exposure given to the cyan matrix (exposed from the red-filter separation negative) is usually used to establish the overall density of the print. With a properly balanced set of dyes, whites, grays, and blacks in the picture will be reproduced as neutrals in the print when all three matrices have equal densities in the white, gray, and black areas. A slight adjustment of color balance may be required at the transfer stage, but the first objective is equal densities in the neutral areas of all three matrices. Compensation for any density differences among the separation negatives must therefore be made in exposing the individual matrices.

Determining Matrix Exposures. Make a test exposure from each new set of separation negatives as follows:

Expose a diffuse white highlight area of the subject from the red-filter negative onto Kodak matrix film, and process the film through the wash-off step. With your fingernail, scratch the white highlight area in the test strip. View the test strip against a dark background by oblique transmitted light. The unscratched area should be just perceptibly darker than the scratched area.

If you lack the experience to make this judgment, dye the test strip cyan and transfer the image onto Kodak dye transfer paper. View the print through a red filter, such as the Kodak Wratten

filter No. 25 or No. 29. The cyan image from a correctly exposed matrix will look like a properly exposed black-and-white print.

With the proper matrix exposure known for the red-filter separation negative, the exposures for the green-and blue-filter negatives can be determined by using a visual or electronic densitometer and the color printing computer in the *KODAK Color DATA-GUIDE,* No. R-19. The *KODAK Graphic Arts Computer,* No. Q-12, can be substituted for the color-printing computer.

Reading Density. On a visual or electronic densitometer without any filters in the beam, read the density of the diffuse white highlight area in the red-separation negative. Turn the computer density scale until this density is opposite the time used to make the good test-strip exposure. The exposure time for each matrix now appears opposite the highlight density value of the corresponding negative.

If there is no diffuse highlight in the transparency that is a good neutral white, locate the step on the accompanying gray scale that is nearest in density to the highlights of the picture. Identify this step in all three color-separation negatives; then use its densities on the computer in the same manner as specified for a diffuse white highlight.

If the magnification or the lens aperture is changed from that used in exposing the test matrix, proceed as follows: Set the density scale as described above and hold it in position. Turn the lens-aperture dial until the lens aperture used for the test exposure appears opposite the magnification used for the test exposure. For any set of negatives, move the density and lens-aperture dials *together* until the lens aperture and magnification to be used appear opposite each other. The exposure time for each matrix now appears opposite the highlight density value of the corresponding negative.

NOTE: If you decide to use a matrix-developer dilution different from that used for the test strip, adjust the calculated exposure times as suggested in the contrast-control table in the matrix film instructions.

Registering Matrix Films. Unless matrices on Kodak matrix film have been exposed in register, they will have to be registered visually after they have been processed, dyed, and dried. To save time, the matrices can be dyed directly after processing and then dried. If matrices are registered prior to

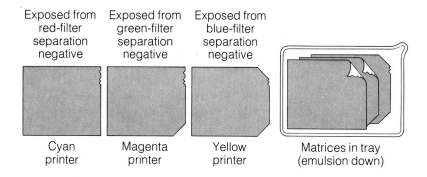

Exposed from red-filter separation negative — Cyan printer

Exposed from green-filter separation negative — Magenta printer

Exposed from blue-filter separation negative — Yellow printer

Matrices in tray (emulsion down)

When preparing for processing, matrices are identified by cutting off the corners. This should be done after exposure.

exposure, the drying step can be omitted. *It is very important to use freshly filtered dyes;* otherwise, foreign particles may become permanently embedded in the soft gelatin relief images. When they have been dried once, the relief images are somewhat more resistant to physical damage.

For dyeing the matrices, carry out steps 1, 2, 3, and 4 as given later in this article in the section on dyeing and transferring when making prints. Then hang the matrices up to dry, taking care to orient all three images in the same direction.

Use of Register Punch. Mount the Kodak register punch in a fixed position relative to an illuminator surface that will support each matrix at the level of the slot in the punch. The slot is ³⁄₁₆ inch above the bottom of the punch. Care should be taken to keep the glass on which the films are registered from becoming too warm. Excessive heat from the illuminator may lead to size changes and subsequent misregister of the dye images. The use of fluorescent illumination and air-spaced sheets of glass over the light source is recommended.

First superimpose the three dye images approximately in register and make sure that the matrices coincide to about ⅛ inch along the edge that is to be punched. If they do not, trim one or two of the matrices as required.

Then tape the cyan matrix in position for punching, emulsion side down, and punch it. Carefully superimpose the magenta matrix over the cyan matrix. With the aid of a magnifying glass, such as the Kodak achromatic magnifier, 5×, check the register at three widely spaced points. Use as guides any small, specular highlights, such as the catchlights in eyes, or cross marks scratched with a sharp knife along two edges of the transparency before the color-separation negatives were made. Secure the matrix with tape that does not overlap the tape used on the cyan matrix. Punch the magenta matrix and remove it without disturbing the cyan matrix. Finally, register the yellow matrix over the cyan matrix and punch it. Simultaneous punching of the three matrices may result in damage to the register punch.

Processing the Matrices

Use a Kodak safelight filter, No. 1 (red) or equivalent, in a suitable safelight lamp with a 15-watt bulb, no closer to the film than 4 feet with matrix film. Pan matrix film must be handled and processed in total darkness.

IMPORTANT: Prolonged exposure of matrix films to humidity conditions higher than those under which the film is packaged may lead to changes in photographic quality. To minimize such changes, open the foil package at the end with the longer tab, tearing off as little foil as possible. As soon as the required sheets have been removed, fold the end of the foil to seal the remaining film.

When the box is opened from the top, the emulsion side of each sheet faces up. Between the top sheet and the stiffener board is a sheet of unusable protective material that should remain in place until all sheets have been used. This protective material is identified by a cutoff corner.

Preparation for Processing. To prepare for processing the matrices, the following steps should be taken.

Matrix Identification. Identify matrices by cutting off corners, *after exposure,* as shown in the accompanying illustrations. Make the cuts as small as is practical for identification.

With the matrices positioned *emulsion down* and the code notch in the upper *right-hand* corner, ready for processing, cut the "lead matrix" (the yellow printer) at both the upper right-hand corner and the lower right-hand corner. During processing, the "lead matrix" refers to the matrix that leads the other two through the processing baths. The next matrix to enter the processing baths (the magenta printer) is cut in the lower right-hand corner only. The last matrix (the cyan printer) does not have any corners cut. All matrices are processed emulsion down.

CAUTION: Kodak matrix film 4150 must not be bent sharply before or during development. Lack of care in this respect may produce nonuniformity or marks in the matrix.

Solutions. Develop Kodak matrix film 4150 in Kodak tanning developer A and B. The two parts of this developer are available separately in prepared powder form.

Use the following volumes of solution for three 16½″ × 21¼″ matrices processed together in a 16″ × 20″ tray.

Total developer* .... 2 quarts
Water rinse .... 2 quarts
Kodak color film liquid fixer
   and replenisher
   (at C-22 dilution) .... 1 quart

*Composed of the required parts by volume of Developer A and Developer B (see accompanying table). Do not use less than 20 ounces of Developer A for three 11½ × 15¼ -inch matrices at any contrast level. To process individual 11½ × 15¼ -inch matrices, approximately one-third of the above volumes can be used.

For other film sizes and for test strips, maintain the above ratio of developer volume to film area as far as possible. Never fill a developer tray to less than one-quarter of its depth.

Contrast Control. The preferred method of contrast control is to develop all matrices to normal contrast; then, if necessary, adjust the contrast of the prints to the desired level by varying the degree of acidity of the dye baths. Directions for making such adjustments are packed with the Kodak matrix dye sets.

A practical range of matrix film contrast can also be obtained by varying the relative volumes of solution A and solution B. *Contrast is increased by increasing the volume of B relative to the volume of A.* Note, however, that the accompanying contrast-control table is not designed to permit the making of a perfectly satisfactory set of matrices from unbalanced separation negatives.

While most separation negatives will produce prints of suitable contrast when the matrices are developed at the "normal" developer ratio indicated in the table, the actual contrast level chosen for developing a given set of matrices will depend on the subject and lighting range, the print preferences of the operator, as well as the nature of the exposing equipment.

Five grades of contrast are given in the table, at levels similar to those available with the different printing grades of black-and-white paper. These grades are based on the use of the normal dye contrast recommended for dye transfer dyes. By interpolating in the table, other combinations of solutions A and B can be used to obtain intermediate contrast.

This contrast-control table is based on the use of a tungsten lamp in a diffuse-type enlarger. With other types of light or optical systems, some adjustment may be required to align the equipment with the contrast-control table. For example, a condens-

CONTRAST CONTROL				
For Development To:	Negative Density Range	Parts by Volume		Exposure Adjustment*
		Solution A	Solution B	
Very low contrast	1.8	1 part	1 part	130%
Low contrast	1.6	1 part	1½ parts	115%
Normal contrast	1.2	1 part	2 parts	100%
High contrast	1.1	1 part	3 parts	90%
Very high contrast	0.9	1 part	4½ parts	80%

*Assuming normal exposure at 1:2 development to be 100%

er-type enlarger may tend to give results of higher contrast.

The processing of matrix films is not difficult, yet it is an exacting operation. Follow instructions in all details, and do not introduce variations based on past experience with other films. Be careful to treat each matrix the same as the others in every step of the process. Use a sweep-hand timer, such as the Kodak timer.

Preparation of Solutions. Place three trays in the sink side by side. Put the required quantity of fixer at approximately 20 C (68 F) in the right-hand tray, and fill the center tray about half full of water at 20 C (68 F). The left-hand tray will be used for developing. If the temperature of the darkroom differs appreciably from 20 C (68 F), provide a water jacket at this temperature for the developer tray.

Measure the proper amount of developer B at 20 C (68 F) into the developer tray. Add the proper amount of developer A at 20 C (68 F). Stir rapidly with a thermometer until the solutions are thoroughly mixed. Check the temperature, and if necessary, readjust it to 20 C (68 F).

The developer starts oxidizing immediately upon mixing, and only a minimum time should elapse before it is used. However, there is a safety margin of 3 to 4 minutes during which the temperature can be adjusted, the room lights turned off, and the matrices prepared for immersion.

IMPORTANT: Use the developer only once and then discard it. It is also very important that the fixer be in good condition. Fresh fixer is recommended for each set of matrices.

Interleafing Agitation. Immediately after placing the final matrix in any solution, lift the notched edges of the top two matrices slightly; pull the bottom or lead matrix out; place it on top; and reimmerse it completely. Leaf the matrices continuously in this manner and use the same type of agitation throughout the process, adjusting the rate so that, at the end of each processing step (up to and including fixing), the lead matrix is on the bottom.

It is important to develop a smooth, reproducible, and moderately rapid leafing technique, and to give special attention to the leafing operation during the first few seconds in each processing bath, taking special care to prevent the adherence of one matrix to another. The emulsion is soft and must be handled carefully throughout.

The lead matrix should be the first matrix in all of the processing steps, and the other two matrices should be given the same treatment as the first in every possible way. The lead matrix can be identified easily because, as each matrix is grasped by the upper right corner, it is the only one with a clipped corner next to the code notch.

Handle the matrices *emulsion down* through all of the processing except the final wash-off and chill operations. During these last two steps, handle the matrices singly, emulsion side up.

1. Developer. Immerse the three matrices in the developer in succession, depressing each one slightly with your hand to assure complete coverage with developer. This process requires about 15 seconds. Time of development is 2 minutes at 20 ± 0.3 C (68 ± ½ F).
NOTE: For maximum uniformity of development, it may be desirable to process large-size matrices individually, emulsion side up. For individual development, use tray-tilt agitation.

2. Rinse. At the end of the development time, place the matrices in the water rinse. Transfer the matrices from the developer to the rinse in the same order and at the same rate as was used for the immersion in the developer. Leaf the matrices through twice in the rinse; to do so takes about 30 seconds. Withdraw the lead matrix, which should be on the bottom; immerse it in the fixer; and follow it in quick succession with the other two.

3. Fixer. Agitate the matrices for 2 minutes in the fixer, using the same leafing procedure as in the developer. The room light can be turned on after 1 minute, and the matrices can be allowed to remain in the fixer until they are given the wash-off treatment. However, do not store matrices in the fixer for longer than 15 minutes. *From this step on, handle the matrices individually, emulsion up.*

Tray-Tilt Agitation. The agitation used throughout the hot-water wash and rinses is similar to that recommended for black-and-white processing. Raise the left side of the tray about 2 inches above the bench top, lower it smoothly, and then immediately raise and lower the near side similarly. Next, raise and lower the right side and then again the near side. These four operations constitute an "agitation cycle," which requires a total time of about 8 seconds.

IMPORTANT: The emulsion is very soft at this stage and should never be subjected to direct streams of water. Direct-spray devices, even those which appear to be gentle, have been found to be harmful, and their use is discouraged.

4. Wash-Off. Place two trays for the wash-off procedure side by side. Fill one tray to about half capacity with water at 49 C (120 F) and place the lead matrix in it, emulsion up. Give the tray moderately vigorous tray-tilt agitation for 1 minute. This treatment removes the bulk of the untanned gelatin and also the backing layer, which appears brown after development.

While agitating the matrix in the first tray of water at 49 C (120 F), fill the second tray to about half capacity with water at 49 C (120 F). At the end of the 1-minute period, place the matrix in the second tray and give it a 30-second rinse with tray-tilt agitation.

At the end of the 30-second period, remove the matrix from the water and wipe the edges and punched holes carefully with your fingernails to remove any loose gelatin particles.

When the edges of the film have been cleaned, empty the first tray and refill it with fresh water at 49 C (120 F). Complete the wash-off with two additional 30-second rinses, each in a fresh volume of water at 49 C (120 F).

5. Chill Rinse. During the last rinse at 49 C (120 F), fill a third tray to half its capacity with water at 20 C (68 F). At the end of the last rinse period, transfer the matrix to the tray of water at 20 C (68 F). During the following 30 seconds, lift the matrix out of the water and drain it three times to remove any surface residue that may still be present. Then immediately hang it up to dry. Do not treat the matrix with a wetting agent.

6. Drying. For quick drying, circulated air can be used, provided it is free from dust and all three matrices of a set are treated identically. Suspend the matrices for drying by attaching clips to two corners in such a way that the orientation of the image on each matrix is the same. Larger matrices may show some tendency to curl, which can be minimized by attaching lightweight clips to the two lower corners. Drying can be expedited by wiping water droplets off the base side of the matrices with a Kodak photo chamois or a soft, wet viscose sponge. Take care not to touch the relief images.

Masking Direct Separation Negatives.

The reproduction quality of direct separation negatives is of a very high order without the aid of color correction masking, since only the unwanted absorptions of the dye transfer dyes are involved. However, when the ultimate in reproduction quality is required, black-and-white masks may be made by contact from the separation negatives in the following manner.

Working in total darkness, expose two sheets of pan masking film by contact from the red-filter separation negative and one from the green-filter separation negative. Process them as described in this article in the section on transparency masking for color correction. The result will be a positive image, the highlight density of which should be approximately 0.20. Register the processed and dried masks, emulsion-to-emulsion, with the separations, unless a register system has been used throughout. Arrange them in the following manner:

> Red-filter separation—red mask
> Green-filter separation—red mask
> Blue-filter separation—green mask

Masked separations tend to be somewhat low in contrast. Therefore, when making the matrices, the contrast can be restored by using the tanning developer at dilutions, 1A to 5B or 1A to 6B.

Transparency Masking

A color transparency is an approximation, although generally a satisfactory and pleasing one, of the original subject. When the transparency is reproduced, there is some loss in reproduction quality because of deficiencies of the dyes used in the photographic processes. A more accurate reproduction of the subject can be obtained by making some correction for these deficiencies. This correction procedure, known as "masking," constitutes an additional step in the reproduction process, but the resulting improvements usually more than justify the extra effort involved.

A single mask corrects relative brightness and saturation errors. With most color transparencies, one mask gives acceptable results. To correct hue-shift errors, two masks are necessary. In addition to such a principal mask or masks, a highlight mask is sometimes necessary to retain important highlight detail. If a highlight mask is needed, it is made first and used with the transparency during exposure of the principal mask or masks.

Contact Highlight Masking. The highlights fall somewhere along the toe portion of the characteristic curve, in many Kodachrome and Ektachrome transparencies; their contrast is therefore lower than that of the middletones. When a print is made, the contrast of the highlights in relation to that of the middletones tends to be lowered further because the highlights again fall on a flatter portion of the characteristic curve.

With subjects containing important highlight areas, it is often worthwhile to correct this error by introducing a highlight mask before making a principal mask or masks. The highlight-masking procedure described here can be used only in conjunction with other masks; in other words, it is supplementary to one of the procedures recommended for use with Kodak pan masking film 4570 (Estar thick base).

Basic Outline of Highlight-Masking Procedure. First, the transparency is printed by contact on Kodalith ortho film 2556, Type 3 (Estar base), with the exposure adjusted so that an underexposed negative is obtained. After development to high contrast in Kodak developer D-11, this negative, the *highlight mask,* will contain densities corresponding to the highlights of the transparency only; other areas will be clear. The highlight mask is registered with the transparency; from the combination, one or more *principal masks* are made. Since the highlights of the transparency have density added to them by the highlight mask, they are printed on the principal mask very much lighter than they would be without the highlight mask.

After the principal mask has been developed, the highlight mask is removed from the transparency and replaced with the principal mask during the exposure of the color-separation negatives. The contrast of the highlights of the masked transparency is now relatively higher than normal. The highlights should therefore reproduce in the print with the desired sparkle and brilliance.

Exposure. As with principal masks, it is convenient to expose highlight masks in a printing frame. The masking film and transparency are exposed emulsion-to-emulsion. The exposure of the highlight mask is fairly critical; an exposure test should be made with each transparency. If the light source is an enlarger that has been set to give an illumination level of 3 footcandles at the exposing plane, with the lens at $f/4.5$, stop the lens down to $f/22$ and add a neutral density of 1.0 (Kodak Wratten neutral density filter, No. 96). With other light sources providing 3 footcandles, use a neutral density of 2.4, which can be assembled from a 2.0- and a 0.40-density Kodak Wratten neutral density filter, No. 96. In either case, give a trial exposure of 6 to 18 seconds with no color filter.

After some experience in highlight-masking work, you will find it is fairly easy to judge whether the correct exposure has been given. If the mask is underexposed, the desired highlight-tone correction in the print will not be obtained. On the other hand, overexposure will extend the increase in contrast to the lighter middletones, and result in a harsh effect in the print. Overexposure will also interfere with accurate register of the highlight mask on the original, and may cause edge effects around the whites in the principal mask or masks.

Processing. Masks on Kodalith ortho film 2556, Type 3, can be developed by inspection. Develop the film, with continuous agitation, for 2½ minutes at 20 C (68 F) in a tray of Kodak developer D-11, full strength. This developer is supplied in prepared powder form. After development, rinse the film for about 10 seconds in Kodak indicator stop bath or Kodak stop bath SB-1a. Fix the film for 2 to 4 minutes in Kodak fixing bath F-5 or Kodak fixer, or for 1 to 2 minutes in Kodak rapid fixer. Wash the film for about 10 minutes in running water. *Use a temperature from 18.5 to 21 C (65 to 70 F) for rinse, fix, and wash.* To minimize drying marks, treat the film in Kodak Photo-Flo solution after washing, or wipe surfaces carefully with a Kodak photo chamois, a soft viscose sponge, a Kodak rubber squeegee, or other soft squeegee. Dry the film in a dust-free place with no more than moderate heat.

Registering the Mask. The developed highlight mask is registered on the emulsion side of the transparency. Unless a pin register system is used, some misregister of the mask may be evident, especially with a transparency that contains larges areas of fine detail. In this case, the mask should be registered most accurately at the most important points in the transparency. The misregister distributed over areas of less importance will be prevented from showing by the diffusion introduced in making the principal mask or masks. After registering the mask, tape it to the original, being careful to let the tape touch only the extreme edges of the transparency.

The mask gives a rather strange appearance to the transparency, but this is perfectly normal. The temporary reversal of the highlights will disappear when the highlight mask is replaced by a principal mask.

NOTE: If a step tablet has been placed beside the original (as recommended), the highlight mask should be cut away from this gray-scale area. Otherwise, the gray scale reproduced in the print will show so few steps in the toe that it will be of little help for judging the color balance of the lighter tones in the picture.

Subsequent Procedure. The principal mask or masks are made in exactly the same way that they would be made if there were no highlight mask on the transparency. After the principal masks have been prepared, the highlight mask is removed and replaced by the principal masks during the exposure of the color-separation negatives.

Since the highlights of the original have been covered by high densities in the highlight mask, they will be relatively light in the principal masks. Large specular highlights in the original transparency will have almost no density at all in the principal masks. As a result, with a principal mask in place, the transparency will appear to have very bright and contrasty highlights. Highlights on faces will even have a greasy appearance, because of their exaggerated contrast in relation to the middletones. When the dye transfer print is made, however, the contrast of this portion of the reproduction curve will be reduced by the toe characteristics of the printing process; only enough contrast will be left to give the desired rendering of highlight areas.

Contact Masking for Color Correction

Arrangement for Exposure. Kodak pan masking film 4570 (Estar thick base) can be used to make the color correction masks. Place the transparency or color negative in a printing frame on the easel. To simplify subsequent register, diffuse the mask during exposure by placing a piece of Kodak diffusion sheet (.003-inch) between the original and the masking film. Consider the matte side of the diffusion sheet as the emulsion side. All three emulsion sides should face the exposing light.

To measure the density range of the mask, place a step tablet beside the original before exposing the mask. (Cut the gray-scale area of any highlight mask away before exposing the principal mask.) In the processed mask, read the two steps where the step tablet matches most closely the highlight and shadow densities of the unmasked original; then subtract one step from the other.

Single-mask procedure: For most transparencies, a single mask exposed with white light is recommended. However, if you want to lighten greens, use a magenta filter, such as a Kodak Wratten filter No. 33, over the light source. If you want to lighten both blues and greens, use a red filter, such as a Kodak Wratten filter No. 29. After you expose and process the mask, tape it in register to the base side of the original transparency. The combination of mask and original is then ready for the making of the three color-separation negatives.

Double-mask procedure: To maintain even better color reproduction (i.e., printing saturated reds and greens in the same picture), two principal masks are needed, one exposed by red light and one exposed by green light.

For making color-separation negatives, the red-filter mask is taped in register with the transparency and left there while the red- and green-filter separation negatives are being exposed. It is then replaced by the green-filter mask for the exposure of the blue-filter separation negative. When the original transparency is one that has been processed in process K-14 (Kodachrome 25 or Kodachrome 64 film), the masking procedure is as follows: For making color separation negatives, the red-filter mask is taped in register with the transparency when the green-filter separation is being exposed. The green-filter mask is taped in register with the transparency when the red- and blue-filter separations are being exposed. NOTE: The red filter in this case is a Kodak Wratten filter No. 24. Use oversize masking film with the Kodak register punch and the Kodak register printing frame.

Exposure. The exposure conditions given assume that a tungsten light source is adjusted to give 3 footcandles at the exposing plane (measured without filters).

EXPOSURE TIMES WITH COLOR CORRECTION MASKS

Color of Exposing Light	Kodak Wratten Filter No.	Exposure Time*
White	96 (totaling 1.20 density)	100 sec.
Magenta	33	100 sec.
Red	29	100 sec.
Green	61	150 sec.
For Process K-14 Films		
Magenta	33	100 sec.
Red	24	50 sec.
Green	61	150 sec.

*If necessary, adjust the exposure time to give just-discernible detail in the darkest shadow area.

Processing. Develop the masks for 3 minutes at 20 C (68 F), with continuous agitation, in a tray of fresh Kodak HC-110 developer, diluted 1 part stock solution to 19 parts water (dilution F); or in a tray of Kodak developer DK-50, diluted 1:4. The density range should be approximately ¼ to ⅓ the density range of the transparency. To obtain more or less contrast reduction, increase or decrease the development time.

Registering the Mask. If the matrices are to be exposed by enlarging the separation negatives, register the mask on the base side of the transparency. Then place the emulsion side of the transparency so that it faces the emulsion side of the separation-negative material, and print either by contact or by enlarging.

If the matrices are to be exposed by contact, register the mask on the emulsion side of the transparency. Then place the transparency so that its base side faces the emulsion side of the separation-negative material and so that the emulsion sides of the mask, transparency, and negative material all face the light source. The separation negatives can be exposed either by contact printing or by enlarging.

Use of register punch: The Kodak register punch is very useful in registering color-separation negatives, masks, and matrices. If separation negatives and masks are to be made by contact from a sheet-film transparency, simply attach a strip of punched film to the original. The image can then be positioned exactly relative to the pins on a register board or in a Kodak register printing frame. If a sheet of masking film is punched and placed on the register pins before exposure, it can be registered with the transparency at any time. Thus, during the exposure of a set of separation negatives, one color-correction mask can be substituted for another, quickly and with assurance of good register. The masking film should, of course, be large enough so that it can be punched along one edge without interfering with the picture.

It is also advisable to punch the separation-negative film before exposure so that the image placement will be the same on each. If the negatives are printed by contact on matrix film that also has been punched, the three images will register automatically. If the negatives are printed by projection, however, the matrices must be registered after they have been processed and dyed, unless, of course, the negative carrier has register pins. If it has, the matrices can be prepunched and exposed on a vacuum register board.

Masking by Projection. Small transparencies can be projected to an intermediate size and separation negatives can be made. When this approach is employed, projected masks can also be made in the following manner.

Project the transparency to the size desired. A register system can be used on the enlarger easel, since the transparency need not be moved during the entire operation. Compose the picture on a register board on the easel of the enlarger. The highlight mask is made first, by punching a sheet of Kodalith ortho, Type 3 and exposing it on the pin system on the easel of the enlarger. A cover glass will be needed. Process the film as recommended for highlight masking, and when it is dry, lay it aside for future use.

Next, expose two color-correction masks in the same manner, using pan masking film. Process as recommended and hang to dry.

Separation negatives are now exposed and processed as outlined in this article in the section on making separation negatives from a color transparency. The following differences in procedure are now observed. The highlight mask is not used at this time, but when the red and green separation negatives are exposed, the red-filter mask is placed on top of the separation film and the transparency is projected through it to the separation film. The blue-filter separation negative has the green mask on top of the separation material when the transparency is projected. The separations are then processed as subsequently outlined.

When the separation negatives are to be projected onto matrix film, the highlight mask is placed in register with each separation in turn. With a registering enlarger, the highlight mask may be left in position for all or for only part of the matrix exposure. This permits varying degrees of highlight masking to be achieved.

Making Separation Negatives from a Color Transparency

Preliminary Steps. Proper identification of the separation negatives is necessary to avoid confusion. One way is to trim the corners with scissors. Usually, the red-filter negative is left untrimmed, one corner is trimmed from the green, and two corners are trimmed from the blue.

Attach a Kodak photographic step tablet to the transparency. If the separation negatives are to be made by enlargement, prepare a mask to accommodate the transparency and the step tablet. When a 35 mm transparency is to be projected, a Kodak photographic step tablet, No. 1A can be used over the sprocket holes. The density steps will then appear in the sprocket holes and will be projected along with the color image.

Newton's Rings. The close contact between transparency and printing-frame glass sometimes produces Newton's rings. One remedy is to use a fine powder in a small polyethylene squeeze bottle with a short tube projecting from it. The end of the tube should have an opening only a few thousandths of an inch in diameter. In the bottle, place about ½ inch of Oxy-Dry offset powder (made by Oxy-Dry Sprayer Corporation) or a similar powder used for preventing offset on the delivery end of printing presses. First, shake the bottle and tilt it so that the nozzle points upward; then squeeze to apply the powder. The resulting spray should be hardly visible and should be applied to only one of the surfaces involved.

Exposure. Use a suitable panchromatic sheet film, such as Kodak Super-XX pan film 4142 (Estar thick base), to make the separation negatives.

The accompanying data are given as a guide for making exposure tests when preparing separation negatives from color transparencies. Adjust an enlarger equipped with a tungsten lamp to give 3 footcandles of illumination at the exposing plane (measured without filters) with the lens set at f/4.5. The exposure suggestions are for average transparencies; use ½ stop more exposure for low-key subjects, ½ stop less for high-key originals.

A density of 3.0 in the transparency should, in a properly exposed separation negative, reproduce with a density of about 0.35 to 0.40.

Processing. Develop at 20 C (68 F) for times given in the table. Adjust times to obtain the desired density range. From normal subjects, a density range of about 1.2 is desirable.

Rinse the film in Kodak indicator stop bath or Kodak stop bath SB-5 at 18.5 to 24 C (65 to 75 F) about 30 seconds with agitation. Then fix it, with agitation, for 5 to 10 minutes in Kodak fixer or Kodak fixing bath F-5; or 2 to 4 minutes in Kodak rapid fixer.

EXPOSURE GUIDE FOR SEPARATION NEGATIVES FROM COLOR TRANSPARENCIES

Color of Exposing Light	Kodak Wratten Filter No.	Use Mask Made with Kodak Wratten Filter No.	Exposure Time at f/8
Red	29	29	25 sec.
Green	61	29	15 sec.
Blue	47B	61	30 sec.
For Process K-14 Films			
Red	24	61	8 sec.
Green	61	24	15 sec.
Blue	47B	61	30 sec.

DYE TRANSFER DEVELOPMENT TIMES

Dye Transfer Process	Kodak Developer*	Development Times (Minutes)			Approx. Gamma
		Red	Green	Blue	
For color-separation negatives made directly from the subject or from masked color transparencies.†	HC-110 (Dil. A)	4 ½	4 ½	7	0.90
For color-separation negatives made from unmasked transparencies.	HC-110 (Dil. B)	4 ½	4 ½	7	0.70

*Tray development at 20 C (68 F) with continuous agitation is recommended.
†Using tungsten illumination as light source.

Wash the film for 20 to 30 minutes in running water at 18.5 to 24 C (65 to 75 F) and hang it in a clean, dust-free place to dry.

Making Direct Separation Negatives

A panchromatic sheet film, such as Kodak Super-XX pan film 4142 (Estar thick base), can be used in a conventional camera to make separation negatives directly from still subjects. The camera must be firmly braced so that no movement takes place during the course of the three exposures. Since film does not always lie in the same plane in different film holders, it is best to use the same holder for all three exposures. The holder should be loaded and unloaded in total darkness.

Lighting. The lighting requirements for direct separation negatives are much the same as those for other types of color photography. Normally, the lighting ratio should be between 2:1 and 3:1. Higher ratios can be tolerated when the subject has a limited range of reflectances or for special effects.

The color quality of the light source affects the filter ratios for the three color filters. Once satisfactory exposure times have been determined for a particular light source, they can be used when other negatives are exposed by the same lighting.

If possible, place a paper reflection scale of neutral-gray steps in the scene. Use a Kodak gray scale (included in the Kodak color separation guides), a Kodak paper gray scale, or the gray scale found in the *KODAK Color DATAGUIDE.* The lighting of the gray scale should correspond as closely as possible to the lighting of the main part of the subject itself. From density readings of the gray scale in the pro-

EXPOSURE CONDITIONS WITH KODAK SUPER-XX PAN FILM 4142

Color of Filter	Kodak Wratten Filter No.	Camera Lens Opening	Exposure Time
Red	29	f/16	15 sec.
Green	61	f/16	12 sec.
Blue	47B	f/16	20 sec.

cessed negatives, you can determine variations in density and contrast. The gray scale should be located in such a position that it can be trimmed from the final print.

Exposure and Processing. When Kodak Super-XX pan film 4142 (Estar thick base) is used in a conventional camera to make separation negatives directly from the subject, typical exposure conditions with 450 footcandles of tungsten illumination (3200 K) on the subject are as given in the accompanying table.

Develop at 20 C (68 F) for times given in the chart of dye-transfer development times. Adjust times to obtain the desired density range. From normal subjects, a density of about 1.2 is desirable.

Interpretation of Gray Scales

A color-balanced set of separation negatives should have the same contrast, as well as approximately equal densities, in corresponding steps of the gray scale. In order to evaluate the results, the densities of the steps in the three gray scales should be read and plotted. This section describes the evalua-

Dye Transfer Process

tion of separation negatives from a transparency, but the same principles also apply to direct separation negatives.

After the desired densities and contrasts have been consistently obtained in exposing and processing tests, the plotting of each step can then be dispensed with. Instead, the density ranges should be determined from corresponding steps in the three negatives that most closely match those of the diffuse highlight and shadow densities in the red-filter negative.

Interpreting the Curves. The curves for a perfectly balanced set of separation negatives are not only alike in shape and slope, but superimposed. If the curves are parallel but do not coincide, the developing times were correct but the three exposure times were not properly balanced. If the curves are not parallel, the development times were incorrect. If the density range of the transparency recorded in each of the separation negatives is the same, compensation for a slight fault in coincidence can be made by adjustment of the matrix exposures. However, if the lateral displacement is greater than .15 in either direction, the separations should be remade with the proper exposure corrections.

If the densities of the transparency are satisfactorily recorded on the straightline portion of one of the negatives, its exposure need not be changed. The exposure for each of the other negatives can be corrected by measuring the distance, in terms of the units on the horizontal (log exposure) scale, that each of the curves needs to be moved either to the right or left. For example, if two curves are superimposed and the third is displaced to the right by a density difference of 0.3, the exposing time for this negative should be multiplied by 2. The distance that the curves need to be shifted in order to bring the reproductions of a fairly neutral shadow density of the transparency to the recommended minimum density of 0.4 in the negatives is measured along the horizontal scale.

The set of negatives should be remade if there are sizable differences in the slopes of the three curves, because corrections for these differences cannot be made satisfactorily when the matrices are exposed and processed. If the slopes of the lines depart markedly from the recommended gamma, or if the three curves are not closely parallel, the development time should be increased for a negative hav-ing a lower value than the recommended gamma, and decreased for a negative having a higher value.

Determining the Density Range. Once a set of well-balanced color-separation negatives has been obtained, determine the density range of the negatives. From the two points on the horizontal scale corresponding to the highlight and shadow densities in the original transparency, draw lines vertically until they intersect the curves of the color-separation negatives. At these points, extend the lines horizontally to the left toward the vertical (Density) scale. The difference between these values, which is the density range of the negatives, should be about 1.2 for a transparency with a long brightness range. In the Kodak dye transfer process, however, compensation for separation-negative density ranges as low as 0.9 or as high as 1.8 can be introduced by altering the composition of the developer.

Making Prints

Making prints efficiently by the dye transfer process requires adequate working space, including a sink area and a transfer area. Seven trays are needed for the working solutions. For production work, an automatic tray rocker for the dye baths is recommended.

The transfer area should be well lighted (at least 50 footcandles), preferably with the same type of illumination that will ultimately be used to view the prints, so that the print quality and color balance can be judged properly. Illumination of color quality corresponding to a color temperature of 3800 to 5000 K serves well for judging prints. This color quality is approximated by several types of fluorescent lamps (in fixtures), including General Electric Deluxe Cool White, Macbeth Prooflite, Sylvania Deluxe Cool White, and Westinghouse Deluxe Cool White.

Mixing Solutions. Some of the chemicals for the Kodak dye-transfer process are available in prepared form. Follow carefully the mixing directions on the containers. Always use distilled water in making up the working dye baths. If the available tap water has been determined to be unsuitable, you must also use distilled water to make up the first acid rinse bath.

All of the other solutions can be made up with ordinary tap water. When tap water is used in the first acid rinse bath, white highlights and margins in prints may show a tint of color. If this trouble occurs, it can often be eliminated by adding 10 to 40 millilitres of Kodak matrix highlight reducer R-18 per gallon of 1 percent acetic acid rinse. Depending on the hardness of the water, it may be necessary to use much larger quantities.

Conditioning Paper. Use Kodak dye-transfer paper of the next size larger than the picture size. This paper is furnished in double-weight F and G surfaces. For best results, do not attempt to treat more than six sheets at a time.

First, to eliminate any loose gelatin specks along the edges of the paper, rinse each sheet in running water for 30 seconds with agitation; then drain it thoroughly. Second, immerse the sheets, emulsion down, in the working solution of Kodak dye-transfer paper conditioner, immediately interleafing them a few times. Agitate the tray periodically. If available, an automatic tray rocker provides agitation conveniently. The time range for conditioning the paper is 10 minutes to 2 hours.

If unused paper remains in the bath when printing is finished, it can be squeegeed, to remove the excess conditioner, and dried. It will then require only resoaking in the conditioner before use.

When the volume of the paper-conditioner bath becomes insufficient to allow the paper to be completely immersed and to float freely, a fresh bath should be prepared. With extended use, the working solution may accumulate solids, such as paper or gelatin fragments and dust particles. In such cases, the conditioner should be either filtered or replaced.

Conditioning Film. Kodak dye transfer film 4151 (Estar thick base) is supplied in sheets larger than the corresponding paper sizes by 1 inch of length and width. This film has a white, translucent appearance; pictures on it can be viewed either by reflected light or a combination of transmitted and reflected light. The "emulsion,"or mordanted, side is identified by a notch in the conventional position. The film is also supplied in rolls, wound mordanted (emulsion) side in. This film requires less conditioning time and less transfer time than Kodak dye transfer paper. To condition it, immerse one sheet of film in the paper conditioner, mordanted side up. Agitate the film initially and periodically. After 1 to 2 minutes, the film is fully conditioned. Do not extend the time beyond 3 minutes. Also, keep the transfer times for the matrices at a minimum. Times

of 2 minutes for the cyan, 3 minutes for the magenta, and 1 minute for the yellow matrix are usually sufficient. Fast drying also helps to retain maximum image sharpness.

Care of Solutions. Dye baths and paper conditioner in trays should not be left uncovered for extended periods of time, since evaporation will change their chemical composition. Covers will also help prevent the solutions from accumulating dust and dirt, which may necessitate spotting work on the prints. For long storage periods, bottles with caps or stoppers are recommended. Do not use glass bottles that have previously been used to store strongly alkaline solutions.

Dyeing and Transferring. Uneven wetting may cause permanent damage to the matrix films. Handle the matrices emulsion side up while they are in trays.

If matrices on Kodak matrix film are to be dyed to facilitate register before punching, carry out steps 1, 2, 3, and 4. Then hang the matrices up to dry; orient all three images in the same direction.

1. Expand Matrices. To bring the matrices to full expansion, soak them for 1 minute or more in individual trays filled with water at 38 to 49 C (100 to 120 F).

2. Dye Matrices. Remove the matrices from the hot water, drain them briefly, and place them in the working dye solutions. Dye the red-filter positive cyan, the green-filter positive magenta, and the blue-filter positive yellow. The time of treatment is at least 5 minutes at room temperature; longer dyeing does no harm. Agitate the trays frequently until dyeing is completed; an automatic tray rocker will be convenient.

The magenta and yellow matrices can be left in their respective dye baths while the cyan matrix is being transferred.

3. First Acid Rinse. Remove the cyan matrix from the dye bath and drain it until the dye solution begins to form droplets. Place the matrix in a 1 percent solution of acetic acid at room temperature and agitate it for 1 minute before draining and placing the matrix in the second acid rinse. Discard this first acid rinse solution after use.

4. Second Acid Rinse. Place the matrix in a larger tray filled to about three-quarters of its depth with 1 percent acetic acid solution. Lift and reimmerse the matrix at least twice to wash off first acid rinse solution adhering to the surface of the matrix. This bath can be reused until it strongly discolors.

The second acid rinse is often known as the "holding bath," because matrices are left in it for a time ranging from 30 seconds up to several minutes. During this period, the paper is positioned on the transfer surface or, in the case of the magenta and yellow transfers, the preceding matrix is removed from the paper.

5. Position Paper. Raise the clamps on the register board. Position the paper on the board, emulsion side up, in such a way that the image will fall on the paper when the matrix is registered over the pins. Squeegee the paper lightly several times to flatten it and remove excess paper conditioner.

To prevent bleeding of the dyes, sponge off the transfer surface around the paper with a sponge dampened with 1 percent acetic acid. Also rinse any paper conditioner off your hands with 1 percent acetic acid before handling matrices, but do not use the second acid rinse bath for this purpose.

6. Position Matrix. Remove the matrix from the second acid rinse and drain it. With the matrix emulsion down, first locate the smaller punch hole over the pin on the register board and press the film down over the pin. Holding the matrix by the end which is away from the punch holes, locate the elongated hole over the other pin. Run your hand across the film between the holes to smooth the punched edge of the matrix into position and lower the two clamps.

During these operations, be sure to keep the matrix raised sufficiently to prevent the image from touching the paper. At the same time, it is important that a bead of second rinse solution is formed between the punched edge of the matrix and the paper. During the next step, this liquid will help expel air bubbles and provide good contact between matrix and paper.

7. Roll Matrix into Contact. Use a Kodak master print roller of a size larger than the width of the matrix. Lay the roller on the matrix near the pins of the register board and roll it firmly over the matrix *once,* toward the hand that is still keeping the matrix from contact with the paper ahead of the roller. Do not pull hard on the matrix with your hand; use only enough tension to keep the matrix from the paper until the roller makes the contact. The weight of the roller plus a slight manual pressure gives adequate

contact between the wet matrix and the paper. The proper pressure is just enough to allow the resilience of the soft rubber roller to be felt. Excessive pressure may cause register difficulties due to creeping of the paper. Also, if a vacuum register board is used for the transfer operation, excessive pressure may cause markings to appear in the picture directly over the vacuum channels.

The cyan image transfers in about 4 minutes, depending on the amount of dye carried by the matrix. While it is transferring, prepare the magenta matrix for transfer. Remove the magenta matrix from the dye bath, drain it, and rinse it in a fresh bath of 1 percent acetic acid (step 3). Agitate it in the same second acid rinse bath used for the cyan matrix (step 4), and leave it there while proceeding to step 8.

8. Remove Matrix. Lay the roller on the matrix at the edge farthest from the pins and roll it back far enough so that you can grasp the edge of the matrix. Then pull the matrix back slowly, allowing it to push the roller back as far as the pins. Raise the clamps and carefully disengage the matrix from the pins. Start step 10 and proceed immediately with step 9.

9. Transfer Magenta. As soon as cleaning of the cyan matrix has been started (step 10), transfer the magenta matrix, repeating steps 6 and 7. The image transfers in 4 to 5 minutes, depending on the amount of dye carried by the matrix. While the magenta dye is transferring, prepare the yellow matrix for transfer, repeating steps 3 and 4.

10. Clean Matrix after each Transfer. Wash the matrix for a minute or so in running water at 38 C (100 F) before draining it and returning it to the dye bath. If water deposits cause dye buildup in the matrices, treat each matrix in Kodak matrix clearing bath CB-5. Agitate the matrix in the clearing bath for 30 seconds, and wash it for 3 minutes in running water at 20 to 22 C (68 to 72 F). After a clearing-bath treatment, rinse the matrix briefly in the holding bath before returning it to the dye bath. The clearing bath should be replaced at the end of each day, or more often if it becomes strongly discolored in use.

With either treatment, *drain each matrix thoroughly before returning it to its dye bath.* The purpose of this precaution is to minimize dilution of the dye baths. To avoid difficulties in register and color balance, treat all matrices of a set identically.

11. Transfer Yellow Matrix. Remove the magenta matrix (step 8), and put it in the warm water (step 10). Then transfer the yellow matrix, repeating steps 6 and 7. The image transfers in 2 or 3 minutes. When transfer is complete, remove the yellow matrix (step 8) and clean it (step 10).

After the yellow transfers have been completed, it is good practice to swab off with damp absorbent cotton the first two prints from a set of matrices on pan matrix film. This procedure will remove any unhardened gelatin adhering to the prints, thus preventing any veiling of highlights in the picture.

12. Dry Print. Remove excess moisture from the surface of the print with a squeegee or windshield wiper blade. Squeegee both sides of the print with firm strokes and immediately hang the print up or lay it on a frame covered with plastic screening or cheesecloth. *Rapid drying gives maximum sharpness.* Shrinkage of a paper print during drying can be minimized by removing excess moisture, and then fastening all four edges of the print to a shellacked board with decorator's tape.

Prints on the F surface of Kodak dye transfer paper can be hot-ferrotyped in the normal manner, provided excessive heat is avoided. *Ferrotype such prints immediately after the yellow transfer.*

Subsequent Procedure. Additional prints are made by repeating the dyeing and transfer procedure as many times as necessary. In most cases, some improvement in print quality can be obtained by using the control techniques described in the following section:

Quantity printing. By using 5-minute dyeing and transfer times for all matrices, one operator can print two subjects simultaneously on separate transfer boards. A time cycle is easily arranged.

Life of matrices. The number of satisfactory prints that can be made from a set of matrices depends almost entirely on the care with which the matrices are handled during the dyeing and transfer operations. By keeping the solutions clean and avoiding physical damage to the relief images, as many as 100 prints or more can be made from a single set of matrices.

Storage of matrices. After the last print has been made, wash each matrix for 1 minute in running water at 37.8 C (100 F), and hang it up to dry. The best place to store the dry matrices is the box in which the film was originally packed. Place each matrix in a separate fold of interleaving paper.

Store the printing data with the matrices so that information about the dye contrast and any control solutions used in the first acid rinse is readily available if printing is resumed. This information can be entered on sheets taped on the outside of the film box or recorded directly on the box.

Controlling Color Balance. Usually, some change in the first print is desirable, either to correct for small errors in exposure or processing, or to satisfy personal preference as to print quality. Briefly, overall print density can be reduced by adding sodium acetate to the rinse bath, or it can be increased slightly by adding acetic acid. Density in the highlights can be reduced by adding Kodak matrix highlight reducer.

Reducing Print Density. One of the most useful controls in the dye transfer process is the addition of sodium acetate to the first rinse of one, two, or all three matrices. Equal treatment of all three matrices in the modified rinsing bath results in a lighter print.

However, suppose that a print shows an overall magenta cast. The density of the magenta dye image can be reduced by adding 5 percent solution of sodium acetate only to the first acid rinse bath used with the magenta matrix. Add 1 to 10 millilitres of the 5 percent sodium acetate solution per 150 millilitres of the standard rinse solution. Dye the magenta matrix in the usual manner. When lifting the matrix from the dye bath, drain it until the dye solution begins to run off in droplets before putting it in the acid rinse containing the sodium acetate. Agitate the dyed matrix for 1 minute in the rinse; then put it in the second acid rinse. More sodium acetate or a longer time can be used to reduce the density further.

In this example, only the rinse for the magenta matrix should contain sodium acetate. Depending on the direction in which the print is off balance, it may be necessary to add sodium acetate to the first acid rinse bath used with two of the matrices, perhaps with a difference in the sodium acetate concentration or in the time of treatment.

Rather large amounts of dye can be removed from matrices by the use of sodium acetate. However, there is a serious decline in photographic quality if you attempt to salvage a definitely overexposed or unbalanced set of matrices by this means.

Dye Transfer Process

Since it has the capability of color balance and contrast control in every step of the process, dye transfer offers unique possibilities for unexcelled photographic quality. These magnificently colored pumpkins are reproduced here from a paper-based reflection image made by the dye transfer process. Photo by June Alexander.

To make sure of consistent results, the sodium acetate solution should be mixed fresh daily.

Reducing Density in Highlights. When the test print is in good balance but the highlights are tinted, add 5 to 10 millilitres of a solution of Kodak matrix highlight reducer R-18 per 150 millilitres of the first acid rinse used with the matrix carrying the color that tints the highlights. Agitate the matrix for 1 minute in the first acid rinse before placing it in the second rinse. If the use of sodium acetate is also necessary, the matrix highlight reducer can be used in the same first rinse bath, and either the time of rinsing or the highlight reducer concentration can be varied as required to produce the desired contrast.

Changing Contrast. As stated in the instructions packaged with the matrix films, the preferred method of contrast control is adjustment of the degree of acidity of the dye baths. However, contrast can also be increased slightly by adding acetic acid to the first acid rinse bath. Add 3 to 10 millilitres of 28 percent acetic acid per 150 millilitres of the first acid rinse bath. When removing the matrix from the dye bath, transfer it directly, *without draining,* to the tray containing the rinse with excess acid. The object is to carry over a little dye into the rinse, so that the rinse bath becomes, in effect, a second dye bath. Agitate the matrix for 1 to 5 minutes in this bath, depending on the increase in contrast needed, and transfer it to the second rinse. As in reducing contrast, it may be necessary to modify the first acid rinse baths used with one, two or all three of the matrices.

Assuming that the calculations involved in making a set of matrices were correct to within 5 or 10 percent, the use of extra acid usually provides adequate correction. If a greater contrast change is needed in one (or more) of the dye images, the matrix can be dyed in a modified dye bath described on

To illustrate the technique used in the dye-transfer process, areas of this print have been marked off to show the three matrices—cyan, yellow, and magenta. Because each color is printed separately, considerable latitude is possible in color control.

the sheet packaged with the Kodak matrix dye set.

When many prints are being made, the color balance of the dye baths is maintained by use of the replenishment technique which is also described in the data sheets packaged with the dyes.

Special Procedures. The following are special procedures that may be used when making prints.

Extra Rinse Treatments. Sometimes a print shows a gradual shift in color balance from one side of the print to the other. This effect, known as "wedging," is usually the result of processing that is not uniform.

Uniform color balance can sometimes be restored by additional rinsing of one or more matrices in an auxiliary 1 percent acid rinse containing sodium acetate and Kodak matrix highlight reducer R-18. For example, if one side of the print is too yellow, the corresponding side of the yellow matrix can be given extra rinsing in the auxiliary rinse bath after completion of the normal first acid rinse. The time of the extra rinse treatment can be varied across

the film by dipping the matrix in gradually and withdrawing it gradually. The action of the extra rinse can be stopped at any time by placing the matrix in the second rinse bath.

When a print shows good color balance but has an excess of one color in a localized area, the chances are that one of the negatives or matrices did not receive full development in that area. Again, the correction is to rinse out some of the dye held by the corresponding matrix. The rinse solution can be applied locally with a camel's-hair brush. Alternatively, it can be applied with a washing bottle of the type sold by scientific supply houses for use in chemical laboratories.

Extra Transfers. Instead of removing dye by an extra rinse treatment, it is sometimes advantageous to put additional dye into the picture. The contrast of any of the dye images can be increased greatly by a second transfer from one of the matrices. It is, however, seldom desirable to transfer a second image of full strength. The amount of dye carried by

Dye Transfer Process

the matrix can be adjusted by *one* of the following procedures:

1. Redye the matrix briefly. A dyeing time in the range of 10 to 30 seconds is usually satisfactory.
2. Redye the matrix completely, but rinse it afterward in water to remove the dye from all areas except deep shadows. Then rinse it briefly in the holding bath.
3. Instead of redyeing the matrix, return it to the first acid rinse bath, to which 10 to 15 millilitres of 28 percent acetic acid per 150 millilitres of rinse solution has been added. The rinse bath already contains dye carried over from the dye bath; if necessary, add a few additional millilitres of the dye solution. Agitate the matrix in the rinse bath for 3 to 4 minutes.

When additional color is required only in certain areas, the following procedure may be useful: After the first transfer, clean the matrix as usual, but do not return it to the dye bath. Instead, use a soft brush of suitable size to put dye solution on the matrix in the areas where it is needed. Depending on the amount of additional color necessary, either a diluted dye solution or the working dye solution can be used. In either case, the application of dye should be followed by the usual first and second acid rinses before the additional dye is transferred to the print.

Black Printing Dye. You can make a black printing dye for producing black-and-white prints from a single matrix, or for creating special effects in a full-color print, by dissolving the neutral component of Kodak retouching colors in 1 litre (34 fl oz) of warm water. Add 5 millilitres of a 5 percent sodium acetate solution and 5 millilitres of a 28 percent acetic acid solution. Dye and transfer the black matrix the same way you would the separation matrices of a color print. If you wish higher contrast from the black dye, double the amount of acetic acid.

Selective Dye Bleaching. Occasionally, it may be desirable to bleach individual dyes in prints. The following procedures work fairly well for experienced operators.

To remove cyan dye, use a weak solution of potassium permanganate (about ¼ percent). Do not add acid to the solution and do not use a permanga-nate concentration high enough to leave a brown stain. You can remove a slight brown stain with 1 percent sodium bisulfite solution.

To remove magenta dye, use undiluted Kodak Photo-Flo 200 solution. Apply the solution with a cotton swab.

To remove yellow dye, use a 5 percent solution of sodium hypochlorite. Alternatively, use a commercial bleach, such as Clorox or 101, full strength.

After any of these bleach treatments, rinse the treated area with ¹⁄₁₀ percent acetic acid and then blot it off.

Formulas for Special Dye Transfer Solutions

One Percent Acetic Acid Solution. Add 1 part Kodak glacial acetic acid to 100 parts water or 1 part 28 percent acid to 27 parts water. Use 10 ml of glacial acetic acid per 1000 ml of water (1¼ fl oz per gallon) or 37 ml of 28 percent acetic acid per 1000 ml of water (4¾ fl oz per gallon).

***Kodak* Matrix Highlight Reducer R-18.** Add 1.2 grams (18 grains) of sodium hexametaphosphate or Calgon to 1 litre (32 fl oz) of water at about 32 C (90 F). (Modify according to the hardness of your water supply.)

***Kodak* Matrix Clearing Bath CB-5.** To prepare stock solution, add 120 grams (4 oz) of Kodak anti-calcium and 48 millilitres (1.6 fl oz) of ammonium hydroxide to 1 litre (32 fl oz) of water at 32 C (90 F). To prepare working solution, dilute 1 part stock solution in 11 parts water.

Five Percent Sodium Acetate Solution. Dissolve 5 grams of Eastman sodium acetate (anhydrous) (Cat. No. I227)* in a small amount of warm water and add water to make 100 millilitres; or dissolve 1 oz of sodium acetate in a small amount of warm water and add water to make 20 fl oz.

Further Reading: Borowsky, Irvin, J. *Handbook for Color Printing.* Philadelphia, PA: North American Publishing Co., 1974; Coote, Jack H. *The Photoguide to Color Printing from Negatives and Slides.* Garden City, NY: Amphoto, 1976; Engdahl, David A. *Color Printing.* Garden City, NY: Amphoto, 1970.

*Unlike photographic products, which are distributed soley through photo dealers, Eastman organic chemicals are available through laboratory supply houses or on direct order from Eastman Kodak Company, Eastman Organic Chemicals, Rochester, New York 14650. There is a minimum charge of $25 on direct orders from the United States and Canada, and a minimum charge of $50 on direct orders from other countries. These chemicals are neither intended nor sold for household use. Catalog numbers should be given in the order.

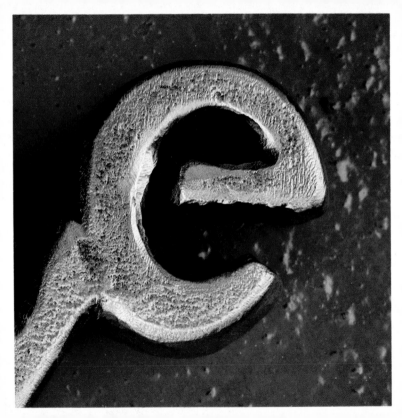

Easel

A printing easel is a device that holds print material flat and in place while enlarging exposures. Related devices used to hold the material being photographed in position for a copy camera are usually called copyboards.

An easel consists of a backing board, a means of holding the print material in place, and usually, for the purpose of providing borders, some method of masking the area in which the image is to be printed. Most commercially manufactured easels are designed for horizontal use under vertical projection enlargers. Vertical easels for use with horizontally projected images are often improvised by using push-pins in a soft board or strip magnets on a metal plate.

Easels may be of a fixed size, or adjustable for use with a variety of paper sizes. Masking is accomplished by using adjustable blades or by overlay masks with fixed-format openings. The backing board is usually white or a cream-yellow so that the projected image can easily be seen for positioning and focusing. (Some photographers prefer—especially when making color prints—to cover the easel surface with black to avoid any effects of light reflected through the back of the print material during exposure. However, any such effects are negligible in

The four adjustable masking blades of this commercial easel can be moved to have any desired print size and format. This easel is produced by Saunders/Omega.

The Kodak Vacuum Register Board is operated by pumping air out of the interior of the easel. The negative is focused within the register marks on the board, depending upon print size needed. The vacuum below causes printing paper to be pressed flat to the board by air pressure from above.

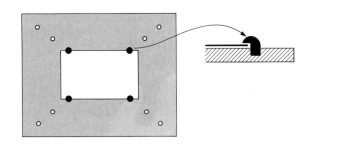

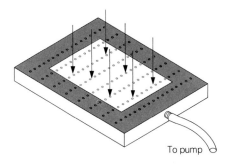

To pump

(Left) One kind of borderless easel uses rubber or plastic tabs to hold the paper at only a few points. The tabs can be positioned for various standard paper sizes. Edges can be trimmed, or overlapped spots can be spotted-in to eliminate them after processing. (Right) A vacuum easel uses a pump to remove air from the interior of a hollow board; unused openings should be covered. Air pressure from above forces appear flat against the easel. Truly borderless prints are obtainable with this device.

practice.) A sheet of white paper is inserted in the easel for focusing.

Easels commonly use one of three methods to hold the print material in place:

Pressure. Blades, lips, magnets, or other devices press down on the edges of the paper. They typically cover about ¼-inch of the paper, producing borders of that width around the developed image; some may be adjusted for various size borders. So-called borderless easels of this type use a minimum overlap or hold the paper at only a few points. A cover glass that presses the paper against a resilient backing can be used for truly borderless prints. Although this method is often used in vertical copyboards, it has limited value for enlarging easels. The glass presents

Easel

the problem of an extra surface to be kept free of dust, reflections, and scratches.

Adhesion. The easel board is covered with adhesive material that grips the back of the print paper. Few such easels are commercially manufactured; they are usually improvised by using rubber cement or spray adhesive on a suitable board. Although this method can be used for borderless prints, it has a number of disadvantages. The adhesive must be frequently renewed; it collects dust and dirt unless constantly protected; some of the adhesive may come off on the print and physically or chemically interfere with the image of the print during processing.

Vacuum. A vacuum easel is a hollow board with holes or narrow slots in its upper surface. A vacuum pump pulls air out of the interior, with the result that air pressure on the surface of the print holds it flat against the easel. The unused openings around the paper must be covered to make the vacuum efficient.

A step-and-repeat easel consists of a board that moves below a masking cover so that the paper can be shifted to print the same image several times on a single sheet without overlapping.

• *See also:* ENLARGERS AND ENLARGING.

Eastman, George

(1854–1932)
American industrialist and philanthropist;
founder of Eastman Kodak Company

At the age of 14, George Eastman was forced to leave school in Rochester, New York, to help support his widowed mother and two sisters. He worked variously as a messenger, office boy with an insurance firm, and finally as a bank clerk. At 24, he

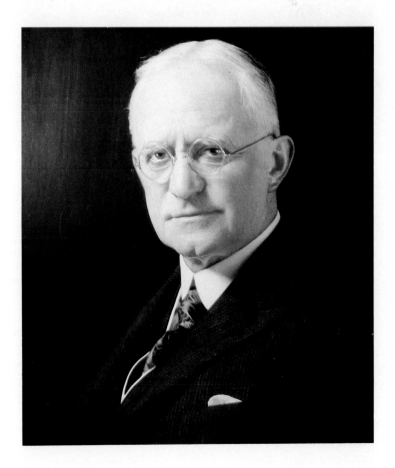

George Eastman, founder of the Eastman Kodak Company and the first great popularizer of amateur photography. Photo courtesy of the International Museum of Photography at George Eastman House.

learned the collodion wet-plate process in anticipation of taking pictures on a vacation trip. This led to a growing fascination with photography. After several years of research and experimentation carried out at night after work and on weekends, he not only perfected his own dry plate formula, but he designed and patented the apparatus to coat dry plates. In this way, he was able to manufacture them in quantity with uniform quality so they could be sold at a reasonable price. He began to manufacture Eastman dry plates in 1880.

The fledgling company almost collapsed in the first year when his dry plates started to lose sensitivity on dealer's shelves because the first plates delivered to stock were the last sold, and the emulsion had deteriorated with time. Eastman recalled all the plates and replaced them.

Eastman wanted to make the camera as easy to use as a pencil. The dry plate was a step forward from the wet plate; the next logical step was roll film. In 1884 the company introduced the Eastman-Walker roll holder in various sizes for use with standard studio and field cameras. The film was a continuous roll of gelatin emulsion coated on paper which, after development, was made transparent enough for printing by treating it with hot castor oil. In 1885, Eastman American film was introduced. The paper backing was stripped off after development, leaving a thin film negative which was then mounted on glass or thick gelatin to use in making prints.

An enormous success came to the Eastman Company in 1888 when the No. 1 Kodak camera was placed on the market. The camera made it possible for virtually anyone to take pictures. A series of instructional ads emphasized that taking a picture took only four steps:

1. *Aim the camera*
2. *Pull the string* (to cock the shutter)
3. *Press the button* (to make the exposure)
4. *Turn the key* (to advance the film)

Other ads featured celebrities as well as the general public testifying: *It's so easy to get the pictures I want, with a Kodak camera.*

The No. 1 Kodak camera used Eastman American film, the paper-backed stripping film. The camera was purchased already loaded with film for 100 exposures; the price was $25.00. Although the user could cut off exposed lengths of film for home processing, the real appeal was that the Eastman Dry Plate and Film Company offered processing—the photographer could have all the fun of photography without any of the work. The camera was sent to Rochester where, for $10.00, the pictures were developed and printed, and the camera was reloaded with another 100-exposure roll. The simplicity and service were advertised with the slogan: *You press the button, we do the rest.*

Exterior and interior of the No. 1 Kodak Camera, first produced in 1888. Photo courtesy of the International Museum of Photography at George Eastman House.

Eastman, George

(Left) Snapshot made by an unknown amateur with a Kodak camera, c. 1890. (Right) Fred Church photographed George Eastman on the S.S. Gallia in 1890; Eastman is holding an early Kodak camera. Photos courtesy of the International Museum of Photography at George Eastman House.

The trademark *Kodak* had been chosen because it was short, memorable, and would be pronounced the same in almost any major language. The pictures themselves were round, 2½ inches in diameter, and mounted on square cards. Eastman reasoned that amateurs could see that a lens formed a circular image, and that they would want every bit of picture they had paid for.

Results were improved by the introduction of roll film on a transparent celluloid (nitrate) base in 1889; the need to return the camera for processing was eliminated in 1891 when a daylight-loading spool was first offered. Subsequent models of the Kodak box camera, a succession of folding Kodak cameras, and a $1.00 box Brownie camera for children maintained interest in the field of amateur photography, which the Eastman Kodak Company had created virtually single-handed. With a growing line of films, papers, and processing chemicals, Kodak entered the field of professional photography. A series of products intended for scientific and technical applications followed.

In 1889, Thomas Edison's Kinetoscope camera used the new Eastman celluloid strip film for the first motion pictures in America. Reversal-process 16 mm black-and-white film and a daylight-loading camera for amateur movies were introduced in 1923. A lenticular film for amateur color movies followed, in 1928.

The growth of the Eastman Kodak Company not only benefited stockholders, but also Kodak employees in some of the first profit-sharing and insurance programs in American industry. During his life, George Eastman gave away over $100 million, much of it anonymously—to establish dental clinics in the United States and Europe; to provide a department of music, a theater, a symphony orchestra, and a School of Medicine at the University of Rochester; to aid the expansion of the Massachusetts Institute of Technology; to support facilities and programs at Hampton and Tuskeegee Institutes for the education of black Americans; and to assist many other organizations, institutions, and charitable causes.

George Eastman became one of the greatest philanthropists of 20th-century America. At the time of his death in 1932, the *New York Times* paid him tribute in an editorial:

> Eastman was a stupendous factor in the education of the modern world. Of what he got in return for his great gifts to the human race he gave generously for their good; fostering music, endowing learning, supporting science in its researches and teaching, seeking to promote health and lessen human ills, helping the lowliest in their struggle toward the light, making his own city a center of the arts and glorifying his own country in the eyes of the world.

• See also: CAMERAS; EMULSIONS; HISTORY OF PHOTOGRAPHY.

Eclipse Photography

An eclipse occurs when a viewer sees a celestial object partially or completely obscured by another body. The most spectacular eclipses that we see from the earth are those of the sun and the moon. These events can easily be photographed on black-and-white or color film.

A solar eclipse is seen when the shadow of the moon passes over an observer on the earth. Since the sun and moon have nearly the same apparent size, the nature of the eclipse depends on the distance of the moon from the earth. If the moon is close to the earth, it completely blocks the bright solar disk, allowing an observer standing in the narrow shadow path to see the faint coronal atmosphere surrounding the sun. An observer within the much wider penumbra sees the sun only partly covered by the moon. The corona cannot be seen.

If, however, the moon is at its most distant point from the earth, it appears too small to completely cover the sun. During an eclipse, light from the sun is seen as a narrow, very bright, annular ring around the dark disk of the moon. The corona cannot be seen.

Solar Eclipse

WARNING: PROTECT YOUR EYES DURING A PARTIAL SOLAR ECLIPSE! Blindness will result from looking at the sun, either directly or through the viewfinder. Never look at the sun without adequate protection. Protecting your eyes adequately will reduce exposure to ultraviolet and infrared radiation, which can severely burn your eyes instantaneously without your immediately being aware of it. Also, adequate protection will increase eye comfort by reducing the intensity of the visible sun rays. No filter is used during the total eclipse.

Viewing Filter for Partial Phases. Always use a filter that will absorb *equally* and *sufficiently* the ultraviolet, visible, and infrared energy of the sun.

Medical authorities indicate that a neutral density filter of metallic silver, such as developed black-and-white photographic film, of 6.0 density will provide protection.

Such filters are not suitable for photographic use because they scatter light, causing a slightly unsharp image. It is convenient to staple the filter behind a slot cut in cardboard and hang the assembly on a string around your neck. Place the filter IN FRONT OF your eyes before facing the sun. Such a filter can be made with two thicknesses of *black-and-white* photographic film, such as Kodak Verichrome pan film, which has been completely exposed and developed to maximum density. Expose the film by unrolling it in daylight; develop the exposed film fully, according to the manufacturer's recommendations. NOTE: Do not use color film or crossed polarizing material as a viewing filter.

A lunar eclipse occurs when the shadow of the earth falls on the moon. During an eclipse the moon is illuminated only by the red rays from the sun that are refracted into the shadow by the earth's atmosphere, therefore it appears reddened and dim. At mid-eclipse the moon may disappear from view completely.

The following sections describe how to photograph solar and lunar eclipses using your camera and small telescopes.

Focal Length of the Lens. The high light intensity of the sun permits you to use any camera. However, the size of the sun or moon image depends on the focal length of the camera lens. You can estimate the actual image size on the film by dividing the focal length by 110. For example, with a camera lens having a focal length of 4 inches (100 mm), the image size would be about 4/110 inch (1 mm) in diameter—the thickness of a dime. However, many good pictures of eclipses have been made with 35 mm cameras equipped with lenses of 2-inch (50 mm) focal length. So don't put your camera away because you don't have a long-focal-length lens.

In movies of the eclipse, the image will be enlarged when projected on the screen. Assuming a magnification of 110 diameters on projection, the diameter of the image of the sun on the screen will be approximately equal to the focal length of your camera lens.

Camera Protection. The sun can burn holes in focal-plane shutters, warp the leaves of between-the-lens shutters, and melt composition shutter blades. Use neutral density filters that are made *for photographic use.* If your camera must be pointed toward the sun throughout the eclipse, shade it between exposures. It is wise to shade the camera from direct sunlight at all times to avoid overheating film and camera.

Aiming Your Camera. WARNING: NEVER LOOK AT THE SUN THROUGH A CAMERA VIEWFINDER WITHOUT SUITABLE FILTERS. This is especially important with single-lens reflex cameras, both still and movie. The best policy is to aim your camera without using its viewfinder. If you must use the viewfinder, use filters made from black-and-white film, as previously described, held in front of the viewfinder or, with a single-lens reflex camera, in front of the camera lens.

Filters made for photographic use give *no visual protection.* Therefore, use the exposed-film filters for visual aiming and change to neutral density filters made for photographic use to take pictures of the eclipse. Once you have changed to filters for use on your camera, do not look through the viewfinder.

Exposure. The light from the sun's surface is so intense that in order to photograph the partial phases of the eclipse, you must reduce the sun's light by 10,000 to 100,000 times. Neutral density filters (ND) provide the most convenient way of cutting down the light to allow normal camera exposures.

During the partial phases, the light intensity of the surface of the sun is the same as it is when there is no eclipse.

Here is a simple formula for determining the correct exposure for the partial phases:

$$f^2 = S \times t \times 10^{\,7-D}$$

where

f is the lens opening
S is the ASA speed of the film
t is the shutter speed in seconds
D is the density of the neutral density
    filter in use

For example, with a neutral density filter of 5.0, Kodachrome 64 film, shutter speed of 1/125 sec., you would use a lens opening of $f/8$; with a shutter speed of 1/30 sec., you use a lens opening of $f/16$.

Additional exposure information is given later in this article. If you are taking pictures with a simple nonadjustable camera, use Kodak Verichrome pan film and a 6.0 ND (neutral density) filter during the partial phases. Remove the ND filter during totality.

The brightness of the sun does not change during the eclipse, so your exposure during partial phases should remain constant as long as sky conditions remain constant. Most camera exposure meters average the reading over some area. If the visible portion of the sun does not cover all of this area, the meter will indicate more exposure than needed.

If you have a camera with automatic exposure control, consult your camera manual to override the automatic exposure system; or see your local camera dealer.

What to Photograph During a Solar Eclipse.
Partial Phases. Beginning about one hour before totality, you can see the moon gradually encroaching on the sun's disk; for about one hour after totality, the shadow gradually retreats. You can obtain an interesting record of the eclipse by mounting your camera on a firm support and making a series of exposures at five-minute intervals on the same frame of film, starting a half hour before totality and continuing for a half hour after. For this technique, you'll need to use a camera which will let you take more than one exposure on the same frame of film. Check your camera manual to see if you can do this with your camera.

The period over which you can make such a record on a single frame depends on the angle of

A record of the eclipse from partial phases through totality can be obtained by making a series of exposures on the same frame of film. The period of time over which such a single-frame record can be made will depend on the angle of view of the camera lens.

view of your camera lens. The position of the sun will change about 15 degrees per hour. A normal-focal-length camera lens will cover a sufficient angle for exposures over a two-hour period. Watch your local newspaper for the timing of the progress of the moon across the sun disk; then plan your camera position and exposure schedule accordingly.

Shadows Under Trees. All during the partial phases, the sunlight filtering through the leaves of trees forms images of the eclipsed sun on the ground. You can photograph these crescents easily with normal exposures for the film you are using.

Shadow Bands. During the last few seconds before totality, you may see wave-like shadows called

shadow bands moving over the ground. They average from one to two inches in width and are five or six inches apart. They are most easily visible on a white background, such as a bed sheet.

This phenomenon is *very difficult* to photograph because of the low illumination and the speed of movement. With a white sheet on the ground to obtain as high a reflectance as possible, you can expose Kodak Tri-X pan film in rolls or Kodak Royal pan film 4141 (Estar thick base) in sheets at 1/125 sec. with lens opening of *f*/2. If the largest lens opening on your camera is *f*/3.5, you can use Kodak recording film 2475 (Estar-AH base) or Kodak Royal-X pan film to record the shadow bands.

Landscape During Totality. The intensity of the available illumination varies rapidly during the minute just before and the minute just after totality. At the darkest period (during totality), an exposure of about 1/4 sec. at *f*/8 on Kodak Ektachrome 200 professional film should give good results for landscape photography.

During totality, you may not be able to see the settings on your camera. Carry a pocket flashlight so that you can check or change your camera settings.

Total Eclipse. Totality usually lasts less than five minutes. Therefore, it is a good idea to go through a few practice runs, and time yourself so that you can take several pictures during this brief period.

Baily's Beads. For an instant just before totality and again just as the sun emerges, light breaks through the valleys on the rim of the moon, forming what looks like a beaded necklace along the edge of the moon. This brief display is very spectacular.

For still cameras, use a shutter speed of 1/500 sec., no filter, and the same lens opening recommended for partial phases in the exposure table found at the end of this section on solar eclipse. For movie cameras, remove the filter and expose at the highest frame rate.

The diamond-ring effect can be achieved by adjusting exposure for the prominences and removing the neutral-density filter the instant before taking the picture.

WARNING: *Do not* remove the filter too soon! If you do, severe eye damage can result.

Baily's Beads, photographed with a six-inch telescope with an effective focal ratio of f/16. A Barlow lens was used to protect the image on the film. Photo by Dennis Cassia.

Corona. At totality, the corona appears around the sun as a beautiful halo, decreasing in brightness from the moon's rim outward. Points of interest to observe and photograph in the outer corona are the equatorial streamers, which may extend several diameters from the sun superimposed. On the inner corona are solar prominences, scarlet, tongue-like jets shooting outward from the sun's surface.

Since the intensity of the corona fades rapidly away from the solar limb (edge of the sun's apparent disk), the distance to which the photograph will show the corona depends on the exposure—the longer the exposure, the greater the extension. However, if you attempt to record the faint outer streamers, then the inner corona will be overexposed. The most colorful results are often obtained with a shorter exposure gauged to record the inner corona.

Telescope or a Binocular. You can use a small telescope or binocular in conjunction with an ordinary camera. The image size obtained with such a combination will be equal to that obtained with your

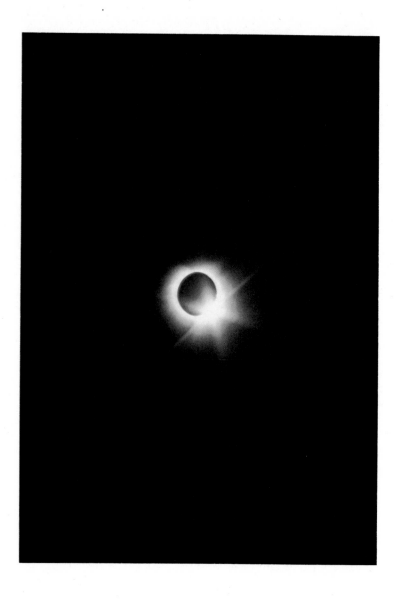

This "diamond ring," was photographed using a hand-held camera with a 135 mm lens. The photo was taken at 1/125 sec. on Kodak high speed Ektachrome film. Photo by Dennis Cassia.

Eclipse Photography

The sun's inner corona appears here as a bright area, the outer corona as a reddish haze (caused by airborne dust). Equatorial streamers are also visible. This photograph was made with a six-inch f/4 reflector on a camera set at the prime focus. Exposure was two seconds on Kodacolor-X film. Photo by Dennis Cassia.

camera alone, multiplied by the power of the telescope or binocular. It is best to build some type of rigid support to hold your telescope and camera in alignment.

You can arrive at the best focus and exposure for the partial phases experimentally by photographing the sun prior to the eclipse. Make an approximate focus setting by focusing the telescope or binocular on an object at a great distance. Then set your camera lens at infinity, and focus at the largest lens opening.

Join the camera and telescope, covering the space between the camera lens and the eyepiece of

the telescope with a black cloth to cut out stray light. See: ASTROPHOTOGRAPHY.

Camera Support. For a series of pictures of the partial phases, mount your camera on a tripod or other rigid support to prevent movement between exposures. Also, with long-focal-length lenses, a telescope, or a binocular, a solid support is essential to avoid loss of definition due to camera motion.

Because of the earth's rotation, solar images one inch in diameter or greater will show significant movement on the film during exposures of 1/2 sec. or more. For these and longer exposures, use an equatorial mounting with a clock drive. If your ex-

A small telescope used in conjunction with a camera may be used for astronomical photography. The image size obtained will equal that obtained with the camera multiplied by the power of the telescope.

posures exceed 1 second and no drive mechanism is available, the diameter of the solar image should be proportionately smaller as the exposure times are increased.

Filters. The use of neutral-density filters is a convenient way of reducing the excessive light intensity for photography during the partial phases. You can quickly remove the filters from in front of the lens at totality. The viewing filters described previously are not suitable for photographic use.

The Kodak Wratten neutral-density filter No. 96 (gelatin) is available in the following densities: 0.10, 0.20, 0.30, 0.40, 0.50, 0.60, 0.70, 0.80, 0.90, 1.00, 2.00, 3.00, and 4.00. You can obtain intermedi-

ate densities or higher densities, such as 4.5 or 5.0, by combining two of the standard filters.

However, if you use more than two at one time, image sharpness will be reduced. These filters are available through photo dealers.

WARNING: Filters made for photographic use give *no visual protection.* Do not try to observe a solar eclipse through such filters because they transmit infrared energy which can burn your eyes.

Although gelatin-film neutral-density filters are protected by a thin lacquer coating, you should handle these filters only by the edges or at the extreme corners. The Kodak gelatin filter frame, a two-part metal frame, is a convenient accessory for handling gelatin-filters. You can use the filter frame with the

NEUTRAL DENSITY FILTERS

Neutral Density	Filter Factor	Reduces Exposure by (f-stops)
0.1	1¼	⅓
0.2	1½	⅔
0.3	2	1
0.4	2½	1⅓
0.5	3	1⅔
0.6	4	2
0.7	5	2⅓
0.8	6	2⅔
0.9	8	3
1.0	10	3⅓
2.0	100	6⅔
3.0	1,000	10
4.0	10,000	13⅓
5.0	100,000	16⅔
6.0	1,000,000	20

Kodak gelatin filter frame holder, which you attach to your camera lens with an appropriate adapter ring. The filter frame holder is convenient to use because you can change filters rapidly, but it is not a necessity. You can attach the filter frame, or even the filters alone, to the lens with small strips of pressure-sensitive tape.

When you use neutral-density filters, be sure you don't confuse their density values. For example, a 0.50 neutral-density filter reduces the light by three times while a 5.0 neutral-density filter reduces the light by 100,000 times.

Some neutral density filters are identified as 2X, 4X, 8X, and 10X. These designations indicate the filter factor and are equivalent to the following densities: 2X=0.30, 4X=0.60, 8X=0.90, and 10X=1.0. The filter factor indicates how many times the filter reduces the light. For example, a filter factor of 4 means that the filter reduces the light by 4 times.

SOLAR ECLIPSE EXPOSURE RECOMMENDATIONS FOR STILL AND MOVIE* CAMERAS

ASA Speed	Partial Phases		Totality (Prominences)		Totality (Inner Corona)		Totality (Outer Corona)	
	Still	Movie	Still	Movie	Still	Movie	Still	Movie
25–32	f/5.6 5.0 ND 1/125	f/11 5.0 ND	f/3.5 No Filter 1/125	f/8 No Filter	f/3.5 No Filter 1/15	f/2.8 No Filter	f/3.5 No Filter 1/2	f/1.4 No Filter
40–50	f/6.3 5.0 ND 1/125	f/13 5.0 ND	f/4.5 No Filter 1/125	f/9.5 No Filter	f/4.5 No Filter 1/15	f/3.5 No Filter	f/4.5 No Filter 1/2	f/1.9 No Filter
64–80	f/8 5.0 ND 1/125	f/16 5.0 ND	f/5.6 No Filter 1/125	f/11 No Filter	f/5.6 No Filter 1/15	f/4 No Filter	f/5.6 No Filter 1/2	f/2 No Filter
125–160	f/11 5.0 ND 1/125	f/22 5.0 ND	f/8 No Filter 1/125	f/16 No Filter	f/8 No Filter 1/15	f/5.6 No Filter	f/8 No Filter 1/2	f/2 No Filter
200–250	f/16 5.0 ND 1/125	f/9.5 6.0 ND	f/11 No Filter 1/125	f/22 No Filter	f/11 No Filter 1/15	f/8 No Filter	f/11 No Filter 1/2	f/2.8 No Filter
400–650	f/16 5.0 ND 1/250	f/11 6.0 ND	f/16 No Filter 1/125	f/11 1.0 ND	f/16 No Filter 1/15	f/9.5 No Filter	f/16 No Filter 1/2	f/4 No Filter
1000–1250	f/16 5.0 ND 1/500	f/16 6.0 ND	f/16 No Filter 1/250	f/16 1.0 ND	f/16 No Filter 1/30	f/13 No Filter	f/16 No Filter 1/4	f/5.6 No Filter

*The lens openings given for movie cameras are based on a normal camera speed of 16 or 18 frames per second.
Note: ND indicates neutral density filter.

Exposure for the eclipse, especially during totality, can vary considerably without loss of picture quality. These three photographs, all made using a 35 mm SLR camera with a six-inch Newtonian reflecting telescope as the lens (the equivalent of a 600 mm f/4 telephoto) were taken at different shutter speeds: (above left) 1/60 sec.; (above) 1/15 sec.; (left) ¼ sec. Note that longer exposures produce greater extension of the corona. Photos by Bruce Lundegard.

Exposure Table. The exposure recommendations in the table on page 921 are based on results obtained in actual solar-eclipse photography with clear viewing conditions. So much depends on atmospheric conditions, however, that you should regard these exposures only as approximate guides.

Exposure, for each phase of the eclipse, especially during totality, can vary over a wide range and still produce good photographs. If you take several pictures at different exposure times and settings, each picture should show different details of the eclipse. Therefore, for the best coverage, bracket the suggested exposure. Take pictures at the estimated exposure and at 1, 2, and 3 stops less exposure and more exposure than the estimate.

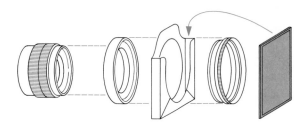

The Kodak gelatin filter frame holder and a Kodak gelatin filter frame provide a convenient means for attaching gelatin-film neutral-density filters to your lens. These filters are not for visual use.

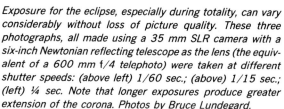

You can calculate exposure times for lens openings other than those given in the table. Suppose the effective lens opening of your lens is $f/32$ and the table suggests $f/8$. Divide 32 by 8 and square the answer: $32 \div 8 = 4$ and $4^2 = 16$. Therefore a lens opening of $f/32$ will require an exposure 16 times as long as that required at $f/8$.

The exposure time for movie cameras operating at a normal camera speed of 16 or 18 frames per second is about 1/35 sec.

Films. For the partial phases, you can use any film intended for general photography. For the most interesting phases of an eclipse, those occurring during totality, a high-speed film is most desirable. You can use the ASA speeds with the exposure table and formula given.

Lunar Eclipse

A lunar eclipse occurs when the moon passes through the shadow of the earth. When the moon is

The moon in penumbra, its position before or after it is totally covered by the earth's shadow, reveals considerable topographic detail.

within the umbra part of the earth's shadow (see accompanying illustration), it is illuminated only by light refracted through the earth's atmosphere. This light is usually orange or brick-red. Totality, the length of time the moon is totally within the umbra, may last as long as 1 hour and 40 minutes. Before the moon moves into the umbra, it passes through an area of partial illumination, called the penumbra. In the penumbra, the moon appears nearly the same as when it's in the full light of the sun.

It is easy to photograph a lunar eclipse. However, because the moon is so dim during totality, you should use a high-speed film. During totality, use the largest lens opening possible. This allows you to use shorter exposure times to stop the moon's motion in your photographs.

The moon may appear large to you, but when photographed through a lens of normal focal length, it will be a very small spot on the film. Use the lens with the longest focal length available for your camera, and support the camera on a steady tripod.

To record details on the moon, take your pictures through a telescope, spotting scope, or a binocular. (*See:* ASTROPHOTOGRAPHY; BINOCULARS, TAKING PICTURES THROUGH.)

Exposure. By making multiple exposures of the moon at regular intervals, you can obtain an interesting sequence showing the progression of the

Photographs of the terrestrial landscape may be taken by moonlight. Here, the photographer aligns his telescope in preparation for observing a total lunar eclipse. The photo was taken with a 135 mm f/2.8 telephoto lens coupled to a 2X telextender; exposure was ½ sec. Photo by Bruce Lundegard.

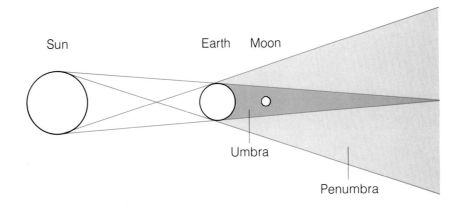

Sun   Earth   Moon

Umbra

Penumbra

Light refracted through the earth's atmosphere illuminates the moon when it is within the umbra of the earth's shadow.

LUNAR ECLIPSE EXPOSURE RECOMMENDATIONS

Stage of Eclipse	ASA Film Speed						
	25–32	64–80	100–125	200	400	800–1000	1250–1600
Full moon, clear sky	1/250 f/5.6	1/250 f/8	1/250 f/11	1/250 f/16	1/250 f/22	1/500 f/22	1/1000 f/22
Moon deep in penumbra up to FIRST contact and after FOURTH contact	1/60 f/5.6	1/60 f/8	1/60 f/11	1/60 f/16	1/125 f/16	1/250 f/16	1/500 f/16
At SECOND and THIRD contacts	2 f/2	1 f/2	1 f/2.8	1 f/4	1/4 f/2.8	1/8 f/2.8	1/15 f/2.8
MID-TOTALITY	8 f/2	4 f/2	2 f/2	2 f/2.8	1 f/2.8	1/2 f/2.8	1/4 f/2.8

Note: All exposure times are in seconds or fractions of a second. With Kodacolor films use ½ stop larger lens opening than indicated in the table.

eclipse all in one photograph. To try this technique, you can either use a camera that allows you to make multiple exposures on the same frame of film; or you can alternately cover and uncover the lens. Check your camera manual. You should use a normal-focal-length lens so that you can get the whole series in one picture. Aim your camera so that the picture will include the path of the moon as the earth's rotation moves it across the sky from east to west.

To capture the sequence, begin taking pictures as the moon moves into the umbra. Make exposures at six-minute intervals so that the images of the eclipse will be evenly spaced across the film frame. A normal-focal-length lens will cover an angle of view sufficient for about a two-hour series of exposures. Since the images of the moon will be quite

small, you may want to have an enlargement made. (See accompanying illustration.)

Determining Exposure. A time-lapse motion picture record of the eclipse is interesting. Attach the movie camera and telephoto lens to a sturdy tripod or two-axis telescope mounting. Expose five seconds of film every five minutes, carefully placing the image in the same place in the frame for each exposure. Lunar eclipses vary in duration and differ greatly in apparent brightness and color. Variations in atmospheric conditions and in the distance of the moon above the horizon may affect the moon's apparent brightness, making exact recommendations impossible. Use the exposures suggested in the accompanying table as guides only. If the sky is hazy

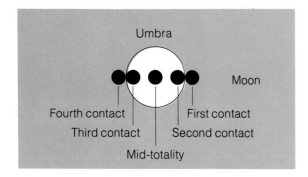

or if the moon is low in the sky, try doubling the recommended exposure time.

When you're taking single pictures of the moon, it's a good idea to bracket the estimated exposure for more assurance of properly exposed pictures. Try one and two stops more and less exposure than what is recommended.

When the moon is partially in the umbra, where you can see a definite shadow line across its surface, select the exposure for either the umbra portion or the penumbra portion. The film cannot properly record both areas at the same time.

Gradually increase the exposure from the second contact to mid-totality; decrease the exposure from mid-totality to the third contact (see exposure table).

Exposure with Various f-Stops. You can calculate exposure times for *f*-numbers other than those given in the table. Suppose your largest lens opening is *f*/5.6 and the table suggests *f*/2.8. Divide 5.6 by 2.8 and square the answer: 5.6 ÷ 2.8 = 2, and $2^2 = 4$. This means the *f*/5.6 lens opening will require an exposure 4 times as long as that required with a lens opening of *f*/2.8. For example, if the table suggests 1 second at *f*/2.8, you can use 4 seconds at *f*/5.6.

The moon appears to move a distance equal to approximately half its diameter in one minute. If the exposure time with a normal-focal-length lens is longer than 10 seconds, the moon motion is likely to be evident in the photograph. If you use a telephoto lens or a telescope with your camera, the maximum exposure time must be even shorter.

$$\frac{\text{Focal length of normal lens}}{\substack{\text{Focal length of telephoto}\\\text{lens (or telescope)}}} \times 10 = \substack{\text{Maximum}\\\text{exposure time}\\\text{in seconds}}$$

You can use the formula to determine the approximate maximum exposure time for sharp pictures of the moon with a telephoto lens or telescope.

For example, suppose the normal lens for your 35 mm camera has a focal length of 50 mm and you want to use a telephoto lens of 400 mm. Then, 50/400 × 10 = 1.25. The answer, 1.25, means that the maximum exposure time for sharp pictures of the moon with the 400 mm lens is about 1 second.

Of course, longer exposure times can be used if you put your camera onto an equatorial telescope mounting that is driven to compensate for earth rotation.

• *See also:* ASTROPHOTOGRAPHY; BINOCULARS, TAKING PICTURES THROUGH; FILTERS; MOON, PHOTOGRAPHY OF; MOONLIGHT PICTURES; NEUTRAL DENSITY; SUN, PHOTOGRAPHY OF.

Further Reading: Cortright, Edgar M., ed. *Exploring Space with a Camera.* WA, DC: Scientific and Technical Information Division, Office of Technology, Utilization, NASA, 1968; Keene, George. *Star-Gazing with Telescope and Camera.* Garden City, NY: Amphoto, 1967; Paul, Henry E. *Outer Space Photography,* 4th ed. Garden City, NY: Amphoto, 1976; Rackham, T. *Astronomical Photography at the Telescope,* 3rd ed. London, England: Faber and Faber, Ltd., 1972; *Sky and Telescope (magazine).* Cambridge, MA: Sky Publishing Corporation.

 ## ECPS (Effective Candlepower-Second)

ECPS is a unit of measurement of light intensity of a source in a reflector. It is derived by averaging the intensities over a specified beam angle, often the angle subtended by the points of half-intensity on a horizontal plane. Beam candlepower-second (BCPS) measurements are similar, but are taken directly on the axis of light output rather than across a beam angle. ECPS and BCPS ratings of electronic flash units with self-contained reflectors are usually so nearly equal that they give identical guide numbers. The electronic flash duration is nearly always shorter than any camera shutter speed. With focal plane shutters, the shortest shutter speed at which the curtain is fully open is usually used; this is 1/60 to 1/125 sec. Most blade shutters can be syn-

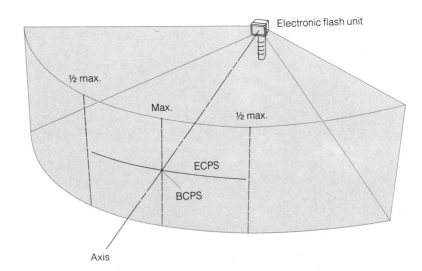

The beam candlepower-second (BCPS) rating indicates the maximum intensity of electronic flash output along the beam axis at a standard distance. An effective candlepower-second (ECPS) rating indicates the average intensity measured through a horizontal angle from the maximum to the half-maximum output on either side of the beam axis. BCPS and ECPS values are usually within 10 percent of each other, so, for practical purposes, they may be used interchangeably.

chronized with electronic flash up to their fastest speed. If the ECPS or BCPS of an electronic flash unit is known, the guide number can be calculated as follows:

$$\text{Guide number} = \sqrt{\frac{\text{ECPS (or BCPS)} \times \text{ASA film speed}}{20}}$$

This guide number is for calculating the distance in feet. To find the metric guide number, divide the foot guide number by 3.28 (or multiply by .304).

ECPS/BCPS ratings are more useful for calculating exposures than a watt-second (joule) rating, which refers to the power requirement of a flash tube. Although light output may be roughly correlated with watt-second requirements, the effect of a reflector and the spread of the output are not taken into account in watt-second ratings.

ECPS/BCPS ratings vary directly with light output; thus, a doubled rating indicates a light increase equivalent to one additional stop of exposure.
• *See also:* BCPS; ELECTRONIC FLASH; GUIDE NUMBERS.

Edge Effect

Edge effect, or adjacency effect as it is sometimes called, is one of a number of image effects that may occur during film development. The edge effect arises at the boundary between an area of high density and an area of low density, such as those corresponding to adjacent light and dark subject areas.

During development, the developer is exhausted rapidly in the high-density area. At the border, some of the exhausted developer (along with some development by-products) diffuses into the low-density area. This reduces the developer concentration and activity level so that less development takes place on the low-density side of the border. Simultaneously, some fresh developer diffuses across the border from

Edge effect: (A) High density area; (B) Low density area; (C) Border effect area of increased development; (D) Fringe effect area of decreased development. The density difference between (C) and (D) is greater than the density difference between (A) and (B).

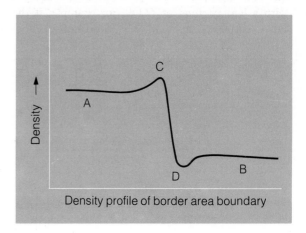

Density profile of border area boundary

the low-density to the high-density side, producing extra development just inside the high-density area. The line of overdevelopment is called the border effect; the line of underdevelopment is called the fringe effect. (See the accompanying diagram.)

The net result is a greater difference between the two densities as measured at the border than as measured in other portions of the two areas. The increased density range makes the edge or boundary more distinct and thus increases the apparent edge sharpness or acutance. Although some acutance developers employ the edge effect, they rely on a small degree of agitation to be useful. In general, agitation minimizes the edge effect because it promotes even diffusion of fresh developer throughout all areas of an emulsion. The edge effect accounts for the modulation transfer factors of films exceeding 100 percent response in the relatively low frequency ranges.

A related effect, the Eberhard effect, causes small image areas to develop to a higher density than larger areas that have received the same exposure and development.

• *See also:* IMAGE EFFECTS.

Edgerton, Harold E.

(Born 1903)
Electrical engineer; Institute Professor Emeritus, Massachusetts Institute of Technology

Dr. Harold Edgerton is internationally recognized for achievements in stroboscopy and ultra-high-speed photography. In the late 1920's he developed several useful stroboscopes, with ample output, for the study of synchronous motors by means of photographic techniques. At the same time, a line of stroboscopes were perfected and made available by the General Radio Corp. From these devices he developed larger repeating flash units for photographic use, and a variety of single-discharge electronic flash units. He has designed and built a variety of underwater flash units for Jacques Cousteau, and has participated in several of Cousteau's expeditions. He developed an early form of high-speed motion-picture camera, which was produced by the General Radio Corp. He is also involved in the development of improved sonar devices for underwater exploration at great depths.

Edison, Thomas Alva

(1847–1931)
American inventor

Thomas Edison held more than 1000 patents on a wide variety of subjects. In 1891, he invented the Kinetograph and Kinetoscope, for taking and viewing images in motion. With George Eastman, he developed the first practical motion-picture film, and devised the system of perforation which is still in use in a more refined form for 35 mm motion-picture film. Edison made a number of early attempts at combining a phonograph with a motion-picture projector to produce talking films. Although the demonstrations were convincing, the process never was commercially practical, because of the lack of an amplification system. The Edison Projecting Kinetoscope, demonstrated at Koster & Bial's Music Hall, was actually designed and built by Thomas Armat and C. Francis Jenkins. The inventors arranged for the use of Edison's name and factory for commercial production of the Kinetoscope.

• *See also:* HISTORY OF PHOTOGRAPHY.

Thomas Edison (right) with George Eastman. Edison's Kinetograph, 1891, first made motion pictures a practical reality through the use of perforated celluloid film, produced by the Eastman Kodak Company. Photo courtesy International Museum of Photography at George Eastman House.

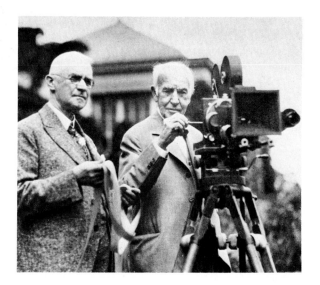